The Creative Industries

SAGE has been part of the global academic community since 1965, supporting high quality research and learning that transforms society and our understanding of individuals, groups, and cultures. SAGE is the independent, innovative, natural home for authors, editors and societies who share our commitment and passion for the social sciences.

Find out more at: **www.sagepublications.com**

The Creative Industries
Culture and Policy

Terry Flew

Los Angeles | London | New Delhi
Singapore | Washington DC

First published 2012

Apart from any fair dealing for the purposes of research or private study, or
criticism or review, as permitted under the Copyright, Designs and Patents Act,
1988, this publication may be reproduced, stored or transmitted in any form, or by
any means, only with the prior permission in writing of the publishers, or in the
case of reprographic reproduction, in accordance with the terms of licences issued
by the Copyright Licensing Agency. Enquiries concerning reproduction outside
those terms should be sent to the publishers.

SAGE Publications Ltd
1 Oliver's Yard
55 City Road
London EC1Y 1SP

SAGE Publications Inc.
2455 Teller Road
Thousand Oaks, California 91320

SAGE Publications India Pvt Ltd
B 1/I 1 Mohan Cooperative Industrial Area
Mathura Road
New Delhi 110 044

SAGE Publications Asia-Pacific Pte Ltd
33 Pekin Street #02–01
Far East Square
Singapore 048763

Library of Congress Control Number: 2010942978

British Library Cataloguing in Publication data

A catalogue record for this book is available from the British Library

ISBN 978-1-84787-575-4
ISBN 978-1-84787-576-1 (pbk)

Typeset by C&M Digitals (P) Ltd, Chennai, India
Printed and bound in Great Britain by TJ International Ltd, Padstow, Cornwall
Printed on paper from sustainable resources

For Charlotte.

Contents

List of Tables

List of Figures

Preface

I would like to acknowledge the support of people who have helped me in the development of *The Creative Industries, Culture and Policy*. Thanks to my colleagues in the Creative Industries Faculty at QUT, particularly to Stuart Cunningham, John Hartley, Axel Bruns, Christy Collis, Christina Spurgeon, Michael Keane, Lucy Montgomery and Brad Haseman. Thanks to those who have worked with me on preparation of the manuscript and research for the book, particularly Mimi Tsai, Tanya Nitins, Adam Swift, Emma Felton, Mark Ryan and Angela Lin Huang. While writing the book, I had the opportunity to spend time at the Department of Telecommunications, Indiana University: thanks to Mark Deuze for being my host, and to Betsi Grabe and David Waterman for their hospitality during that visit. The ideas developed in the book have also been refined through presentations at Monash University, Murdoch University, RMIT University, Beijing University and the Communications University of China, and I thank those who invited me. I have also benefitted from conversations with Mark Gibson, Terence Lee, Kate Oakley, Jiannu Bao, Gay Hawkins, Jason Potts, Julian Thomas, Elinor Rennie, Trevor Barr, Michael Curtin, Joshua Green, Tony Bennett, Dwayne Winseck, Jason Wilson, Melissa Gregg, Nick Couldry, Danny Butt, Jack Linchuan Qiu, Brendan Harkin, Megan Elliott and many others. I would also like to thank Mila Steele, Sarah-Jane Boyd, Rachel Hendrick, Imogen Roome, Chris Rojek and the team at Sage for overseeing the project to fruition, and their unwavering support for the book.

Acknowledgements

I am grateful to the following authors and publishers for permission to use their work in this book:

Table 1.1, Department of Culture, Media and Sport, *Creative Industries Mapping Document*, 1998; Table 1.2, Department of Culture, Media and Sport, *Creative Industries Economic Estimates 2007: Statistical Bulletin*; Table 4.1, Design Institute of Australia, *What is a Designer?* <http://www.dia.org.au/index.cfm?id=186.>; Table 7.3, Arts Council of England, published in Helen Jermyn, *The Arts and Social Exclusion*, 2001, p. 13.

Figure 1.1, National Endowment for Science, Technology and the Arts, for *Creating Value: How the UK can Invest in Creative Businesses*, 2006, p. 55; Figure 1.2, The Work Foundation, for *Staying Ahead: The Economic Performance of the UK's Creative Industries*, p. 103; Figure 2.1, KEA Economic Affairs, for *the Economy of Culture in Europe*, p. 3; Figure 2.2, The World Bank, for Indermit Gill and Homi Kharas, *An East Asian Renaissance: Ideas for Economic Growth*, p. 49, p. 49; Figure 2.3 and Figure 2.4, United Nations Educational, Scientific and Cultural Organisation, *Understanding Creative Industries: Cultural Statistics for Public Policy-Making*, p. 80 and p. 81; Figure 2.5, United Nations Trade, Aid and Development, *Creative Economy Report 2008*, p. 14; Figure 3.1, United Nations Educational, Scientific and Cultural Organisation, for *The 2009 UNESCO Framework for Cultural Statistics*, p. 20; Figure 4.1, Australian Research Council Centre of Excellence for Creative Industries and Innovation, for Peter Higgs, Stuart Cunningham and Janet Pagan, *Australia's Creative Economy; Basic Evidence on Size, Growth, Income and Employment*, CCI Technical Report, 2007, p. 10; Figure 4.2, National Endowment for Science, Technology and the Arts, for Peter Higgs, Stuart Cunningham and Hanan Bakhshi, *Beyond the Creative Industries: Mapping the Creative Economy in the United Kingdom*, Technical Report, 2008, p. 6; Figure 5.1, Sage, for Colin Hoskins, Stuart McFadyen and Andy Finn, *Media Economics: Applying Economics to New and Traditional Media*, p. 145; Figure 7.1, National Academies Press, for William Mitchell, Anal Inouye and Marjory Blumenthal, *Beyond Creativity: Information Technolgoy, Innovation, and Creativity*, 2003, p. 25.

About the Author

Terry Flew is Professor of Media and Communications in the Creative Industries Faculty at the Queensland University of Technology (QUT), in Brisbane, Australia. He is the author of *New Media: An Introduction* (OUP), which has gone into three editions (fourth edition forthcoming), and *Understanding Global Media* (Palgrave).

He is a leading international figure in creative industries research, having played a key role in establishing the world's first Creative Industries Faculty at QUT, and undertaking invited presentations on creative industries in China, Japan, Korea, Taiwan, the United States and New Zealand. He has edited special issues of the journals *International Journal of Cultural Studies* and *The Information Society* on creative industries.

He is a Chief Investigator in the ARC Centre of Excellence for Creative Industries and Innovation, the leading humanities and creative arts research centre in Australia, where he has been engaged in research into creative industries and cities in China and East Asia. He has also headed research projects into citizen journalism and the role of suburbs in creative industries development.

He has published over 30 book chapters and over 50 scholarly journal articles, in leading international publications in the fields of communication, media and cultural studies, journalism and digital media.

He has been President of the Australian and New Zealand Communication Association, and is active in the International Communications Association. He has provided expert advice to the Organisation for Economic Co-operation and Development, the National Academies Forum, the Australian Federal government and the European Science Foundation.

During 2011–12, he headed the National Classification Scheme Review, undertaken by the Australian Law Reform Commission for the Australian Federal Government.

Introduction

One of the hit television programmes of the late 2000s was the series *Mad Men*. First broadcast on the AMC channel in 2007, the program is set in a New York advertising agency in the early 1960s, and provides a fascinating snapshot of how advertising as a creative industry at that time balanced creativity and commerce, and artistic aspirations with the stated desire to manage consumers' purchasing decisions on behalf of their corporate clients. Some aspects of *Mad Men* are appealingly anachronistic, like the fashions, the three Martini lunches, and the high tolerance for smoking in every workplace, domestic and entertainment environment. Others serve as reminders of how society has moved on since the early 1960s, with the rigidity of gender roles in both the home and the office being an obvious case in point. But surrounding the show is a pervasive sense of a world about to change. This is seen in events external to the Sterling Cooper ad agency, such as the Cuban missile crisis, the Kennedy assassination, the civil rights marches and the intensifying war in Vietnam. But even within Sterling Cooper, changes are afoot. Some male staff declare themselves to be homosexual, while others remain in the closet, fearing (with some justification, as it turns out) that 'coming out' could cost them their careers. Peggy Olsen is going ahead as the sole female creative in Don Draper's team, but this comes at a cost to her relations with her mother, and with the disapproval of her Catholic priest, as well as some rejection from her female secretarial peers and hostility from some of the men in the office. The character of Betty, Don Draper's long suffering wife, would appear to be a prime candidate to join the women's movement once it emerged, having had her desires and ambitions suppressed in the name of Don's career advancement, and having put up with his serial womanising.

The Sterling Cooper advertising agency is a fictitious entity. But if it really existed in Manhattan, New York, in the 1960s, it would not have been far away from Andy Warhol's Factory. The 1960s saw Warhol become one of the world's leading artists, but the decade would also see him branch out into movies and rock music: in the 1970s, Warhol would have his own television programme. Around Warhol emerged a diverse cohort – to put it mildly – of celebrities, musicians (such as Lou Reed and the Velvet Underground), gays, transsexuals, drug users, artists and others, who made The Factory their home, and who produced some of the most exciting and eclectic creative work of its era. The art scene around The Factory did not buy into the modernist assumption of the need to separate art and commerce – Warhol had a background in advertising and interior design, and was a quite savvy businessman – but it did consistently challenge and confound the social and cultural orthodoxies of the time. The lived bohemianism of Warhol's 'Superstars' would be one of the factors that would make New York the centre of the cultural universe by the early 1970s, and this creative impulse continues to be as central to the identity of New York as a global city as its banking and finance industries.

Creative industries is somewhat unusual as a concept in social and cultural theory as it has its origins in policy discourse. Nonetheless, the discourse of creative industries draws upon a range of academic disciplines, from cultural studies to economics, and from geography to policy studies to critical theory and sociology. This book analyses creative industries at two levels. It undertakes a historical account of creative industries as a discursive concept, tracing how it has been used in both academic theory and public policy in different parts of the world from the 1990s to the present. It traces developments from the term's origins with the 'New Labour' governments of Tony Blair and Gordon Brown in the UK to its contemporary uses by international bodies such as UNESCO and UNCTAD, as well as its uses in both advanced industrial and developing economies. The book also undertakes an empirical account of the key concepts related to the creative industries, including production, consumption, markets, trade, creative labour, globalisation, creative cities, cultural policy and intellectual property.

In order to understand how the concept came into being, and why it is significant, we need to consider different traditions of thinking about the relationship between contemporary cultures and public policy. A key element involves the rise of cultural studies. From the late 1950s to the present day, cultural studies has developed from its origins as a critique of British intellectual and political culture associated with the work of Raymond Williams, Richard Hoggart, Stuart Hall and others, to become an international 'project to democratise our understanding of culture' (McGuigan, 2009a: 2). Cultural studies has provided a point of intersection for what had been a discrete and somewhat disconnected set of intellectual fields involved with the project of studying culture – from anthropology to literary criticism, and from sociology and mass communications to philosophy, art theory and linguistics – but it also came to constitute the field that it was designed to study.

Cultural studies came with a set of underlying assumptions and priorities that have come to define ways of thinking about culture. These include: the attention given to popular culture and the desire to see such forms as having cultural value; concerns about how more traditional frameworks for analysing culture, such as aesthetics, can act to perpetuate social and cultural hierarchies; aligning the study of culture to a political project that sought the democratisation of knowledge and the challenging of socio-economic inequalities; and the whole idea that the study of culture is in fact political, as questions of power are embedded in systems of cultural production and consumption. We find today that such questions are raised in arts and humanities courses throughout the world, and are increasingly central to school curricula in areas such as English literature, in ways that were inconceivable even 20 years ago. Concepts associated with cultural studies serve to raise new questions about issues such as national or cultural identity, and have given a new dynamic to our expectation that any single cultural artefact or text – a term which itself changes its meaning with the rise of cultural studies – can be open to multiple meanings and interpretations. Indeed, even those who reject these questions being the focus of the study of culture, such as conservative critics in the 'culture wars', start from the premise that cultural studies has been winning in the so-called 'long march' to politicise the humanities (Gibson, 2007).

An important debate that emerged within cultural studies was whether the field can, or should, gain greater practical purchase by focusing on questions of public policy, particularly as they relate to the arts, culture, media and new technologies. Drawing upon the later work of Michel Foucault on governmentality and the modern liberal state (Foucault, 1991a; Gordon, 1991), authors such as Tony Bennett (1992, 1995, 1998), Ian Hunter (1988, 1994) and Stuart Cunningham (1992, 2010) proposed that culture in its modern sense emerged 'as both the object and the instrument of government' (Bennett, 1992: 26 – author's emphasis), and that this was overlooked in contemporary cultural studies due to its rhetorical commitment to a radical anti-statism, in ways that undermined its potential political efficacy. While there were many who rejected this reformist turn as an unacceptable form of political revisionism, it was nonetheless argued that cultural policy studies could in fact enable critical intellectuals to have a greater capacity to influence progressive social change, by tapping into social democratic politics and emergent discourses of cultural citizenship. This would entail cultural critics focusing their energies on cultural fields where their interventions could make a difference (media policy, education policy and museums were three areas identified as potential sites for such a cultural politics), and by learning to speak the language of policy makers and cultural bureaucrats. Tony Bennett put it more formally in proposing that 'intellectual work [should] be conducted in a manner such that, in both its substance and its style, it can be calculated to influence or service the conduct of identifiable agents within the region of culture concerned' (Bennett, 1992: 23).

The cultural policy debate has waxed and waned since the early 1990s. Two points that were apparent from this debate were that national histories and political-institutional formations mattered in terms of getting influence and traction for such ideas – there is a much richer history of cultural policy in the countries of the European Union than the United States, for example – and that the form of government and its dominant ideological motifs also mattered. For those Australian cultural theorists who advocated a turn towards cultural policy studies, the rise and fall of cultural policy in the transition from Labour to conservative governments was a salutary reminder that the policy field is by no means politically neutral. Nonetheless, the 'cultural policy moment' indicated that there were debates to be had about the relationship between cultural studies and public policy, even among those who would hold to both a more critical perspective on the liberal-capitalist state and a more radical conception of the role of intellectual work in the humanities (McRobbie, 1996; Miller and Yúdice, 2002).

If cultural studies has been both a set of concepts and an intellectual formation that have been transforming how we understand, interpret and act upon contemporary culture, this book points to another such moment, which has its origins in the 1970s but accelerates in significance from the late 1990s onwards, and that is creative industries. Narrowly defined, creative industries was the term used by Tony Blair's 'New Labour' government when it came to power in Britain in 1997 to develop new policies for industries associated with the arts, media, design and digital content. But the uses of the term have always been more ambitious than is suggested by these origins in policy discourse, and the ideas that underpin creative industries have broader and deeper roots than would be suggested by the pragmatic politics of the Blair and Brown governments. While this book begins with an overview of the British experience with creative industries, and how it evolved as a policy discourse, it is a contention of this book that creative industries has captured a set of trends of much wider global provenance than these origins would suggest. Like cultural studies, creative industries is a concept that is reshaping how we think about culture, and particularly about the forms of public policy that are being developed in relation to the areas that come to be within its purview. While it is noted that terminology changes across countries, with some referring to the cultural industries, the copyright industries, the digital content industries, and even the cultural and creative industries or – as in China – the cultural creative industries, the underlying questions that have been opened up by creative industries debates are not a genie likely to be put back in the bottle, or even a term that disappears with such erstwhile staples of the 1990s and 2000s as 'New Labour', the 'Third Way', the 'new economy' or 'Cool Britannia'. Chapter Two discusses the differential international uptake of the concept of creative industries, at the level of nation-states, regional entities such as the European Union, and supranational institutions such as UNCTAD and UNESCO.

Two of the lasting legacies of cultural studies are the proposition that the cultural forms and practices associated with the mass of the population are worthy of critical scrutiny and intellectual understanding, and that these cultural forms and practices are best thought about as operating in tandem with, rather than in isolation from, other spheres of social activity, particularly those pertaining to politics, economics, social relations and law. The attempt to hold these propositions together often generates binary oppositions within cultural studies, and arguments for one set of ideas and theorists against others. Among the many examples that can be provided of this include: the distinction made by Stuart Hall between the 'culturalist' and 'structuralist' traditions of critical thought (Hall, 1986); Tony Bennett's opposition between cultural criticism and cultural policy (Bennett, 1992); Andrew Milner and Jeff Browitt's contrast between 'materialist' and 'utilitarian' approaches to cultural studies (Milner and Browitt, 2002); John Hartley's contrast between the 'struggle' and 'democratisation' traditions of cultural studies (Hartley, 2003); Mark Gibson's contrast between 'power' and 'communication' as competing touchstones in the field (Gibson, 2007); and the dichotomy that Jim McGuigan has drawn between 'cultural populism' and 'critical intervention' (McGuigan, 2009a). My interest here is not so much in who is right or wrong in these debates – many of these accounts work from the premise that one approach is right and the other wrong – but rather from the ways in which the recurring dichotomies seem themselves to be part of what constitutes the field of cultural studies.

The contemporary cultural forms and practices that are the mainstays of cultural studies are of course produced and consumed, and the more popular the cultural forms and practices are, the more likely it is that their production and consumption is tied up with wider economic structures and relations. It is precisely the relationship between these cultural forms and relations and the economic structures, relations and institutions through which they are produced and consumed that creates the field that creative industries is concerned with. This exists at two levels. First, it concerns the industries themselves, the products and services, the markets through which they are brought and sold, the forms of labour involved in their production, the applications of technology associated with production, distribution and consumption, and the social needs and desires that are being addressed through decisions to purchase and consume these cultural goods and services. The industrialisation of culture has been a recurring theme of twentieth century critical theory, most notably in the Frankfurt School's moral and philosophical critique of the culture industries and the incorporation of art into the ideological system of monopoly capitalism. From the 1970s, however, the usefulness of this account of the arts and culture under capitalism itself came under sustained critique, both from cultural studies theorists questioning its apparent disdain for mass/popular culture, and from political economists who argued that there was a pressing need for progressive theorists with a policy orientation to better understand the economic dynamics of what they referred to as the cultural industries. This work, which is best accounted for and summarised by Hesmondhalgh (2007a), provides an important backdrop to contemporary debates about creative industries, and is discussed at length in Chapter Three of this book.

The rise of the creative industries also introduces a second layer of questions concerning the changing relationships between economics and culture, which have both a descriptive and a normative dimension. At the empirical level, there is a growing body of work on cultural economy, coming from political economists (Hesmondhalgh, 2007a; Winseck, 2011), cultural economists (Throsby, 2001; Towse, 2010), a growing group of social theorists interested in the cultural economy from perspectives such as cultural studies, sociology and geography (du Gay and Pryke, 2002; Amin and Thrift, 2004; Scott, 2008a, 2008b), as well as commissioned studies aiming to map the creative industries in terms of their work force, industry dynamics, locational geography and export potential (Higgs et al., 2007; de Propris et al., 2009). Such work has generally found that there has been significant growth in the industry sectors that constitute the creative industries, and they are in many ways the paradigmatic new growth industries of post-industrial capitalist economies.

Much work needs to be done to better measure the size and significance of the creative industries sector, not only to get better agreed benchmarks as to what constitutes these sectors (see Throsby, 2008a for an overview of these debates), but also because Standard Industrial Classification (SIC) data was designed for manufacturing-based economies rather than those where services and knowledge-intensive industries predominate. Moreover, there are unique characteristics of the creative industries workforce, such as high levels of self-employment, people having a 'primary job' in a different industry, and a blurring between the waged workforce and a large and growing number of 'pro-am' participants in these industries (Leadbeater and Miller, 2004). The latter tendency is rapidly accelerated by the generalised diffusion of the Internet and digital media technologies (Hartley, 2009). The extent to which such dynamics are changing the traditional paradigm of cultural economics can be gauged from Ruth Towse's (2010) textbook of the field, which is split between an overview of 'traditional' arts and cultural economics, and the new set of concepts and models – particularly those related to contracts, trade, new technologies and intellectual property – associated with the creative industries. Chapters Four and Five of this book outline elements of the study of the creative industries as industries, with a focus in Chapter Four upon its products and services, production processes, distribution systems and labour markets, while Chapter Five considers consumption, consumer markets, the impacts of new technologies and international cultural trade.

Debates about creative industries have, however, been shrouded in a normative dimension that goes beyond empirical questions as to the accuracy of the data that has been gathered and the policy utility of the arguments presented. This has not been so prominent in economic work on the creative industries, as economists typically start from the perspective of the good or service being bought or sold, with the 'industry' being a shifting canopy used to aggregate these individual production and consumption decisions. From this perspective, whether one refers to 'cultural industries' or 'creative industries' is not a major issue. In the critical humanities and cultural studies, however, it has become a massive issue, with creative industries being viewed as a kind of 'Trojan Horse' through which to smuggle neo-liberal discourses into the field, and subvert the critical mission of cultural studies and related fields of humanities scholarship. Many examples of such arguments are cited in the book, and I won't recount them in detail here. At the time of completing this book, however, a representative example could be found in Jim McGuigan's *Cultural Analysis* (McGuigan, 2009a). For McGuigan, creative industries as both a policy framework and an intellectual discourse marks the 'convergence of consumerist Cultural Studies with "cool capitalism"', and the theory and practice of creative industries involves cultural studies making 'its journey from the humanities and social science faculties all the way over to its resting place in the business school' (McGuigan, 2009a: 145–146). Such a perspective is seen as the culmination of a tendency within cultural studies with a longer history that focuses on questions of consumption and identity over the more traditionally Marxian anchor-points of production and class, engaging in what McGuigan refers to as 'uncritical populism', or the positive valorisation of current forms of popular culture as expressions of consumer preference and active engagement. McGuigan opposed this populist tendency to what he terms 'critical intervention', or the interrogation of such popular cultural forms for their underlying ideological content. For McGuigan, then, creative industries is a manifestation of neo-liberal 'cool capitalism', where expressions of dissent and rebellion are incorporated back into a form of what Jeremy Rifkin referred to as cultural capitalism (Rifkin, 2000), displacing the classical Marxist model of industrial capitalism based upon alienated labour, which has increasingly moved from the advanced capitalist economies to the developing world, most notably China.

These debates are unlikely to simmer down. Indeed, one striking feature of critiques of creative industries is their protean form, whereby it can simultaneously be proposed that creative industries advocates have been overstating the size of these sectors and 'cooking the books' by including ICTs and software in their calculations (Garnham, 2005), **and** that creative industries mark out the proto-typical forms of global capitalism based upon flexible production and legitimated through neo-liberal ideology (Harney, 2010). The general message is, however, quite clear: to talk of creative industries in anything other than highly critical terms is to cede too much ground to the business school and to economics, and the critical vocation of cultural studies and related fields of the humanities needs to draw its ethical and moral compass from deconstructive critique of the underlying ideologies that frame creative industries discourses.

Chapters Six and Seven make some attempt to unpack these debates in less conceptually charged terms. Chapter Six considers the argument that creative industries have emerged in the context of globalisation, and as the world's population has become increasingly urbanised, and whether cities provide unique incubators for the development of the creative industries. It notes that theories surrounding creative cities and creative clusters have drawn upon such claims, although in the chapter I question the degree of correlation between such theories and the actual development of creative industries in cities. It is noted that the 'world cities' hypothesis provides one possible alternative explanation, and the chapter also critiques claims – most famously associated with economic geographer Richard Florida – that the creative industries require hip, inner-urban *milieux* in order to flourish. In doing so, the aim is to identify forms of urban policy that may generate more sustainable development of creative industries in cities, that draw upon the whole range of resources of a city – such as those who live and work in suburbs as well as in inner city areas – and which can develop more locationally-specific accounts of such developments that are not derived from what British urban analyst Kate Oakley has termed 'cookie-cutter' models of urban cultural policy (Oakley, 2004).

Chapter Seven addresses the significance of changes to media and cultural policy that have been associated with both globalisation and the rise of creative industries. Noting that twentieth-century cultural policy was often defined by its distancing of the arts from commercial markets, and by extension regulatory regimes for broadcast media, it identifies a series of drivers of change from the 1970s onwards that relate to technological changes, shifting economic circumstances, new political discourses, international trade agreements, and a revaluation of the economic significance of culture. Much turns on the latter, as we have noted, around the issue of whether the 'culturalisation of the economy' is linked to the rise of neo-liberalism as a set of policy discourses, or whether it marks a more profound shift in the global economy to which creative industries policies mark out one set of responses. Put in Marxist terms, are creative industries primarily a component of the ideological superstructure of contemporary global capitalism, or are they now a core element of its economic base? Drawing upon Michael Foucault's 1978–79 lectures, which are now published in English as *The Birth of Biopolitics* (Foucault, 2008), it is argued that we need a more subtle and context-sensitive analysis of how creative industries policy discourses are being embedded into regimes of cultural management and cultural policy than the relatively blunt analysis provided by neo-Marxist accounts of how neo-liberalism captured the nation-state, and redirected public policy from pro-social and reformist ends to the malign set of consequences associated with 'a radically free market' (Brown, 2003) and 'the commodification of everything' (Fuchs, 2008: 109).

The intensity of debates surrounding creative industries mark out in many ways a recurring set of tensions that will arise from critically apprehending changing relations between economy and culture. To return to the earlier discussion of cultural studies, we can see how the demand from cultural studies to take popular culture seriously has produced a schism that has come in some ways to constitute the field, between those who see popular culture as an essentially democratising force in society and those who understand it in more critical and ideological terms. A similar schism can be identified in creative industries debates. If it is acknowledged that these sectors are of growing economic significance, and that it is therefore important to better understanding their economic dynamics, then the question arises as to whether the purpose of doing so is to advise policy makers and those in these industries how they may work better in terms of economic indicators such as employment, sales and exports, or whether the purpose is to better understand the creative industries in order to more effectively critique their social and cultural impacts. Such a discussion is overlaid by the relationship of the higher education sector to the creative industries, which is by no means a purely intellectual one. Through programmes in media and communication, digital media, design, film and television, journalism, public relations, advertising and other fields, universities are increasingly engaged in providing professional training for graduates to work in the creative industries, just as the more traditional areas of the creative and performing arts are also increasingly attuned to the employment outcomes of their graduates. Moreover, these are the growth sectors in the arts and humanities. In Australia, enrolments in media and communication courses grew by 16 per cent between 2002 and 2007, or eight times the total growth of domestic student enrolments (Cunningham and Turner, 2010), and this continues a long-term trend whereby such courses are increasingly displacing more traditional liberal arts disciplines as being at the core of contemporary arts and humanities enrolments (Flew, 2004a).

The argument of this book is that active engagement with creative industries as theory, policy discourse and as industries where graduates ultimately find work does not require one to abandon cultural studies or the humanities and to find refuge in the business school. Indeed, there are those within business schools who would argue that cultural studies has provided better insights into contemporary features of global business, such as the evolution of brands, than the work coming out of business school disciplines such as management and marketing (Kornberger, 2010). Creative industries as a concept certainly challenges a long-standing academic division of labour between cultural studies and economics, and we are only at the early stages of working out what new paradigms that link the two may look like.[1] What does come out of such work is, at the same time, an appreciation of the increasingly complex ways in which economy and culture are intertwined, and this book aims to map out that territory in ways that are of relevance to policy makers and industry participants as well as the scholarly communities who are engaged with such questions.

Endnote

1   One means of resolving the culture–economy tension has been through Marxism, which has provided both a political-economic and a socio-cultural analysis of capitalist societies. To take one famous example, Fredric Jameson's 1984 essay 'Postmodernism, or the Cultural Logic of Late Capitalism' (Jameson, 1984), proposed that postmodernism was the dominant cultural form of the era defined by the Marxist economist Ernest Mandel as 'Late Capitalism' (Mandel, 1975), just as realism was the dominant cultural logic of market capitalism and modernism the dominant cultural logic of monopoly capitalism. This reading works with what is known as the base/superstructure metaphor in Marxism, where a particular economic framework gives rise to cultural forms that are reflective of it, and in this case flexible accumulation generates the fragmentary narratives characteristic of postmodernism (cf. Harvey, 1989). From the perspective of cultural studies, the difficulty with such arguments is that they reflect a reductive logic associated with Marxist theories of culture which many of the founders of cultural studies largely rejected and sought to challenge. As Stuart Hall put it, 'I entered cultural studies from the New Left, and the New Left always regarded Marxism as a problem, as trouble, as danger, not as a solution ... the things that Marx did not talk about or seem to understand were our privileged objects of study: culture, ideology, language, the symbolic' (Hall, 1992: 279). Whether cultural studies became more Marxist in the 2000s, with the rise of neo-liberalism as a generic explanation for all manner of cultural forms and practices, is an interesting question to consider. On the complex relationship between cultural studies and Marxism, see Gibson (2007).

1 Origins of Creative Industries Policy

Introducing Creative Industries: The UK DCMS Task Force

The formal origins of the concept of creative industries can be found in the decision in 1997 by the newly elected British Labour government headed by Tony Blair to establish a Creative Industries Task Force (CITF), as a central activity of its new Department of Culture, Media and Sport (DCMS). The Creative Industries Task Force set about mapping current activity in those sectors deemed to be a part of the UK creative industries, measuring their contribution to Britain's overall economic performance and identifying policy measures that would promote their further development. The Creative Industries Mapping Document, produced by the UK DCMS in 1998, identified the creative industries as constituting a large and growing component of the UK economy, employing 1.4 million people and generating an estimated £60 billion a year in economic value added, or about 5 per cent of total UK national income (DCMS, 1998). In some parts of Britain, such as London, the contribution of the creative industries was even greater, accounting directly or indirectly for about 500,000 jobs and for one in every five new jobs created, and an estimated £21 billion in economic value added, making creative industries London's second largest economic sector after financial and business services (Knell and Oakley, 2007: 7).

The UK Creative Industries Mapping Document defined the creative industries as 'those activities which have their origin in individual creativity, skill and talent and which have the potential for wealth and job creation through the generation and exploitation of intellectual property' (DCMS, 1998). The Creative Industries Mapping Document identified 13 sectors as constituting the creative industries, shown in Table 1.1.

In launching the Mapping Document, the Minister for Culture and Heritage, Chris Smith, made the observation that:

> The role of creative enterprise and cultural contribution ... is a key economic issue. ...
> The value stemming from the creation of intellectual capital is becoming increasingly
> important as an economic component of national wealth. ... Industries, many of them

Table 1.1 DCMS's 13 Creative Industries Sectors in the UK

Advertising	Interactive leisure software (electronic games)
Architecture	Music
Arts and antique markets	Performing arts
Crafts	Publishing
Design	Software and computer services
Designer fashion	Television and radio
Film and video	

Source: DCMS, 1998.

new, that rely on creativity and imaginative intellectual property, are becoming the most rapidly growing and important part of our national economy. They are where the jobs and the wealth of the future are going to be generated. (Smith, 1998)

This theme that creative industries were vital to Britain's future was a recurring one for Labour under Tony Blair and, from 2007, Gordon Brown. Tony Blair observed that his government was keen to invest in creativity in its broadest sense because 'Our aim must be to create a nation where the creative talents of all the people are used to build a true enterprise economy for the 21st century – where we compete on brains, not brawn' (Blair, 1999: 3). Chris Smith, in launching the second DCMS Mapping Document in 2001, argued that 'The creative industries have moved from the fringes to the mainstream' (DCMS, 2001: 3), and continuing work in developing the sector saw related policies being developed in areas such as education, regional policy, entrepreneurship and trade. This theme continued with the change in Prime Ministership, with Gordon Brown arguing that 'in the coming years, the creative industries will be important not only for our national prosperity, but for Britain's ability to put culture and creativity at the centre of our national life' (DCMS, 2008a), although – as we will see later – the economic ground shifts very rapidly in Britain during the time of Gordon Brown's Prime Ministership.

The DCMS mapping of the UK creative industries played a critical formative role in establishing an international policy discourse for what the creative industries are, how to define them, and what their wider significance constitutes. In Michel Foucault's (1991b) classic account of discourse analysis, a discourse can be identified in terms of its:

1 Criteria of formation: the relating between the objects identified as relevant; the concepts through which these relations can be comprehended; and the options presented for managing these relations;
2 Criteria of transformation: how these objects and their relations can be understood differently, in order to generate what Foucault refers to as new rules of formation (Foucault, 1991b: 54);
3 Criteria of correlation: how this discourse is differentiated from other related discourses, and the non-discursive context of institutions, social relations, political and economic arrangements etc. within which it is situated.

In the field of policy studies, discourses are understood as 'patterns in social life, which not only guide discussions, but are institutionalised in particular practices' (Hajer and Laws, 2006: 260). In this way, as Foucault observed, relations between discourses and institutions, or between social reality and the language we use to represent it, become fluid and blurry. From a research point of view, policy discourse analysis enables one to get 'analytic leverage on how a particular discourse (defined as an ensemble of concepts and categorizations through which meaning is given to phenomena) orders the way in which policy actors perceive reality, define problems, and choose to pursue solutions in a particular direction' (Hajer and Laws, 2006: 261). Policy discourse constitutes a core element of what Considine (1994) refers to as policy cultures, or the relationship within a policy domain between shared and stated values (equity, efficiency, fairness, etc.), key underlying assumptions, and the categories, stories and languages that are routinely used by policy actors in their field, and help to define the policy community, or those who are 'insiders' within that policy field.

Understood in terms of policy discourse, we can see some of the central contours of the approach to creative industries adopted by the Blair Labour government and the DCMS in Britain as it emerged in the late 1990s. The new government took the opportunity provided by its election mandate and a large parliamentary majority to reorganise policy institutions. In this case, it took what had been the Department of National Heritage and reorganised it as the Department of Culture, Media and Sport, bringing the arts, broadcast media and (somewhat oddly in retrospect) sport together within the one administrative domain. But such an administrative change would have little significance if it had not been accompanied by a series of related discursive shifts. By bringing together the arts and media within a department concerned with the formation of culture, the Blair government was signalling a move towards more integrated approaches to cultural policy that have characterised European nations, rather than the more fragmented, *ad hoc* and second-order approaches to cultural policy that have prevailed in much of the English-speaking world (Craik, 1996, 2007; Vestheim, 1996). But the second, and perhaps more significant, discursive shift lay in the way that creative industries drew upon the then-new concept of convergence to argue that the future of arts and media in Britain lay in a transformation of dominant policy discourses towards a productive engagement with digital technologies, to develop new possibilities for the alignment of British creativity and intellectual capital with these new engines of economic growth. This association of creative industries with the modernisation project of Tony Blair's 'New Labour' was strong, and is discussed in more detail below. The final key point was that creative industries promises a new alignment of arts and media policies with economic policies, and by drawing attention to the contribution of these sectors to job creation, new sources of wealth and new British exports, there would now be a 'seat at the table' for the cultural sectors in wider economic discourses that had become hegemonic in British public policy under the previous Conservative governments.

As a policy discourse, creative industries was itself a successful British export. Wang (2008) has identified the term 'creative industries' as a successful British marketing exercise, and Ross has observed that 'few could have predicted that the creative industries model would itself become a successful export' (Ross, 2007: 18). In the next chapter, we

Table 1.2 Economic Contribution of UK Creative Industries, 2004

Industry	Contribution to UK GVA (%)	Annual rate of growth 1997–2004 (%)	Value of exports (£ million)	Number of people employed
Advertising	0.7	3	1,100	223,400
Architecture	0.5	2	570	108,200
Art and antiques	0.06	7	2,200	22,900
Crafts	n/a	n/a	n/a	95,500
Design	0.5	n/a	550	n/a
Designer fashion	0.05	2	n/a	115,500
Video, film and photography	0.3	0	940	63,800
Music and the visual and performing arts	0.5	2	150	236,300
Publishing	1.2	2	1,500	253,300
Software, computer games and electronic publishing	2.7	9	4,700	596,800
Radio and television	0.9	8	1,300	108,700
Total	7.3	5% average	13,000	1,824,400

Source: DCMS, 2007.

will consider the take-up of creative industries policy discourse in other parts of the world. What needs to be considered is how in practice the economic value of the creative industries was determined. While the definition of the sectors constituting the creative industries has evolved over time, a list-based approach to creative industries has remained a hallmark of the original DCMS model, where the overall size and significance of the creative industries to the UK economy has been taken to be measurable as the aggregate output of its constituent sub-sectors. Early documents were engaged with mapping the creative industries, but this was more a cognitive mapping than a geographical one, seeking to determine what the objects of creative industries policy were, what were their relationships with one another, and how to relate the measurement of their size and significance with the broader public policy goals which had now been enunciated for arts and media policy under the creative industries policy rubric. How this worked in practice can be seen from the Creative Industries Economic Estimates for 2004 data in Table 1.2 provided, which measured the size of the UK creative industries in terms of their contribution to national income (Gross Value Added – GVA), their average annual rates of growth, their contribution to exports, and the number of people employed in these industries.

In an early commentary on this list-based approach, I described it as being *ad hoc* (Flew, 2002), as it was not clear what the underlying threads were that linked a seemingly heterogeneous set of sub-sectors as the creative industries. The categorisation draws together industries that are highly capital-intensive (e.g. film, radio and television) with ones that are highly labour-intensive (art and antiques, crafts, designer fashion, music, the visual and performing arts). It also combines sectors that are very much driven by commercial imperatives and the business cycle, such as advertising and architecture, with those that are not. From a policy point of view, the static economic performance of the UK film industry over 1997–2004 indicated by these figures would be a major concern to government due to the size of Britain's audiovisual trade deficit with the United States, which is not compensated for by a comparatively strong performance in the art and antiques markets.

Critics of the DCMS approach such as Garnham (2005) argued that inclusion of the software sector in the creative industries artificially inflated their economic significance in order to align the arts to more high-powered 'information society' policy discourses. It is certainly the case from the figures above that the sector defined as 'Software, computer games and electronic publishing' accounted for 37 per cent of the economic output of the UK creative industries, 36 per cent of its exports, and 33 per cent of creative industries jobs; the question of its inclusion or exclusion bears heavily on wider claims made about the economic significance of the creative industries. As well as questions of inclusion, there are also questions of exclusion, with some asking why sectors such as tourism, heritage and sport were not in the DCMS list (Hesmondhalgh, 2007a). The exclusion of sport is interesting given that so much energy had been expended on bringing sport within the Department, but perhaps more telling is the reluctance to consider the economic contribution of what has come to be termed the GLAM (Galleries, Libraries, Archives and Museums) sectors in these original policy documents. Since the economic value of Britain's cultural institutions (British Museum, National Gallery, British Library, Tate Modern, Victoria and Albert Museum, etc.) cannot be questioned, one suspects that it reflected the modernisation drive of the Blair era to understand Britain in terms other than those of an 'old country' (Wright, 1985). Finally, there is a well-known paradox in trying to determine the size of the creative industries workforce. Many people working in those industries defined as creative industries are in jobs that would not normally be considered to be 'creative' ones (e.g. an accounts manager at an advertising agency), while there are others who have been termed 'embedded creatives' (Higgs and Cunningham, 2008) who are pursuing creative work in other sectors (e.g. website designers for a bank or financial services company). Many of these issues take us to the utility of the concept of creativity as a definer of industries and sectors, and these debates will be returned to later in this chapter as they have played themselves out in the British context.

Cultural Planners and Cool Britannia: UK Creative Industries Policy in the Context of 'New Labour'

The creative industries concept maintained an ongoing relevance as a policy discourse in the United Kingdom from the mid-1990s to the late 2000s. This period was one of concurrent Labour governments in the UK, headed by Tony Blair from 1997 to 2007, and by Gordon Brown from 2007 to Labour's electoral defeat in May 2010. It has certainly been the case in the English-speaking world that left-of-centre governments tend to adopt a more activist stance towards questions of cultural policy than conservative ones, but at the same time creative industries policies differed significantly from traditional cultural policy in their stronger focus on economic wealth generation, and the significance given to creative entrepreneurs and the private sector rather than publicly funded culture. Creative industries as a concept was consistent with a number of touchstones of the redefining of the British Labour Party as 'New Labour', as it was spearheaded by Tony Blair and his supporters within Labour, with its recurring concerns with economic modernisation and Britain's post-industrial future. Its focus on the role of markets as stimuli to arts and culture was consistent with the notion of a 'Third Way' between Thatcher-era free market economics and traditional social democracy, which was nonetheless more accommodating of the role of markets and global capitalism than traditional British Labour Party philosophy and doctrine (Giddens, 1998). Promotion of the creative industries was also consistent with empirical realities of the late 1990s where 'Britain's music industry employed more people and made more money than did its car, steel or textile industries' (Howkins, 2001: vii), and it marked out one response to the common theme of de-industrialisation facing the traditional manufacturing powerhouses of Western Europe.

Labour came to power in Britain after 18 years of Conservative governments, headed by Margaret Thatcher and John Major, that had relentlessly pushed the privatisation of state-run enterprises, user-pays principles for access to government services, a self-reliant enterprise culture, and a general devaluation of the role of the public sector in British economic and social life. This had been a particularly cold climate for the arts, with peak funding bodies such as the Arts Council of Great Britain feeling underfunded and beleaguered. Moreover, artists themselves had become targets for scorn in the popular media, with works that had a critical, counter-cultural or avant-garde element being routinely derided as a 'waste of taxpayers' money'. It had no longer been sufficient to defend the value of the arts in their own terms, and from the late 1980s onwards it had become common to argue the case for public support for the arts in terms of their economic contribution (Myerscough, 1988). While the shift in power from the Conservatives to Labour in 1997 was strongly welcomed in the arts and cultural sectors, it had by this time become common to argue for the value of the arts and culture in Britain in economic terms, and creative industries marked in one respect a more innovative and influential way of doing that.

Creative industries also tapped into a wider *Zeitgeist* of the early Blair years about how to link the question of what would be the jobs and industries that would replace traditional mining and manufacturing sectors with a drive to re-brand Britain as a new nation – 'Cool Britannia' to use the parlance of the times – rather than a once-great power whose traditional industries, values and global influence were now in terminal decline (McGuigan, 1998). This modernising project of the Blair government overlapped with an emergent academic and policy literature on the 'new' or 'weightless' economy, promoted by policy think-tanks such as DEMOS and Comedia, which was identifying creativity as being at the cornerstone of success for post-industrial cities, regions and nations in the globalised economy (Mulgan 1997; Coyle 1998; Landry 2000). One influential book from this period was Charles Leadbeater's *Living on Thin Air: The New Economy* (Leadbeater 1999), which pointed to a 'new economy' and a 'knowledge society' driven by globalisation and information technology, but also by individual creativity, social and cultural entrepreneurship, and a meritocratic spirit.

Yet the concept of creative industries remained significant in Britain even after Tony Blair's political star began to wane, and as 'Cool Britannia' became as passé as 'Britpop'.[1] Why this has been the case related to two factors. The first was that Britain, like most advanced industrial economies, is continuing to face critical questions about what will be the new industries it can develop as globalisation sees many parts of manufacturing and services shift to lower-wage economies, as improvements in communication and transportation make such shifts more seamlessly integrated into global production networks, and as developing economies such as those of East Asia, China and India are moving up the value chain as their enterprises have become directly competitive with European and North American firms. The Cox Review of Creativity in Business (HM Treasury, 2006) identified the nexus between creativity, innovation and design as an area in which Britain needed to develop a competitive edge over the next five to ten years as a matter of urgency, before the developing economies enhanced their local research, education, technical and creative capacities to the point where they would out-compete Britain not only in low-wage, low-skill industries, but in high-technology industries where skills are at a premium.

The second factor promoting creative industries in the UK was the fact that, at a local level, city and regional governments had been responding to the challenge of a post-industrial future for at least 15 years prior to the Blair government's election in 1997. As Britain's industrial cities, such as Liverpool, Manchester, Glasgow, Sheffield and Bradford, faced the loss of traditional manufacturing in the 1980 and 1990s, they responded with strategies to give culture a new role in the local economy (Lewis 1990; Greenhalgh 1998; O'Connor 1999, 2007). Interestingly, given that creative industries is often criticised for being a surrender of the arts and creativity to neo-liberal values, it is notable that the origins of creative industries policy can be found in local councils in UK cities dominated by left-wing Labour governments in the 1980s, whose approach to the question of democratising cultural policy often led to answers that blurred traditional dichotomies between the arts and commerce, markets and planning, and intervention and enterprise. These have all been hallmarks of creative industries as a policy discourse as it has evolved in the UK from the 1990s to the present.

Local Socialism in the UK: A Precursor to Creative Industries?

The concept of 'local socialism' has a history as a minority strand in left-wing British political thought, favouring participatory democracy and local solutions over the dominant post-1945 Labour consensus favouring centrally delivered solutions and national economic planning (Gyford, 1985). The election of the Thatcher Conservative government in 1979 saw a parallel trend towards the election of Labour councils in numerous UK cities, which in many cases were committed to programmes to promote local economic development as well as progressive agendas on women's rights and those of minority groups.

(Continued)

(Continued)

The most prominent of the left-wing Labour councils was the Greater London Council (GLC), headed by 'Red' Ken Livingstone from 1981 to its abolition by the Conservatives in 1986. Bianchini (1987) observed that the GLC developed two distinctive approaches to local cultural policy: promotion of ethnic and community arts to empower under-represented minorities in the cultural sphere; and development of a Cultural Industries Strategy through the Greater London Enterprise Board (GLEB) to promote new enterprises and more effective public sector intervention in commercial cultural industries and markets. Drawing upon the work of political economist Nicholas Garnham, the Cultural Industries Strategy put forward a number of important changes and provocations in relation to public policy towards the cultural sectors:

1   It argued against deficit financing of existing arts organisations and practices, seeing this as reflective of policies which '[place] artists at the centre of the cultural universe ... [and] define the policy problem as one of finding audiences for their work ... when audiences cannot be found ... the market is blamed and the gap is filled by subsidy' (Garnham, 1987: 24);

2   Such approaches were reflective of an 'idealist' tradition in cultural policy that rejected the role played by markets in the allocation of cultural resources. Garnham argued that 'while this tradition has been rejecting the market, most people's cultural needs and aspirations are being, for better or worse, supplied by the market as goods and services' (Garnham, 1987: 25);

3   The alternative approach proposed for cultural policy was to better understand how the cultural industries worked as 'institutions in our society which employ the characteristic modes of production and organisation of industrial corporations to produce and disseminate symbols in the form of cultural goods and services generally, although not exclusively, as commodities' (Garnham, 1987: 25);

4   Strategies for the media industries needed to have a central role in cultural policy, due to their prominence as employers of cultural labour, their nature as commodities that account for large amounts of consumers' time spent in cultural consumption, and their relationship to the diffusion of new technologies;

5   Cultural industries strategy should therefore focus upon the whole value chain of cultural production, distribution and consumption, and upon strategies to promote new cultural enterprises, better understand audiences, and better market and promote cultural goods and services that receive public financial support, in order to 'concentrate ... interventions not on production but on distribution in the widest sense' (Garnham, 1987: 36).

While the impact of the Cultural Industries Strategy within the GLC was ultimately limited (Bianchini, 1987), it was highly influential in rethinking the relationship of the cultural industries to local economic development in cities, and the policy strategies to be adopted by local governments. As many cities in Britain faced the decline of their traditional manufacturing industries – a process that accelerated under the Thatcher government policies of the 1980s – culture was identified as playing an increasingly important role in both the 're-imagining' of these cities, and the cultural industries were seen as providing new opportunities for economic and employment growth (O'Connor, 2007).

The music industry provided an interesting case study in these new policy approaches. In cities such as Sheffield and Manchester, initiatives were undertaken to harness and promote their vibrant and diverse (and internationally successful) popular music cultures as part of the re-branding of the city as a destination for events, tourism and new investment. Policy initiatives included: the development of council-funded rehearsal spaces; 'Cultural Industries Quarters' in parts of the city where clusters of bars, nightclubs and music recording facilities had emerged; and improvements to physical infrastructure and changes to licensing laws that better fitted the notion of a 'night-time economy' that was central to the music industry (O'Connor and Lovatt, 1995; Brown et al., 2000). This presented new challenges for economic development policy, as popular music as an industry was often seen as 'soft' and ephemeral, lacking in the large-scale investments in physical infrastructure associated with manufacturing and service industries. It also required a rethinking of arts and cultural policy, as popular music industries and scenes developed outside, and sometimes in spite of, the activities of local governments and cultural planners, reflecting both what has been referred to as the 'Darwinian inheritance' of popular music – a few succeed commercially, but most don't – and the fact that it is hooked into national and global cultural circuits as well as having an element that is locally driven. Frith et al. (2009) provide a valuable account of some of the tensions involved in developing policies for music as a creative industries, with particular reference to work undertaken in Scotland.

Critiques of the DCMS Definition of Creative Industries

For a policy document issued from within a new government department, the DCMS Mapping Documents gained remarkable traction and ongoing significance. They were also subject to widespread critique. As creative industries was presented as something of an *ex nihilo* category capable of encompassing a heterogeneous set of industries and practices, critiques of the DCMS model of creative industries in the UK have often been bundled up with other discussions, such as: whether the arts are, or should be, associated with economic discourses focused on wealth creation (Caust, 2003; O'Connor, 2009); whether or not there exists what urban policy advocate Richard Florida termed the 'creative class' (Florida, 2002); and the general directions of public policy under 'New Labour' in Britain and the political philosophy of the 'Third Way'. 'New Labour' in particular has been subject to a range of caustic critiques, which saw its policies as essentially a continuation of the neo-liberal economic and social programmes of the Thatcher era with a social democratic gloss, or 'Thatcherism with a human face'. In the words of leading academic critic Stuart Hall, New Labour and the 'Third Way' entrenched a neo-liberal project whereby 'Slowly but surely, everybody – kicking and screaming to the end – becomes his/her own kind of "manager" [and] the market and market criteria become entrenched as the modus operandi of "governance" and institutional life' (Hall, 2005: 327). From such a perspective, the UK model of creative industries can be critiqued as '"old wine in new bottles" – a glib production of spin-happy New Labourites, hot for naked marketisation but mindful of the need for socially acceptable dress' (Ross, 2007: 18), or as 'a reactionary model insofar as it reinforces the status quo of labour relations within a neoliberal paradigm' (Rossiter, 2006: 111). Some of these root-and-branch issues concerning the legitimacy of the creative industries concept will be considered in later chapters, particularly Chapter Three, where the concept of 'creative industries' is counter-posed to that of 'cultural industries'.

A range of critiques of the DCMS definition of creative industries emerged from a more applied, policy-oriented perspective. The most common of these related to the validity of 'creativity' as a policy concept capable of bringing together the diverse set of industries and practices associated with the creative industries, and the inherent difficulties involved in differentiating these industries from others on the basis of their application of creativity. Bilton and Leary (2002) observed that the DCMS definition could not in itself explain what was distinctive about the creative industries, since:

> Every industry would surely lay claim to some measure of individual creativity, skill and talent; equally, it is difficult to think of a product which does not exploit some intellectual component in the form of patents, design elements or other intangible, symbolic properties which make that product unique. (Bilton and Leary, 2002: 50)

Pratt (2005: 33) echoed this point, observing that 'it would be difficult to identify a non-creative industry or activity'. The resulting danger was that of stretching the concepts of culture and creativity 'beyond breaking point' (Hesmondhalgh and Pratt, 2005: 6), since 'any innovation – including scientific and technical innovations – of any sort in any industry is creative, and, in such terms, any industry is, therefore, potentially a "creative industry"' (Galloway and Dunlop, 2007: 19). Howkins (2001) was critical of the UK DCMS initiatives in precisely these terms, arguing that it restricted creativity to the domains of the arts and culture, excluding the sciences and engineering, and technological innovation more generally.

These were examples of what Pratt (2005) referred to as the *breadth question* in definitions of cultural and creative industries, and it has two elements. The first is that of inclusion and exclusion. The DCMS definition of the creative industries was seen by critics as being simultaneously too broad and too narrow. O'Regan (2002) questioned the one-sided focus on that which was 'new' and commercially oriented, arguing that such an approach risked losing sight of the complex cultural ecology through which commercially-oriented and publicly-subsidised forms of cultural production were linked, as well as the links between digital and tangible arts and media forms. The DCMS approach was sometimes seen as a politically pragmatic one, driven by the way in which the Mapping Documents 'opened a door to Treasury funding and gained an economic respect for the sector it had never had before as simply "the arts lobby"' (Pratt, 2005: 33). Pratt observed that the significance of the new creative industries analysis was that it provided a new way of collecting and aggregating data around the cultural sectors that had been neglected under Standard Industry Classifications (SIC) models, so that:

> For policy makers, it is as if suddenly a successful new industry has arrived from nowhere. Although the constituent industries (film, television, advertising etc.) are widely recognised, previously they had been seen either as part of the state-supported sector, or viewed as somewhat peripheral to the 'real economy'. (Pratt, 2004a: 19)

At the same time, questions remained about what was excluded from the creative industries definition. As noted above, the apparent exclusion of cultural institutions from the GLAM (Galleries, Libraries, Archives and Museums) sector appears odd, as does the absence of cultural heritage and cultural tourism. At the same time, the focus on crafts and antiques may in itself be more reflective of Britain as an 'old country' where TV programmes such as *Antiques Roadshow* are part of the national patrimony and global image (Wright, 1985; Bonner, 2003), rather than their centrality to national cultural and economic policy. Moreover, it can be argued that the logic of creative industries production and organisational practices extends its trajectory outwards to sectors such as telecommunications, sport and entertainment, and to knowledge-intensive service industries more generally (Cunningham, 2002).

The second element in the breadth question surrounding creative industries is that creative industries policy discourse has emerged in a context where the symbolic and cultural dimensions of all aspects of the economy have acquired a greater significance. Creativity has been identified by businesses worldwide as an increasingly important source of sustainable competitive advantage in a globalised, knowledge-based economy where the barriers to reproduction of ideas, concepts and products have been dramatically reduced. Moreover, the growing significance of cultural and symbolic dimensions to the economy overall has proceeded apace, through processes originally identified by sociologists such as Featherstone (1991) as the 'aestheticisation of everyday life', and what Lash and Urry described as the 'culturalisation of the economy', where 'ordinary manufacturing industry is becoming more and more like the production of culture' (Lash and Urry, 1994: 123). The resulting policy problem with the 'everything is creative' definition of the creative industries is that it fails to identify the distinctive and specific aspects of cultural sectors, and generates a resulting tendency towards a 'one size fits all' or generic 'cookie cutter' approach to media and cultural policy. Critics argue that such generic approaches that lack a grounded understanding of the specificities of the industries concerned, and thus the most effective policy interventions to further their development (Oakley, 2004; Pratt, 2005; Galloway and Dunlop, 2007).[2]

Garnham (2005) argued that the DCMS definition of creative industries was developed in a way that was not only politically pragmatic in promoting the cultural sectors as economically important, but also strategically aligned to the more prestigious policy domains associated with the information society and the knowledge economy. Garnham argued that the focus on creative industries was part of 'an attempt by the cultural sector and the cultural policy community to share in its relations with the government, and in policy presentation in the media, the unquestioned prestige that now attaches to the information society and to any policy that supposedly favours its development' (Garnham 2005: 20). Garnham argued that this definitional shift has had two major consequences for the development of arts, media and cultural policy in the UK. One was that it promoted a strengthening of copyright protection that has benefited the so-called copyright industries such as the software, media and entertainment industries, through an alliance with cultural workers and small-scale cultural entrepreneurs around the importance of intellectual property (IP) protection to the creative industries generally. This is despite the limited evidence that exists for arguments that such IP protection benefits content creators as distinct from copyright owners, and the possibility that strong IP regimes can act as a fetter on innovation, particularly in the digital content domain (Flew, 2006). The propensity to promote stronger intellectual property regimes on the basis that they would assist the British creative industries could also be seen in later policy documents such as *Digital Britain*, where it was argued that strong intellectual property laws are a pillar of creative industries development since 'strong rule of law is vital for industries that depend on respect for intellectual property' (DCMS/DBIS, 2009: 105).

The second consequence, for Garnham, has been that it has shifted the policy focus away from regulation over distribution of cultural products and services towards a supply-side, artist-centred notion of 'creativity' as the primary driver of cultural policy, through extrapolating the idea of the artists as a 'model creative worker' towards education and human capital formation for the economy as a whole. As well as the observation that this may in fact resurrect the view of 'creativity based on individual exceptionalism' that may be least useful for the economic development of the creative industries (Bilton and Leary, 2002; Bilton, 2007), it also runs the risk, as critics such as Andrew Ross (2007) have argued, of promoting precarious work and employment conditions that often characterise the position of creative artists into a 'new entrepreneurial paradigm' for the knowledge workforce.

Further Elaborations of UK Creative Industries Policy: Regionalisation, the Arts and Mainstreaming

Some of the criticisms made of the early DCMS approach to creative industries, as found in the Mapping Documents were responded to in further elaborations of the policy. Three major developments in creative industries policies in the UK in the 2000s were:

1 More explicit incorporation of a regional dimension to creative industries policies, in partial recognition of the limits of top-down, 'one size fits all' policy prescriptions;
2 A reassertion of the distinctiveness of the arts in cultural and creative industries policy;
3 A mainstreaming of creative industries policy discourse, which sought to establish the relevance of themes and concepts derived from analysis of the creative industries to the British economy as a whole.

In considering these developments, it is notable that there was no turning away from development of the creative industries as a core policy theme. It survived not only the decline in earlier animating concepts such as 'Cool Britannia' and the 'new economy', but also the fall in the personal popularity of Tony Blair – particularly after Britain committed troops to the war in Iraq in 2003 – and his replacement by Gordon Brown as Prime Minister. How it is being reconfigured in the shift from Labour to the Conservative/Liberal Democrats coalition is discussed later in this chapter, but early signs were that the new government retained a commitment to developing these sectors in their current institutional form, with the senior Conservative MP Jeremy Hunt becoming the Secretary of State for Culture, Olympics, Media and Sport in May 2010.

Pratt (2004a) argued that the major change in creative industries policy in the UK in the early 2000s was regionalisation. He noted that 'despite the inclusion of "mapping" in the title there are no maps in the UK [DCMS] report; moreover, there was no attempt to address regional or local variations, or to benchmark findings against those of other nation states' (Pratt, 2004a: 20). This gap was acknowledged in the second Creative Industries Mapping Document in 2001, which coincided with the establishment of the Scottish Parliament and the Welsh Assembly in 1999, as well as the development of new forms of regional governance such as Regional Development Agencies (RDAs). Monitoring of the regional dimensions of public policy was a recurring concern of Labour governments, due in part to their electoral strength in Northern England, Scotland and Wales, but also to the perception that the Conservatives had presided over a 'Two Nations' Great Britain, with a prosperous south where new service industries were based, and a damaged and de-industrialised north.

The regionalisation agenda, and the associated development of Regional Cultural Consortia by DCMS to work with the RDAs and Regional Arts Boards, produced a series of studies into the creative industries in the various UK regions. Significant creative industries networks were identified in various cities and regions, as seen, for example, in work on South-East England (Pratt, 2004a), Northern Ireland (Jeffcutt, 2004) and Nottingham and the East Midlands (Shorthose, 2004a). It also produced a range of initiatives to promote cultural quarters and creative clusters (Jayne and Bell, 2004; Roodhouse, 2006). Kate Oakley argued that these were driven by a vision of 'culture-led regeneration … as the last great hope of cities with economic or social problems' (Oakley 2004: 68), although she observed that in practice the outcome was often 'cookie cutter approaches' to creative industries developed without suitable attention being given to place specificity:

> Rather than trying to understand the difference between the creative economy of Glasgow and that of Cornwall, we currently seem hell bent on trying to replicate a single creative industries model across the country. It appears that everywhere needs a university, some incubators and a 'creative hub', with or without a café, galleries and fancy shops. (Oakley, 2004: 73)

Where success has been monitored, it was often associated with factors not considered in the standard DCMS policy template, such as the role of 'vernacular creativity' in Nottingham

(Shorthose, 2004a) or tacit knowledge networks in Manchester (O'Connor, 2004), whereas 'engineered' attempts by city authorities to develop creative industries quarters in cities such as Leicester and Stoke were less successful (Jayne 2004; Shorthose, 2004b). At the same time, London continued to be the centre of Britain's creative industries, being particularly dominant in the media, music, fashion, advertising, electronic games and publishing industries (De Propris et al., 2009). This was not because it had the best policy frameworks, but because its history, infrastructure, status as a global city, and links to the financial and business services sectors meant that 'it alone can afford to "specialise" in creative industries employment, providing the infrastructure of commissioning, distribution, management and other professional functions that enable these sectors to get their products to market' (Knell and Oakley, 2007: 8). The inability to redistribute creative industries jobs away from London over the life of the Blair and Brown governments could be seen as a wider metaphor for the failure to redress the class-based and regional inequalities of British society during the 'New Labour' years.

A second major development has been the reassertion of priorities associated with developing the arts within DCMS. O'Connor (1999) and Pratt (2004a) alluded to the unresolved question of the relationship between DCMS and its predominantly economic focus and remit, and that of more established bodies such as the Arts Council of Great Britain (now the Arts Council of England), and between 'the Department's economic and commercial constituencies', with the commercial creative industries being 'considered by many in the arts establishment to be in opposition, in aim and purpose, to "the arts"' (Pratt, 2004a: 21). The DCMS Mapping Documents were described as 'nothing less than a new manifesto for cultural studies' (Hartley, 2003: 118), as they flattened the traditional hierarchies of cultural authority and privilege, sitting art alongside architecture, software with Shakespeare, and Big Brother with the British Museum as the advancing global flagships of 'British creativity'. Alas, it was not to last. Tessa Jowell, the Secretary of State for Culture, Media and Sport from 2001 to 2007, sought to disavow DCMS's reputation as the 'Ministry for Fun' – acquired during the Chris Smith years – with a personal essay on *Government and the Value of Culture*, where she made it clear that while she did not find the term 'high culture' very useful, she did consider 'great art' to be an instantiation of the sort of 'complex culture' that could lift all Britons out of a 'poverty of aspiration', and hence warranted large-scale public subsidy (DCMS, 2004). A distinction between 'culture' and 'entertainment' thus re-emerged in DCMS policy discourse, and Tessa Jowell's successor, James Purnell, commissioned a study into excellence into the arts, and how best to 'free artists and cultural organisations from outdated structures and burdensome targets, which can act as millstones around the neck of creativity' (DCMS, 2008b). While the recommendations of *Supporting Excellence in the Arts – From Measurement to Judgement* (the McMaster Report) would enable some in the arts sector to benefit from the capacity to base future funding decisions upon expert judgement of how they had obtained excellence, rather than 'simplistic targets', other recipients of DCMS funding would continue to be evaluated against its Performance Indicator Framework, needing to demonstrate a 'balanced scorecard' against a range of indices to have their funding renewed from one year to the next (Eckersley, 2008). As Garnham (2005) suggested, moves towards an artist-centred, supply-side framework for supporting cultural creativity brought the paradigm of excellence, and its associated claims for public subsidy independent of public accountability, back to the centre of British cultural policy.

The final major development with UK creative industries policy in the 2000s was the development of strategies to mainstream it around the concept of Britain as a creative economy. There had long been a critique of the creative industries strategy as based upon assumptions that overstated the extent of decline of the manufacturing sector, and with it traditional working-class jobs, in order to promote Britain as a post-industrial economy and more 'classless' society (e.g. Heartfield 2000; Elliott and Atkinson, 2007). The Cox Review of Creativity in Business (HM Treasury, 2006) was explicit in its focus on how creative capabilities were at the core of Britain's capacity to compete with emerging economies over the next five to ten years. It identified the capacity to link creativity and innovation through the effective deployment of design capabilities, combined with the promotion of greater innovation among Britain's small-to-medium enterprise (SME) sector, as the key supply-side challenges to the British economy as a whole. The 2008 DCMS policy paper, *Creative Britain: New Talents for the New Economy* (DCMS, 2008a) reinforced the proposition that 'The creative industries must move from the margins to the mainstream of economic and policy thinking, as we look to create the jobs of the future' (DCMS, 2008a: 6). It promoted a vision for Britain, backed by targeted policy initiatives, where 'in ten years' time … the local economies of our biggest cities are driven by creativity', and where 'the creative industries … have become central to our national identity and brand' (DCMS, 2008a: 6, 63). The 2009 *Digital Britain* report, jointly developed by the DCMS and the Department for Business, Innovation and Skills, had a similar refrain, proposing that policies to promote digital infrastructure could enable Britain to 'be a global centre for the creative industries in the digital age, delivering an ever wider range of quality content, including public service content, within a clear and fair legal framework' (DCMS/DBIS, 2009: 1).

Revising Creative Industries: NESTA and The Work Foundation

Having considered a number of the critiques of the list-based approach to creative industries first promulgated by the DCMS, I now want to appraise two reports developed for UK policy makers in the 2000s that sought to provide an alternative analytical framework for evaluating Britain's creative industries. The first was that of the National Endowment for Science, Technology and the Arts (NESTA) in its 2006 report *Creating Growth: How the UK Can Develop World Class Creative Businesses* (NESTA, 2006). The second was the 2007 report prepared by The Work Foundation, *Staying Ahead: The Economic Performance of the UK's Creative Industries* (Work Foundation, 2007). Both sought to develop a more nuanced and coherent approach to understanding creative industries as being multi-layered and internally differentiated. Of the two, it has been The Work Foundation's approach, based on what is known as the concentric circles model of the creative industries, and on a differentiation between cultural and creative industries in terms of their cultural inputs, which has been the more influential model, particularly in the uptake of the concept by the European Union (discussed in Chapter Two). My argument, however, is that The Work Foundation's concentric circles model presents a set of recurring problems for understanding these sectors, which tend to push the creative industries concept back towards being a form of *de facto* arts policy.

In its 2006 report *Creating Growth: How the UK Can Develop World Class Creative Businesses*, the National Endowment for Science, Technology and the Arts (NESTA) developed an approach to mapping the UK creative industries that both built upon the DCMS framework and modified it in significant ways (NESTA, 2006). Emphasising that its approach was economically based, and with a focus on the commercial growth potential of creative businesses and commercially focused innovation, NESTA found the DCMS approach to be insufficient in four ways:

1 It found the original 1998 definition to be too broad, and its inclusion of industries such as software and computer services had the effect of artificially inflating the overall figures.
2 Because it did not differentiate between the 13 industry sectors listed, it could not adequately identify those industries whose economic performance was most critical to growth, employment and exports.
3 The creative industries are defined primarily in terms of their outputs, and there is a lack of differentiation between industries in terms of their commercial value chains, market structures, distribution mechanisms and consumption patterns.
4 As a result, the DCMS model did not differentiate between those sectors whose dynamic is primarily commercial, and those whose outputs are partly or primarily generated through public subsidy.

NESTA instead proposed a model that differentiates the creative industries into four interlocking but nonetheless distinct groupings:

1 *Creative service providers*, who earn revenues for devoting time and applying intellectual property (IP) to other businesses and organisations. These include advertising agencies, design consultancies, architecture practices and new media agencies.
2 *Creative content producers*, who invest capital up-front to produce IP-protected outputs that are distributed to consumers/audiences, and who earn revenues through a mix of direct sales, advertising and subscriptions. Creative content enterprises include film, television and theatre production companies, computer and video game development studios, music labels, book and magazine publishers, and fashion designers.
3 *Creative experience providers*, who sell the right for consumers to experience specific activities, performances or locations in a particular time and place. This includes theatre, opera and dance production companies, and live music organisers and promoters, and can be extended to live spectator sports, festivals, cultural institutions and tourist promotions.

Refined model of the creative industries

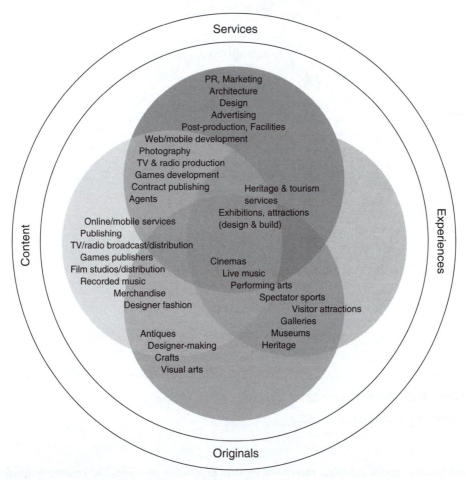

Figure 1.1 NESTA Model of Creative Sectors

Source: NESTA, 2006: 55.

4 *Creative originals producers*, who are involved in the creation, manufacture or sale of physical artefacts, whose value is derived from their perceived cultural or creative value, exclusivity and authenticity, i.e. they are typically one-offs or produced in limited production runs rather than mass produced. This includes much of the visual arts, crafts and designer-makers (e.g. of specialist clothing).

In developing this four-fold typology, it was argued that, from an economic perspective, there was more scope for growth and profitability to be derived from the creative content providers

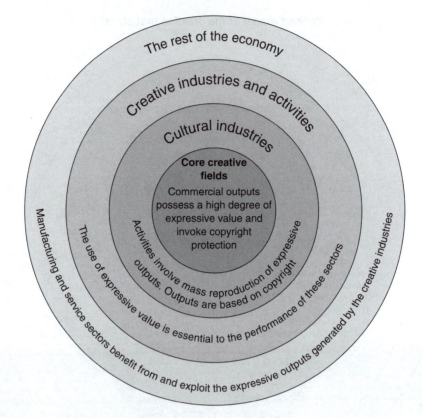

The rest of the economy

Creative industries and activities

Cultural industries

Core creative fields

Commercial outputs possess a high degree of expressive value and invoke copyright protection

Activities involve mass reproduction of expressive outputs. Outputs are based on copyright

The use of expressive value is essential to the performance of these sectors

Manufacturing and service sectors benefit from and exploit the expressive outputs generated by the creative industries

Figure 1.2   The Work Foundation 'Concentric Circles' Model

Source: Work Foundation, 2007: 103.

and creative service providers than from creative experience providers and creative originals producers. It was argued that this model focused on 'the creative industries as industrial sectors rather than as a set of creative activities based on individual talent' (NESTA, 2006: 54), and proposed two reasons for focusing upon creative content producers and creative service providers. First, these sectors – and particularly creative content producers – have a greater capacity to create, own and exploit intellectual property through the ability to distribute and reproduce content on a large scale. The Internet has opened up new platforms and channels for global distribution and export growth, while at the same time presenting new challenges for the ownership and control over IP. Second, there was seen to be stronger potential for employment growth, particularly in the creative service providing sectors, where increases in client demand are typically met by increases in the number of staff to service these clients. For these two reasons in particular, NESTA proposed that the model of the creative industries that they have developed 'better reflects the perspective of private investors' (NESTA, 2006: 55).

The Work Foundation, in its report *Staying Ahead: The Economic Performance of the UK's Creative Industries* (Work Foundation, 2007), identified a link between the rise of the creative industries, trends towards a knowledge economy, and demand trends where 'better educated and richer consumers [who are] looking for experience and psychological reward ... are co-architects of the knowledge economy' (Work Foundation, 2007: 126). In contrast to the NESTA approach, The Work Foundation chose to differentiate creative content, and the industries that produce and distribute it, on the basis of what it referred to as the *expressive value* of creative products and services. It differentiated between what it referred to as a creative core, of the cultural industries, and the creative industries, on the basis of the centrality of expressive value to the resulting outputs, producing what has come to be known as the *concentric circles* model of the creative industries.

Expressive value is defined as 'every dimension (in the realm of ideas) which, in its broadest sense, enlarges cultural meaning and understanding' (Work Foundation, 2007: 96). Derived from the work of cultural economist David Throsby (2001), it is seen as incorporating elements such as aesthetic value, spiritual value, social value, historical value, symbolic value and authenticity value. The term appears to function primarily to differentiate the creative and performing arts from the commercial media on the basis of greater aesthetic value and significance – Shakespeare's plays and Beethoven's Ninth Symphony are of greater cultural value and significance than reality TV and heavy metal music – and to justify public investment in the former and not the latter. If this were the case, it would look much like the familiar distinction between high culture and popular culture and how it has worked in arts policy to validate public subsidy of the former but not the latter (Frow, 1995; Bennett et al., 1999). At the same time, The Work Foundation disavows this distinction, arguing that:

> In the first decade of the 21st century, expressive value is no longer confined to traditional art forms. Expressive value (in the sense of symbolic value) is represented in software programs and video games such as the *Grand Theft Auto* and *Metal Gear* series where engrossing narratives combine with performance-driven play and increasingly naturalistic graphics. Expressive value (in the sense of social value) is represented in the range of interactive, user generated cultural material found on the internet (Work Foundation, 2007: 97).

On the basis of their different levels of expressive value, as compared to functional value, The Work Foundation differentiates between cultural industries, such as film, music, publishing, radio, television and computer games, and creative industries, such as advertising, architecture, design, fashion and computer software. While this distinction has been used in policy documents elsewhere, most notably those developed by the European Union, it is a difficult distinction to maintain, and the concept of expressive value itself does little to clarify the distinction.

The two reports were developed at a time when an inherent tension in the concept of creative industries was becoming apparent in Britain, as to whether it was primarily an economic policy associated with promoting generating successful industries and new forms of IP, or primarily a policy to support the arts and cultural sectors, particularly those reliant upon public sector funding. The NESTA report takes the former approach, although in doing so it can be accused of neglecting the economic significance of what it terms the creative experience sectors to the British economy. This seems reflective of a general problem in the British creative industries policy discourse of overestimating Britain's opportunities in the global digital content industries, and understating the value of events, heritage, cultural infrastructure and built environment, presumably because digital content was seen as representing modernisation whereas cultural heritage was reflective of Britain as an 'old country'. The Work Foundation's report was consistent with the directions for DCMS associated with ministers such as Tessa Jowell and policy documents such as the McMaster Report, that sought to reassert the centrality of the arts to creative industries, and public support for cultural excellence rather than being seen as a 'Ministry for Fun' or a department of applied cultural studies. In seeking to reconcile a very traditional conception of aesthetics as manifested in the concept of expressive value with recommendations about how to grow British creative industries, The Work Foundation presents a divide between cultural and creative industries that in practice always appears highly permeable. Locating the media industries here is particularly problematic, as the question of whether expressive value resides in media content would appear difficult to resolve in terms that are anything other than subjective. Does it reside in genre: in drama and documentary but not in soaps, chat shows or reality TV? Where does British comedy – definitely a successful British cultural export – sit within this schema? If there is expressive value in *Metal Gear*, then why not in *Top Gear*?

Creative Industries in Britain: From New Labour to the ConDems

The Labour government that was led by Gordon Brown from 2007 to 2010 was soundly defeated in the May 2010 General Election, with a 6 per cent swing against it. This marked the end of the 'New Labour' project as it was developed by Blair, Brown, Peter Mandelson and others over the period from the mid-1990s, although the Conservative Party, led by David Cameron, did not gain a majority in its own right, and entered into a coalition with the Liberal Democrats, headed by Nick Clegg. A key factor in the turn against Labour was the dramatic impact of the global financial crisis on the UK economy, with the collapse and subsequent nationalisation of the Northern Rock Bank and the Royal Bank of Scotland, resulting in Britain experiencing one of the more prolonged recessions of the OECD economies over 2008–2009, with ballooning level of public sector debt over this period. The extent of public sector debt meant that the new Conservative–Liberal Democrats government oversaw sharp reductions in the level of government expenditure, leading to cuts in cultural and creative industries spending, including the abolition of Regional Development Authorities and the UK Film Council, as well as a significant reductions in funding to the BBC.

The global financial crisis and the prolonged economic recession in Britain had a deeply pessimistic impact on many involved in the creative industries sectors. The mood was captured in a collection of essays titled *After the Crunch* (Wright et al., 2009), and by a sign outside a shop window in Hackney, East London, referred to at the beginning of the book, saying 'Sorry, we're f***ed'. The crisis also generated a backlash towards many aspects of the 'New Labour' years, ranging from the failure to more stringently regulate the big banks in the City of London, to the concept of creative industries itself, seen by critics as sacrificing the radical potential of art to the blandishments of commerce. This mood is captured by the arts columnist in the *New Statesman*, Alice O'Keeffe, who argued that the arts in Britain during this period were corrupted by money-worship or, as she put it, 'the champagne has flowed and the megabucks have changed hands in ever greater quantities. ... Art has always followed the money, and it was inevitable that hedge-funders, Premier League footballers and Russian oligarchs would want pictures for their penthouse walls'. She described New Labour's embrace of the creative industries as follows:

> I remember, in March 2007, going to see Tony Blair make a speech on the arts at Tate Modern, in which he boldly claimed to have presided over a cultural 'golden age'. The arts, he told the gathered great and good, were a vital component of Britain's continued economic success: 'A nation that cares about art will not just be a better nation. In the early 21st century, it will be a more successful one.' In new Labour parlance, the arts had become the 'creative industries'. Like bankers and stockbrokers, artists were expected to prop up the wobbly edifice of consumer capitalism, to generate profit, attract tourists, help Britain market itself as a cultural – and therefore financial – 'hub'. Placing culture firmly at the service of finance had its advantages for the arts administrators in the audience, too, as it gave them a clear claim on their slice of the government pie. (O'Keeffe, 2009)

O'Keeffe is here identifying the global financial crisis of 2008 and the subsequent job losses in the City of London and the fiscal crisis of the British state as marking the end of this wobbly alliance between the arts and the big end of town. Just as the boom saw art in her eyes being subordinated to the cocaine binges of millionaires grooving to superstar DJs – she quotes one attendee at the Venice Biennale as saying 'No-one comes to Venice for the art, darling' – O'Keeffe concluded by expressing the vague hope that 'the next few years of economic austerity will ring a creative renaissance' (O'Keeffe, 2009).

At one level, this captures the thinking of a strand of the British left that never bought into 'New Labour' ideology, and welcomed the exposure of its failings and its ultimate economic demise.[3] But it was also reflective of a wider cynicism about creative industries prevalent in Britain by the late 2000s, but also apparent elsewhere. In a review of a collection of essays on music titled *Sonic Synergies* (Bloustein et al., 2008), the Australian writer Graham Preston argued that 'with the onset of the global financial crisis in 2008 and its negative impact on creative industries, the material here on the Creative Knowledge Economy seems strangely optimistic and now part of a distinct historical moment which may have passed us by already' (Preston, 2009: 143). In academic journals such as the *International Journal of Cultural Policy*, it was argued that we were in a period 'after the creative industries' (Banks and O'Connor, 2009), and that 'after 10 years, the direction of UK creative industries policy is looking increasingly bleak' (Banks and Hesmondhalgh, 2009: 428).

What arises here is a vitally important question of the extent to which the creative industries can experience autonomous development – they have their own growth and innovation dynamics – or whether their development is inevitably dependent upon stimulus from elsewhere, be it the hyperactive London financial scene that O'Keeffe refers to, or government support and subsidy. If we take Alice O'Keeffe's comments first, it is apparent that she has taken a particular snapshot of a highly visible arts scene – the London visual arts world of the 2000s, with its superstars such as Damian Hirst and Tracey Emin – and transposed it onto British culture as a whole. Not only is this realm rather unique in its relationship between money and motivations (although of course symbolically significant for precisely that reason), but it is also very much a metropolitan perspective. While there is considerable evidence that London predominated in the British creative industries through the New Labour years since 1997 (De Propris et al., 2009), it would be expected that the dynamics of arts and cultural markets in the rest of Britain would be less tied to the rhythms of the financial hub of the City of London, and its associated hedge funders, cocaine dealers, Premier League footballers, pneumatic heiresses and Russian oligarchs. Andy Pratt's early analysis of the impact of the crisis on British cultural and creative industries indicated that they had been among the sectors coming out of the crisis reasonably early, due in part to major projects being fast-tracked as publicly-funded counter-cyclical measures (Pratt, 2009a). Such findings run counter to the assumption that British creative industries rise and sink with British finance capital, that culture is largely associated with consumption rather than production and employment, and that creative industries are not 'proper' industries but are rather reliant upon the surpluses produced elsewhere in the 'real' economy. For Pratt, the continued vitality of creative industries in the face of downturns elsewhere suggests that policy makers and analysts may still not have fully grasped how central the cultural dimensions of goods and services have become, so that '"culture" is not simply an added extra, or candy floss, [but] it is the main action, and as such cannot be removed from the product easily' (Pratt, 2009a: 496).

In the British case, the future of creative industries hinges to a significant degree on the view taken towards them by the Conservative–Liberal Democrat coalition. The language of creative industries was one that Conservatives were prepared to use when in opposition, albeit with a tendency to differentiate them from the arts. The Conservative Mayor of London, Boris Johnson, was keen to support industries such as fashion and games as vital elements of a diversified London economy, and expressed concerns about the impact of large cuts to arts spending. At the same time, the *Ingenious Britain* report prepared for the Conservatives by Sir James Dyson prior to the May 2010 election was a *cri de couer* for the importance of science and engineering to the British economy, warning that 'terms like "post-industrial" and "creative industries" … render invisible the significant contribution of science and engineering to the economy. They must go' (Dyson, 2010: 12). The new government's response to the Browne Review of Higher Education Funding (Browne, 2010), which proposed withdrawing all public grant funding for teaching in humanities, arts and social sciences (HASS) courses, while retaining some public support for science, technology, engineering and mathematics (STEM) courses, indicated a lack of support for creative industries arguments claiming to put the arts and the sciences on an equal footing in terms of their contributions to national well-being. Such policies indicated that the 2010s would be a tough decade for Britain's creative industries sectors.

Any sectors in Britain that are strongly reliant on public sector funding are hard hit by measures to reduce Britain's government deficit and public sector debt, so the 2010s are unlikely to be a flourishing era for many of these industries in Britain. More generally, it may be the case that we are seeing a 'Wimbledonisation' of the concept of creative industries. The term 'Wimbledonisation' refers to areas where Britain retains a strong symbolic association with the field, even where much of the ownership and the action has moved elsewhere (Fay, 1997; Peston, 2009). It was coined in relation to the British financial industry, to describe the role of British figureheads as the public face of banks that were now owned by foreign interests. Its origins lie with the annual spectacle of the Wimbledon tennis tournament, which remains the world's leading tennis event, even though British players rarely feature in the final rounds of the tournament (Andy Murray's recent success notwithstanding). It may well be that, like tennis, creative industries has its origins in Britain, but activity associated with it will increasingly shift elsewhere around the globe, even though Britain will retain some sense of ownership of the origins of the concept. To see whether this is what is happening, we need to consider the take-up of creative industries as a policy discourse elsewhere in the world.

Endnotes

1 'Britpop' was a term used to describe the rise of British bands such as Blur, Oasis, Pulp and The Verve in the mid 1990s. These bands were seen as being influenced by past British guitar-based bands such as The Kinks and The Beatles, and rose to prominence during roughly the same period as New Labour came to power. Tony Blair frequently sought to associate himself with Britpop, inviting Oasis guitarist Noel Gallagher to No. 10 Downing Street, and referring to his own past history in rock bands. An excellent account of the rise and fall of Britpop, and its curious relationship to New Labour, can be found in Harris (2004).

2 This problem becomes most apparent in Howkins' definition of a creative product as 'an economic good or service that results from creativity and has economic value' (Howkins, 2001: x), and his resulting definition of a creative industry as one 'where brain power is preponderant and where the outcome is intellectual property' (Howkins, 2005: 119). Howkins makes valid critiques of the DCMS approach to creative industries, such as the nonsensical consequences of including advertising in the creative industries sectors but excluding marketing (the former does not exist without the latter), and the tendency to define creative industries in opposition to manufacturing, and seeing the rise of the

former as evidence of the decline of the latter. At the same time, his approach leads to both inflated figures about the size of the creative economy and a loss of focus on the cultural dimensions of policy. The claim that the creative economy was worth $US2.2 trillion globally in 2000, or 7.3 per cent of global GDP, is made on the basis of including all scientific and technical research and development in the figure as well as all software development: these two sectors are estimated to be worth over $US1 trillion, and account for 46 per cent of the global creative economy as Howkins calculates it (Howkins, 2001: 116). At the same time, areas specifically related to the arts (art, crafts, music and performing arts) largely disappear from the calculus of the creative economy, being worth $139 billion or only 6 per cent of the global creative economy.

3   An admirably clear statement of such a position, published in the eve of the UK elections, can be found in Wood (2010), which is consistent with the position taken by *New Left Review* throughout the 'New Labour' era.

2 International Models of Creative Industries Policy

This chapter takes up some of the themes developed in the discussion of how creative industries policies developed in the United Kingdom, considering some implications of extending the analysis to other parts of the world. There are five cases considered: the European Union; North America; East Asia; Australia and New Zealand; and strategies for developing countries as proposed by UNESCO and UNCTAD. One clear theme that comes through from this comparative analysis is that a plurality of strategies have emerged under the general rubric of creative industries, so it is difficult – and becoming increasingly so – to speak of a singular creative industries policy template, such as that developed in the UK in the late 1990s. Another theme is that different regions have evolved different approaches to managing the interrelationship between component elements of the creative industries, such as the arts, media, digital content industries and cultural heritage. In very general terms, we can identify the following four models, whose features will be expanded upon in this chapter (cf. Cunningham, 2007, 2009):

- A United States model, where there is a substantive divide in thinking and calculation towards arts and culture on the one hand and the entertainment/copyright industries on the other, and where the bulk of policy initiatives are highly localised and sub-national in their focus, as seen with the rise of the 'creative cities' movement;
- A European model, which emphasises the cultural mission of these industries and strategies for social inclusion for common cultural benefit, and where terms such as 'cultural industries' or 'cultural and creative industries' are generally preferred;
- A diverse range of Asian approaches, which strongly emphasise the role of national socio-cultural and political circumstances, but still identify opportunities for export growth and successful branding of global city-regions in the highly competitive Asia-Pacific region, while at the same time challenging long-held orthodoxies about instrumentalist education and the dominance of the ICT sectors in driving economic growth;

- Developing country models in South America, South Africa, the Caribbean and elsewhere, where questions of cultural heritage maintenance, poverty alleviation and provision of basic infrastructure have precluded overly technocratic conceptions of creative industries being promoted uncritically as the inevitable fruits of the information society.

Finally, these generalised regional models need to be further interrogated to reveal variations that arise from forms of government as well as trajectories of institutional and policy formation. The models developed in Australia, for instance, are strongly influenced by the country's federalist political structure, while developments in the Scandinavian countries differ from those of the European Union models. In Asia, city-states such as Singapore and Hong Kong, with their historic affinities with British culture and ideas, developed policies along the lines of the UK DCMS model, whereas countries such as China, Taiwan and South Korea developed policy along very different paths. These variations can be expected to accentuate, not least because emergent economies such as China, India, Brazil and South Africa will take very different approaches to policy formation to the established post-industrial economies. To give one example, the focus on intellectual property found in the UK case can be expected to be significantly modified in these countries, where there has historically been a more critical relationship to the dominant international intellectual property regimes (Drahos and Braithwaite, 2002).

Europe/European Union

Europe provides an important site for understanding policy debates surrounding creative industries development.[1] Many of the European Union's established member states face comparable issues in their economic and cultural development to those facing Britain. Their strong economic foundations in manufacturing industries have been challenged since the 1970s as production has been moved to other parts of the world through the formation of global production networks, leading to de-industrialisation in particular cities, regions and nations, and rising unemployment in the EU as a whole. There is also the question of uneven development within the European Union, sharpened with the global financial crisis, which has exposed the highly indebted economies of Greece, Ireland, Portugal, Spain, and Italy, who have been forced to undertake major public sector spending cuts in order to secure the euro as a common currency in the eurozone region.

While there has been a decline in employment in traditional manufacturing industries, employment growth in the cultural sectors has been quite marked. The MKW study commissioned for the European Union estimated that annual employment growth in cultural occupations over the 1995–99 period was 4.8 per cent, which was four times the rate of average EU employment growth (MKW, 2001: 87). This study estimated that 4.6 per cent of the EU workforce was engaged in cultural employment in 1999, with the fastest rates of growth being in countries such as Finland, Denmark and Sweden, which were also among the fastest growing EU economies over this period. Moreover, this growing cultural workforce could be seen as being the harbinger of wider change in labour markets and employment relations in the EU since:

- The rate of self-employment of cultural workers in cultural industries (40.4%) was three times the average EU level of self-employment (14.4%);
- The percentage of cultural workers with a tertiary-level education (47.2%) was over twice the average for the EU workforce as a whole (22.5%);
- A comparatively high percentage of this workforce (14.2%) has temporary or contract jobs (MKW, 2001: 85–89).

There are significant definitional and policy dilemmas involved in developing an understanding of cultural or creative industries across the member states of the European Union. The MKW study noted that the adoption of the term 'creative industries' in the United Kingdom was seen as reflecting a historical 'hands-off' approach to relations between culture and the state, which differed from the more activist cultural policy traditions of Austria, France and the Scandinavian countries (MKW, 2001: 20–22; cf. Craik, 1996; Vestheim, 1996). The relationship between culture and industry is also a point of contention. It was noted that, 'in German, the connotations of the word Industries are restricted to mass, industrialised products and, subjectively at least, this was long regarded as almost the antithesis of culture' (MKW, 2001: 27). By contrast, Finland, as a small country, adopted a highly inclusive definition of cultural industries to include all sectors involved in symbolic production, which included sectors such as telecommunications and clothing as well as arts and media (MKW, 2001: 28). The European perspective on cultural sectors is also shaped by its positioning in regional and international politics.

The European Union's political project of unity in diversity among its member states predisposes it to favour an active role for nation-states in the maintenance of cultural and linguistic diversity, as a bulwark against tendencies arising from global cultural markets towards cultural homogenisation, the demise of minority cultures, and the dominance of a single language such as English. It has successfully applied these principles at the level of international law through support for a cultural exception to the application of the principles of the General Agreement on Trade in Services (GATS) to trade in cultural goods and services as well as support for the UNESCO Convention on Cultural Diversity; both of these imply an intrinsic dimension to culture that sets limits to its treatment as a commodity, and a resulting role for public policy in maintaining cultural diversity by setting limits to the operations of global cultural markets (Flew, 2007: 194–197). Finally, culture is seen as an element of European international diplomacy, being regarded as 'an "ambassador" and as a vehicle for European values (tolerance, democracy, diversity and pluralism, etc.) and its "way-of-life"' (KEA, 2006: 29). The European Parliament in 2006 called on the European Commission to 'clarify what constitutes the European vision of culture, creativity and innovation and to elaborate political measures … in order to develop European creative industries, incorporating these in a genuine European strategy for culture' (European Commission, 2010: 4). It is apparent in such a call that the idea that there is a distinctive 'European vision of culture' is as important as the more pragmatic strategies required to 'develop European creative industries'.

The Economy of Culture in Europe, a 2006 study commissioned by the EU and undertaken by KEA European Affairs, identified the cultural and creative sectors as contributing 2.6 per cent to the Gross Domestic Product (GDP) of the European Union in 2003 (KEA, 2006). According to the KEA study, these sectors experienced a rate of growth over 1999–2003 of 8.1 per cent, which was 12.3 per cent higher than that of EU economies as a whole. It observed that 4.7 million people worked in these sectors, or 2.5 per cent of the EU workforce, with an additional 1.17 million employed in cultural tourism. This study found that the contribution of the cultural and creative sector to GDP was largest in France (3.4%), Norway (3.2%), Denmark (3.1%), Finland (3.1%), the UK (3%), The Netherlands (2.7%) and Germany (2.5%), indicating a correlation between the size of the national economy and the contribution of these sectors. At the same time, it found the fastest rates of growth to be in the newest EU member states, most notably those of the former Soviet Bloc of Eastern Europe, such as Lithuania (67.8% growth between 1999 and 2003), the Czech Republic (56% growth from 1999 to 2003), and Romania (29% growth from 1999 to 2003). The KEA study confirmed the distinctive features of employment markets in the European creative economy, such as high levels of self-employment, university-level education, part-time work and people with more than one job (KEA, 2006: 73).

In developing this analysis, the KEA study adopted a model for understanding the sectors that was described in Chapter One as the 'concentric circles' model, developed by Throsby (2001, 2008b) and The Work Foundation (2007). This model places the arts at the centre on the basis of their original and copyrightable form, extending outwards to what are termed core cultural industries whose outputs are exclusively cultural, to the creative industries, classified as having a mix of creative and other inputs and whose outputs are not primarily cultural (e.g. design, architecture, advertising), and finally to related industries whose outputs are not cultural but which enable cultural consumption (e.g. personal computers, MP3 players, and mobile phones). This model includes video games, design, heritage, advertising and architecture in the cultural and creative sectors, but excludes sport, software and related manufactured goods sectors. Cultural tourism as a 'related' industry was included in employment data but not in data measuring the size of the cultural and creative industries sectors. This approach has been continued with the European Commission's Green Paper on Unlocking the Potential of the Cultural and Creative Industries (European Commission, 2010). It defined the cultural industries as 'those industries producing and distributing goods or services which at the time at which they are developed are considered to have a specific attribute, use or purpose which embodies or conveys cultural expressions, irrespective of the commercial value they may have', while the creative industries are defined as 'those industries which use culture as an input and have a cultural dimension, although their outputs are mainly functional' (European Commission, 2010: 5–6). It puts the arts, broadcast media, film, music, video games and publishing in the category of cultural industries, and advertising, design, architecture and fashion in the creative industries category.

Table 2.1 European Union Model of Cultural and Creative Industries

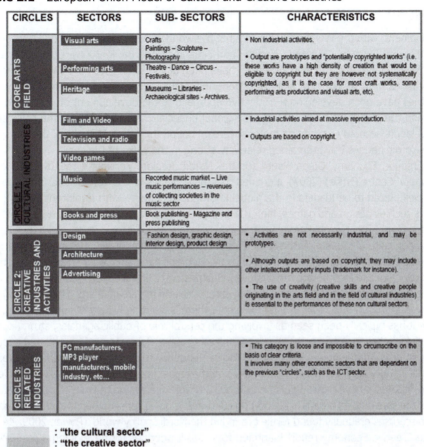

CIRCLES	SECTORS	SUB- SECTORS	CHARACTERISTICS
CORE ARTS FIELD	Visual arts	Crafts Paintings – Sculpture – Photography	• Non industrial activities.
	Performing arts	Theatre - Dance – Circus - Festivals.	• Output are prototypes and "potentially copyrighted works" (i.e. these works have a high density of creation that would be eligible to copyright but they are however not systematically copyrighted, as it is the case for most craft works, some performing arts productions and visual arts, etc).
	Heritage	Museums – Libraries - Archaeological sites - Archives.	
CIRCLE 1: CULTURAL INDUSTRIES	Film and Video		• Industrial activities aimed at massive reproduction.
	Television and radio		• Outputs are based on copyright.
	Video games		
	Music	Recorded music market – Live music performances – revenues of collecting societies in the music sector	
	Books and press	Book publishing - Magazine and press publishing	
CIRCLE 2: CREATIVE INDUSTRIES AND ACTIVITIES	Design	Fashion design, graphic design, interior design, product design	• Activities are not necessarily industrial, and may be prototypes.
	Architecture		• Although outputs are based on copyright, they may include other intellectual property inputs (trademark for instance).
	Advertising		• The use of creativity (creative skills and creative people originating in the arts field and in the field of cultural industries) is essential to the performances of these non cultural sectors.
CIRCLE 3: RELATED INDUSTRIES	PC manufacturers, MP3 player manufacturers, mobile industry, etc...		• This category is loose and impossible to circumscribe on the basis of clear criteria. It involves many other economic sectors that are dependent on the previous "circles", such as the ICT sector.

: "the cultural sector"
: "the creative sector"

Source: KEA, 2006: 3.

A Scandinavian Model?

The Scandinavian countries (Denmark, Norway, Sweden, Finland and Iceland) were leaders in the development of welfare state capitalism in the period since the 1940s, with a combination of economic planning that enabled restructuring in response to changing global markets, a strong focus on partnerships between employers and unions to work together, and a comprehensive welfare state based on high and redistributive taxation (Korpi, 1983; Esping-Andersen, 1990). In the 1990s and 2000s, these countries were world leaders in knowledge economy

(Continued)

(Continued)

development, with the World Bank finding that the world's four leading knowledge economies in 2007 were Sweden, Denmark, Norway and Finland (World Bank, 2008). Companies such as Nokia (Finland) and Ericsson (Sweden) have been at the forefront of the shift of telecommunications from service provision to content and design in the digital economy. The Nordic countries have been developing a distinctive approach to the development of creative industries and the creative economy. While the global financial crisis of 2008 saw the collapse of the Icelandic economy as the first major sovereign nation that was a casualty of the crisis, the other Nordic nations have remained relatively strong in the wake of the crisis.

A Creative Economy Green Paper for the Nordic Region, commissioned by the Nordic Innovation Centre (NICe) (2007), identified that the countries of the Nordic region were potentially well placed to be leaders in the global knowledge economy, with significant strengths in sectors such as design and games, high ICT uptake, a proven capacity to link new technologies to innovative content, highly proactive traditions of state support for culture, and a developing focus upon cultural tourism. At the same time, each individual country in the region is relatively small and distanced from global cultural hubs by geography and language. There has also been some reluctance to incorporate the creative industries into cultural policy, with a perceived tension in some countries between commercial enterprise and the creative arts. Power (2009) has observed that such talk arises in a region where there is a strong history of cultural policy, but where it has typically been seen as involving the central role of public agencies, strong corporatist links between public authorities and interest groups, elaborate welfare-oriented support systems for cultural workers, and 'an ideological tendency to stress egalitarianism as well as national identity agendas' (Power, 2009: 447). At the same time, Power also observed that 'economic discourses have had long historical roots in Nordic debates on the role of culture and the role of the state and its organs in supporting culture. It is not surprising then that creative industries discourses gradually found fertile ground in the Nordic policy world' (Power, 2009: 447).

The Creative Economy report identified four policy priorities for developing a pan-Nordic creative industries development strategy:

1 Entrepreneurship and creativity: moving the strong educational focus upon work-relevant skills to a greater emphasis upon creativity in learning environments, and upon the application of creativity into commercial business knowledge. The Creative Environments Studio in Malmö University (Sweden) is identified as one such site, with its focus on the interplay between interactive media technologies, space and activity, and how physical space and ubiquitous technologies can be used in new ways for multi-user and multi-site interaction (NICe, 2007: 29).
2 Growing creative businesses: shifting the focus of cultural funding from grants to seed-funding investment in new creative businesses, and aligning innovation policies more explicitly to the creative industries.
3 Building creative clusters: there are successful examples of sub-sector cluster development, such as the film cluster in Aarhus (Denmark) and the design cluster

in Göteborg (Sweden). At the same time, cluster development policies have often been overly prescriptive and presented themselves as a state-driven alternative to the market rather than growing organically. It also notes that these often pay too much attention to 'hygiene' factors (new buildings, co-location with university campuses, etc.), and neglect the 'messier' elements of a successful cluster.

4   Creative place making: again, this needs to be driven more by an emergent culture of a city/region rather than by top-down cultural planning focused upon economic and social futures 'desired' by policy makers. The southern city of Malmö in Sweden is important in this respect, as it has sought to turn from a declining industrial city to a post-industrial centre through greater economic integration with the Danish capital of Copenhagen after the completion of the Öresund Bridge in 2000 linked the two cities.

The terms experience economy and experience industries are sometimes also used, particularly in Sweden. Nielsén (2004) estimated that the experience industries accounted for 6.5 per cent of the Swedish labour market, including activities such as event tourism and industries such as the restaurant industry alongside what are elsewhere defined as the creative industries such as film and broadcasting, music, games and architecture. A study commissioned by the Nordic Innovation Centre identified significant spin-off benefits from event tourism that include promotion of a city's image and global 'brand', media coverage and possible future relocation for work by those who visit, alongside more direct benefits to employment, local businesses and urban infrastructure (NICe, 2006).

United States

The United States approach to creative industries has been marked by a notable bifurcation between publicly supported arts on the one hand, and the giant commercial entertainment and software industries on the other. The arts sector has taken up the concept of creative industries, with Americans for the Arts collecting data on businesses and employment in the arts sectors, finding that about 3 million people, or 2.2 per cent of the US workforce, were employed in arts-related activities in 2008 (Americans for the Arts, 2008). At the same time, the International Intellectual Property Alliance (IIPA) collects data on the US copyright industries (Siwek, 2006). The IIPA is an umbrella organisation representing US copyright interests, and acts on behalf of the Association of American Publishers (AAP), the Business Software Alliance (BSA), the Entertainment Software Association (ESA), the Independent Film and Television Alliance (IFTA), the Motion Picture Association of America (MEAA) and the Recording Industry Association of America (RIAA). The IIPA estimated that in 2002 the 'core' copyright industries, or those industries 'whose primary purpose is to produce and/or distribute copyright materials', account for 6 per cent of US GDP and 4 per cent of the US workforce, with 'related' or 'partial' copyright industries accounting for another 6 per cent of US GDP and 4.5 per cent of US employment (Siwek, 2006).

While there is some overlap in the datasets collected by Americans for the Arts and the IIPA, they do not cohere into an overall picture of the US creative industries. In contrast to other parts of the world, the momentum to develop a national creative industries policy for the United States is virtually non-existent. Miller and Yúdice have noted the 'great historical paradox of culture – that its principal exporter, the United States, claims to be free of any policy on the matter' (Miller and Yúdice, 2002: 35). US cultural policy settings are historically divided between a poorly funded and often politically beleaguered National Endowment for the Arts and an arts sector strongly reliant upon private philanthropy, and powerful commercial entertainment interests who can exercise influence through trade and foreign policy institutions and have typically seen themselves as having little connection to the subsidised arts sector. As a result, there is little capacity to translate creative industries analysis into policy action at the national level. This is despite some highly innovative work coming out of the USA on the relationship between cultural creativity and the domains of science and business, and how ICTs enable greater interaction between the arts, business and the sciences around new forms of creative practice (Mitchell et al., 2003).

If creative industries policy discourse has gained little traction at a national level in the USA, the picture is very different at the urban and regional level. Wyszomirski makes the point that the international size and significance of US entertainment industries can obscure the fact that 'another large and important segment [of the American creative economy] is composed of the subsidized and non-profit arts and cultural fields. The United States has a long tradition and exceptionally large set of civil society institutions in the arts and culture' (Wyszomirski, 2008: 200). The 1990s and 2000s saw a boom in the construction and expansion of cultural facilities in American cities, at a time when other sources of state and Federal level funding for the arts and culture were static or being actively cut back. In their survey of this switch towards what Schuster (2002) termed sub-national cultural policy, Grodach and Loukaitou-Sideris (2007) distinguished between two dominant approaches to US urban cultural policy. The first were entrepreneurial urban cultural policy strategies, focused on promoting tourism and new forms of city 'branding' through investment in flagship cultural projects and promotion of private sector investment in cultural infrastructure (cf. Harvey, 2008). The second were creative class strategies, which promote urban cultural and other forms of amenity and quality of life through the development of distinctive arts and entertainment districts (also termed quarters, precincts or clusters (Jayne and Bell, 2004; Roodhouse, 2006)), encouraging apparently footloose employees in the creative and knowledge economy sectors – the 'creative class' – to remain in or relocate to these 'creative cities'.

The publication of Richard Florida's *The Rise of the Creative Class* (Florida, 2002) was associated with a surge of creative cities/creative class urban strategies throughout North America and globally. Florida argued that while the nineteenth and early twentieth centuries were the heyday of industrial capitalism and the mid-late twentieth century was the high point of bureaucracy and managerial capitalism, the 21st century has seen the rise of the creative economy, and with it the creative class. Creativity is seen as the 'decisive source of competitive advantage' in 21st century global capitalism, yet it is a peculiar resource to deploy, since 'creativity has come to be the most prized commodity in our economy – and yet it is not a "commodity". Creativity comes from people. And while people can be hired and fired, their creative capacity cannot be bought and sold, or turned on and off at will'

(Florida, 2002: 5). With the growth of the creative economy comes the rise of the creative class, whose significance to the US economy may be as high as constituting 30 per cent of the total workforce and contributing 47 per cent of new wealth in the US economy. From an urban policy and cultural planning perspective, Florida's arguments about the power of place and its relationship to creativity and innovation in global knowledge-based economies were what proved most influential. Developing his concept of the 'Three T's' of technology, talent and tolerance, Florida argued that creative people are attracted to cities and regions that are culturally vibrant, have distinctive identities and provide a rich array of engaging experiences, and that 'regional economic growth is powered by creative people who prefer places that are diverse, tolerant, and open to new ideas. Diversity increases the odds that a place will attract different types of people with different skill sets and ideas' (Florida, 2002: 249). Florida used American cities such as San Francisco, Seattle, Portland, Boston and Austin as examples of 'second-tier' cities that leveraged their embedded reputations for diversity, tolerance and openness to become dynamic creative economy hubs.

The impact of Florida's creative class thesis on urban policy in the 2000s was substantial. Peck observed that 'in the field of urban policy, which has hardly been cluttered with new and innovative ideas lately, creativity strategies have quickly become the policies of choice, since they license both a discursively distinctive and an ostensibly deliverable development agenda' (Peck, 2005: 740). Florida's own energetic salesmanship for his ideas, combined with a lively and eminently readable account of the lifestyle and consumption preferences of the creative class, saw uptake of creative class strategies as a toolkit for urban revitalisation throughout North America, as seen with the proclamation in 2003 of the 'Memphis Manifesto' by mayors and city planners from 50 US cities, who dedicated themselves 'to helping communities real-ize the full potential of creative ideas' (quoted in Peck, 2005: 743). The creative cities agenda promoted a boom in public art, as forms of cultural infrastructure that were seen as vital to contributing to both place competitiveness and the attractiveness of cities to geographically mobile knowledge workers and the creative class, ranging from bicycle paths to officially defined 'gay districts', as well as the increasingly ubiquitous cultural precincts and quarters.

Due in part to Florida's own high-profile, media-friendly advocacy of his case, he has become a magnet for critics both from the political right – who attack his agenda as being anti-suburban and anti-family (Kotkin, 2006, 2007) – and those on the left, who argue that his agenda is about 'articulating neo-liberal economics with cool culture' (McGuigan, 2009b: 298). A compelling application of elements of Florida's work, and its intellectual precedessor in the urban sociology of Jane Jacobs (1961), is provided in Elizabeth Currid's *The Warhol Economy* (Currid, 2007). Currid attributes the centrality of New York City to both global culture and the global economy as arising from what she terms (after Andy Warhol) the 'Warhol economy', where 'people find success in creative industries by cast-ing a wide net through their networks of weak ties, and by being open to the structured randomness that such ties bring … By engaging their networks, creative people instigate the dynamics that propel their careers and bring them some measure of economic success' (Currid, 2007: 85–86). At the same time, while Currid's account of New York's creative economy is innovative, it is by no means news that New York has a high concentration of creative people and activities. On the more central policy question of whether cities can reinvigorate themselves and become economic powerhouses through investments to support cultural consumption by urban professionals, the evidence is a lot more mixed, and the picture is muddied significantly by a propensity to conflate evidence that city governments have adopted 'creative class' strategies with evidence that they have worked as a form of urban economic policy (Peck, 2005). Pratt (2009b) and Evans (2009) have questioned the focus in such accounts on cultural consumption rather than cultural production networks, arguing that consumption-led strategies for cultural development will always be dependent upon public subsidy of middle-class lifestyles, while Storper and Scott (2009) have criticised the neglect in what they term amenities-led models of urban development of endogenous growth factors that lead some cities to become creative hubs, and the difficulties of transferring these factors from one city to another. Finally, the focus on inner cities as hubs of creative talent in major cities neglects the extent to which a growing proportion of the creative workforce in major cities, like the workforce generally, are located in suburbs rather than inner cities (Collis et al., 2010). Even in the much-discussed case of New York, there has been an accelerated suburbanisation that will need different analytical tools for its relationship to creative industries to be properly understood (Hammett and Hammett, 2007).

East Asia

The circulation of creative industries policy discourse from Britain to the so-called 'Anglosphere' nations could have been anticipated based on prior policy experience (O'Regan, 1998), as could its (contested) uptake in Europe given the common questions facing EU nations about post-industrial economic futures and the scope for culture to provide a new catalyst for employment and economic growth. What has been notable and distinctive has been the uptake of creative industries as a nodal policy concept in East Asia, most notably in the fast-developing 'tiger' economies of Singapore, Hong Kong, Korea, Taiwan and, most recently, China. Gibson and Kong (2005) have observed how this take-up of creative economy strategies took root in urban centres such as Hong Kong, Seoul, Singapore and Taipei in the late 1990s and early 2000s, as it pointed to the intangible markers of place competitiveness in the global economy that enable some cities to become 'hot spots' for attracting an increasingly mobile 'creative class'. This 'normative creative economy script' proved attractive to policy makers in these cities, which had 'already established national broadcasting, arts and cultural industries, but [had] aspirations for "world city" status' (Gibson and Kong, 2005: 550). At the same time, it was apparent that, while governments and policy makers have been giving increasing attention to the creative economy as a new economic growth engine, 'geographies of knowledge on cultural economy are still highly skewed towards Europe and North America' (Gibson and Kong, 2005: 550). Kong et al. (2006) observed that the take-up of this discourse by Asian commentators, academics and policy makers thus involved complex processes of diffusion and translation, with pathways of innovation, adaptation and mutation of these policy 'scripts' to adjust to local circumstances needing to be monitored carefully, as well as non-adoption and non-diffusion of these concepts in particular national and metropolitan contexts, with countries such as Japan and India being less inclined to take up the policy concept.

The general context for the uptake of creative industries in East Asia has been the rapid economic growth, urbanisation and social transformations that have occurred in key urban centres since the 1980s. World Bank economists Yusuf and Nabeshima (2005) identified these enabling factors as including:

1 Rural–urban migration and the declining significance of agriculture as the principal determinant of export performance;
2 The dominance of service industries and activities in urban centres;
3 Expansion of high-value-added business services and ICT-intensive industries as the most dynamic sector of urban economies;
4 Changes in consumption patterns towards higher-value-added goods and services that reduce the need for proximity of urban centres to natural resources;
5 The growing importance attached to product and process innovation as drivers of competitiveness and export growth;
6 The correlation between levels of national innovation and the existence of dynamic knowledge clusters characterised by a skilled workforce, research investment and sophisticated educational and ICT infrastructures;
7 Changes in legal, regulatory and institutional frameworks that promote greater competition, trade and export orientation.

Two further driving factors can be added to this list. The first relates to the cumulative impact on policy thinking of the Asian financial crisis of 1997–98 and the dot.com meltdown of 2001. Both revealed limits to export-led development through state *dirigisme*, by revealing weaknesses in the institutional foundations of Asian state capitalism, as well as the increasingly generic nature of ICTs and the limits of technological 'leapfrogging' of the Western capitalist economies. Both crises pointed to the need for greater attention to be paid to the development of creative human capital and domestic markets. The second factor has been the rise of China as an economic competitor as well as a potential new market. The combination of high technology and low real wages that has made the 'China price' such a challenge for manufacturers in Europe and North America also resonates in the East Asia region, creating the phenomenon of 'co-opetition' between China and its East Asian neighbours: China offers both the largest regional market for goods and services exports as well as highly competitive sites to relocate production, but its businesses compete in the same markets as the East Asian economies (on 'co-opetition', see Progressive Policy Institute, 2002).

Singapore adopted a creative industries strategy in the early 2000s, with the development of a 'Renaissance City' strategy for arts and culture (Kong et al., 2006); the preparation of a Creative Industries Development Strategy in 2002 (Ministry of Trade and Industry, 2003); the creation in 2003 of a Media Development Authority under the 'Media 21' programme (Leo and Lee, 2004: 207); and development of the Design Singapore strategy. The economic contribution of creative industries to the Singapore economy was estimated at between 2.8 per cent and 3.2 per cent of GDP in 2000, and their rates of growth were 70 per cent higher than those for the Singapore economy as a whole over 1990–1999 (Ministry of Trade and Industry, 2003). The Creative Industries Singapore strategy, announced by the Ministry for Information, Communication and the Arts, declared its intention 'to develop Singapore into a New Asia Creative Hub' and double the Creative Industries' contribution to 6 per cent of GDP by 2012. Kong et al. (2006) argued that while Singapore has been an exemplar in adopting and adapting 'Western' discourses of the creative economy and creative industries, it nonetheless links them to a distinctive nation-building project. Leo and Lee (2004) also observed that a strategy to develop the creative industries in Singapore was linked to a wider, and potentially more politically contentious, question of whether political authority can be decentralised and state controls over cultural and media content loosened in order to develop individual creativity and promote Singapore as a creative cluster.

Hong Kong has long been a leader in creative cultural production in Asia, particularly in its film and television industries (Donald and Gammack, 2007). With the handover of sovereignty to China in 1997, and the increasing economic integration of Hong Kong with the Chinese mainland, there has been a push to develop creative industries in Hong Kong, partly to renew some of the economic vigour lost after the handover, but also as something of a 'test-bed' for the adoption of such policies in China (Wang, 2004). Adopting the UK framework with some modifications, the Baseline Study identified creative industries as contributing 3.8 per cent of GDP in 2000, although this figure includes distribution and marketing as well as content creation and production inputs (Hong Kong Centre for Cultural Policy Research (HK CCPR), 2003). It identified a downturn in key sectors between 1996 and 2001, such as film and advertising, which reflected problems arising from the transition to Chinese sovereignty and the development of the Hong Kong Special Administrative Region (HK SAR). Hong Kong researchers have also sought to advance comparative studies of the creative industries and creative clusters by developing metrics to measure creativity in different locations.

Taiwan refers to cultural creative industries and has been particularly focused upon developing its digital content industries, identifying an area of potential strength that matches its advances in the ICT sectors (Tsai et al., 2008). The Taiwanese government developed its 'Two Trillion and Twin Star' programme in the mid-2000s that aimed to promote Taiwan's semiconductor and flat-panel display industries on the one hand, and its digital content industries on the other. It needs to be particularly alert to the dilemmas arising from co-opetition with the People's Republic of China, as China dominated export markets for Taiwanese cultural and creative industries products, and competes in the same markets as Taiwan (e.g. the video games markets); and also, while the political relations between the two states are better than was the case in the mid-2000s, they remain potentially fraught.

Korea (South Korea) is arguably the Asian country that has most successfully developed its creative industries in recent years, but it neither uses the term nor has developed a strong set of policies to develop these industries. What is known as the 'Korean Wave' (*hallyu*) emerged somewhat by accident, arising out of a mix of media liberalisation policies pursued in the 1990s, the need for Korean cinema to become more oriented towards mass audiences after political pressures to remove controls over the distribution of US audiovisual product, and strong policies to develop Korea as an information society and knowledge economy, characterised by levels of Internet uptake and high-speed broadband connectivity that are among the highest in the world (Choi, 2008). Shim (2008) has referred to the 'Jurassic Park factor' as a major catalyst for rethinking Korean economic development strategies in the 1990s, as it was pointed out that the total revenues of the Hollywood movie Jurassic Park were equal to those of 1.5 million foreign sales of Hyundai cars, thereby challenging the orthodoxy that Korea's economic prosperity was only tied to industries such as automobiles, shipping and consumer electronics. Korea has experienced a surge in its exports of films, television program, video games and other forms of digital content over the 1990s and 2000s, and Korean cultural products have come to occupy a central place in East Asian popular culture (Beng Huat and Iwabuchi, 2008). Shim has observed that 'the much feared takeover of Korean culture by foreign images brought by imported media was not realized' (Shim, 2008: 31); instead, Korean creative product has acquired unprecedented levels of recognition and impact in the Asian region and around the world.

East Asian Economic Development: Flying Geese or Fighting Tigers?

The economic transformation of East Asia since the 1970s, which the World Bank has referred to as the East Asian Renaissance (Gill and Kharas, 2007), has perhaps been the most significant global transformation of our times. The region has experienced average annual GDP growth of 5.8 per cent from 1966 to 2004, compared to an OECD average of 2.5 per cent, and 7.7 per cent average annual growth since 1980 (Gill and Kharas, 2007: 49–50). This economic growth saw the number of people earning below $US2 a day falling by 500 million between 1980 and 2004, although about 500 million remain below this poverty line. Korea, Singapore and Hong Kong SAR have joined Japan as high-income economies; Malaysia has become a higher-middle-income economy; and China has become a lower-middle-income economy, likely to be joined in the near future by Vietnam. The economic historian Angus Maddison has observed that while East Asia's share of world GDP was 15 per cent in 1950, it was 33 per cent in 2003, and expected to reach 42 per cent by 2025, the level that it was at in 1820 (quoted in Gill and Kharas, 2007: 49).

According to the World Bank, East Asia has now acquired the dynamics of a middle-income region. It is argued that middle-income economies face unique challenges, as competitiveness based upon low real wages becomes less of an option, but they lack the capacity for innovation that typically characterises high-wage economies. The World Bank proposes that middle-income economies need to make three policy commitments:

1   Greater specialisation in goods and services produced, and increased orientation towards export markets in order to realise scale economies and the benefits of agglomeration or clustering;

(Continued)

(Continued)

Table 2.2 Share of World GDP by Region, 1980–2004

Region	1980–84	1985–83	1990–94	1995–99	2000–04
East Asia and Pacific	7.2	7.8	9.4	6.8	7.2
Latin America and the Caribbean	1.4	2.2	3.6	2.4	2.2
Europe and Central Asia	—	—	−5.2	2.0	5.2
Middle East and North Africa	3.8	1.2	4.6	3.4	4.4
South Asia	5.4	6.0	5.0	5.8	5.6
Sub-Saharan Africa	1.6	2.4	0.6	3.6	3.4

Source: Gill and Kharas, 2007: 49.

2 Promotion of innovation rather than simply new investment as the primary driver of growth, which is associated with a greater attention to quality and commitment to more competitive markets (e.g. lower barriers to entry for new competitors while allowing less competitive enterprises to fail);

3 A renewed focus on tertiary education to promote skills, innovation and the quality of human capital, as basic education and literacy requirements are increasingly met.

The World Bank study observed that the proportion of trade that East Asian economies do within the region continues to grow, reflecting both rising average consumer incomes within the region and the rise of more complex global production networks within the region (as seen in the growth of intra-industry trade). The growth of China has been a critical driver of regional integration since, in addition to the sheer size of its population and economy (and, with rapid economic growth, the spending power of it consumers), it is also a distinctly open economy, with an imports-to-GDP ratio of 34 per cent (three times that of Japan and the United States), and with over 50 per cent of its exports being sourced through multinational corporations (Gill and Kharas, 2007: 6, 87).

Yeung and Lin (2003) have argued that two distinctive contributions of the East Asian experience to global economic geography have been theories of developmental states and the '"flying geese" hypothesis'. Developmental statist theories hold that a distinctive feature of East Asian growth models has been the central role played by the state in economic co-ordination and the alignment of corporate strategies to national development priorities, and this has been as true of states that have democratic elections, such as Japan, Korea and Singapore, as it has been of one-party states such as China (Amsden, 1989; Weiss, 1997, 2003). The '"flying geese" hypothesis' argues that late developers in the global economy learn from the successes and failures of those who have already advanced, and engage in a process of partial institutional emulation, or 'free-riding' on the success of others (Ozawa et al. 2001). The source country for this hypothesis was Japan, which based its industrial development strategy on lessons learnt from Britain, Germany and the United States. In turn, Korea has been able to learn from the successes of Japan from the 1950s to the 1980s in its economic advancement in the 1990s and 2000s, particularly around questions of production quality, global branding, and an emphasis on research and development and the skills of its workforce. It is argued that China can accelerate its economic advancement by learning from Japan, Korea and other 'tiger' economies such as Taiwan and Singapore, as these countries provide more culturally proximate and histori-cally relevant examples than growth models derived from US-led global institutions such as the World Bank.

Hart-Landsberg and Burkett (1998, 2003) argued that the '"flying geese" hypothesis' and other models of 'catch-up' underestimate the extent to which the global economy is based on aggressive competition between nation-states for geographically mobile capital, so that the successes of one national economy may come at the expense of others. In particular, they argue that countries such as Thailand, Malaysia, Indonesia and the Philippines are squeezed by the rise of China, which sets limits to their ability to move from cost-driven growth to models based on specialisation and innovation; this is accentuated by potential protectionist reactions from North America or Europe to their loss of relative economic sta-tus and power. The World Bank itself acknowledges that, even when economic transition to middle-income status occurs, the East Asian growth model generates particular tensions, although it views them as questions of national governance rather than contradiction of global capitalism. These tensions arise from:

1 The rapid growth of cities, as agglomeration and scale economies increase the pro-pensity both of businesses to invest in cities and of people to move from the country-side to the major cities. In the absence of careful management of urban growth, this can lead to greater congestion, rising housing costs, the growth of slum areas, crime and environmental degradation, and a declining urban quality of life.
2 Growing inequalities, particularly urban–rural inequality and inequalities within cities, with a rising income and wealth gap between an emergent middle class, and the majority of the population that remains in low-wage jobs, in the informal economy, or unemployed or underemployed.
3 The potential for corruption, as the 'developmental state' model sees insufficient separation between government and business, and the existence of economic rents which are based on personal connections rather than business performance. Ozawa et al. (2001) argued that the Asian economic crisis of the late 1990s arose in part from institutional rigidities associated with the developmental state model (e.g. misalloca-tion of credit), and that the need for a more innovation-driven economy would require a move away from 'governing the market' and changes towards more market-oriented institutional and policy settings.

China

The 1949 Revolution in China saw cultural and media institutions placed under the control of the state, where their role was a largely political one of providing 'positive' images to the population in order to build 'socialist civilisation', while at the same time 'protecting' the masses from messages that were deemed to be negative or contrary to the goals of the Chinese Communist Party as the representative of the masses. The politicisation of culture in China reached a disastrous nadir with the Great Proletarian Cultural Revolution (1966–76), but the programme of 'reform and opening up' initiated by Deng Xiaoping after 1978 sought to undo the excesses of the Mao years while simultaneously promoting the development of a market economy and an opening up to international trade and investment. The 1980s and 1990s saw rapid growth in commercial popular culture and a greater orientation on the part of state cultural and media institutions towards the market, although this also involved a shifting set of state regulations and controls that sought to differentiate 'entertainment' from 'culture', and a 'separation … within the cultural industries in terms of what ought to be state-owned and what could involve the private sector' (O'Connor and Gu, 2006: 276), which was always linked to the question of what forms of content were deemed to be politically sensitive and which were deemed to be 'safe' (Wang, 1996; Keane, 2007).

A cultural industries (*wenhua chanye*) development strategy was formalised in 2001 as part of the recommendations of the Tenth Five-Year Plan (Wang, 2004). Cultural institutions were increasingly expected to operate on a commercial or enterprise (*qiye*) basis, media industries were partially opened up to foreign investment, and a series of 'Blue Books' were commissioned to measure the size and growth of the various cultural industries (Zhang, 2008). 2001 was also the year in which China finally became a member of the World Trade Organization, and WTO accession placed a renewed focus upon innovation (*chuangxin*). The impact of entry into the WTO was seen by some – including senior government officials – as akin to that of a 'wrecking ball', unleashing a Schumpeterian wave of 'creative destruction' that would force Chinese industry on to a new plane of international competitiveness, while destroying those institutional forms unable to adapt to the realities of a global market economy (Hu, 2002; Jin, 2002).

Creative industries emerged as a policy concept in 2004, gaining particular momentum in the major Eastern cities such as Beijing, Shanghai, Shenzhen and Guangzhao. A series of developments were promoting greater interest in creativity as a 'super-sign' able to address issues as diverse as wealth creation, productivity improvements, environmental improvements, educational reform, and the renewal of traditional cultural resources (Keane, 2007: 128–129). The Hong Kong Baseline Study on the Creative Industries (HK CCPR, 2003) had attracted considerable attention, and discussions were commencing about how to move from a 'Made in China' economic base, centred on low-cost, high-volume manufacturing, to a 'Created in China' paradigm, emphasising innovation, new ideas and concepts, intellectual property, and higher quality goods and services. The creative industries model presented challenges to adapt to a Chinese context. Jing Wang argued that 'the thorniest question triggered by the paradigm of creative industries is that of "creativity" … How do we begin to envision a parallel discussion of something like creative industries in a country where creative imagination and content are subjugated to active state surveillance?' (Wang, 2004: 13). At the same time, macro-trends both in China and in the global economy more generally were promoting new thinking about the relationship between innovation and creativity. Professor Zhang Xiaoming from the Chinese Academy of Social Sciences (CASS) argued that '"innovation" and "creativity" are two concepts closely related to each other. The increasing confluence of information and cultural industries has led to overlapping policies between a national innovation system and the cultural industries, which result in policy-makers in other fields actively adopting the term of "creative industries"' (Zhang, 2008: 191). In 2005, the concept of 'cultural creative industries' (*wenhua chuangyi chanye*) had gained acceptance and, by the end of 2006, creative industries or cultural creative industries strategies were a part of the draft Eleventh Five Year Plans for the cities of Beijing, Shanghai, Chongqing, Nanjing, Shenzhen, Qingdao and Tianjin (Keane, 2007: 136; cf. Hui, 2006, on strategy for the Chaoyang district in Beijing). Speaking to the International Conference on Creative Industries and Innovation held in Beijing in 2005, the Vice-Minister for Education, Wu Qidi, observed that:

> In the era of the knowledge economy, the rate of growth of creative industries already constitutes a breakthrough industrial trend in many developed nations and regions. These nations and regions have made creative industries an important industrial strategy by actively fostering and promoting policies. Nations and cities have raised their core competitiveness. ... The momentum for the development of China's creative industries primarily comes from two directions. First, as society develops, people's spiritual needs are growing and there is a demand for constant renewal of knowledge and ideas. Creative goods and services are able to satisfy such needs. Second, economic globalization means that China's industries are both directly and indirectly drawn into intense global competition. In order to increase international competitiveness and bring about a continuous development strategy, China should re-adjust the national industrial structure and raise industrial levels. Creative industries play a key role in enhancing China's core competitiveness and raising the added value of products and services. (Wu, 2006: 263–264)

Whether China will be able to develop its creative industries in the way that it has developed its industrial sector since 1978 is one of the most interesting questions of our times. The rise of creative industries as a policy discourse points to some tensions in China's economic, political and cultural development. It would seem to point in the direction of liberalisation of the media industries, relaxation of Internet censorship, and the broader tolerance of a culture of questioning and public dissent beyond what have been deemed to be acceptable limits by the Chinese Communist Party-state thus far. It also raises the question of whether China's creative content producers can generate products and brands that are competitive in global markets, given both the history of state control over culture and its comparatively small middle class, who are seen as the drivers of innovation in creative content (Wang, 2008). The rhetorical appeal of the creative industries as harbingers of cultural modernisation raises critical questions about the next wave of development in China, as it seeks to move from being the 'workshop of the world' to being a global leader in the knowledge and creative economies:

> This latest wave of modernization thus again poses problems; no longer a question of how to manage the rapid industrialization of a peasant society, it is now about promoting human creativity. In particular, it involves promoting a new economic sector that more than any other draws precisely on the discourse of cultural modernization itself and demands a whole series of economic, legal and social-urbanistic structures within which it can thrive. (O'Connor and Gu, 2006: 274)

This discussion calls to light a longstanding debate about whether China needs to divest itself of the institutional and ideological apparatus of the Communist Party-state in order to develop its economy beyond its current stage of growth. Will Hutton (2006) has argued that the contradictions of Chinese authoritarian state capitalism are growing, and what is needed is transition towards what he refers to as an 'Enlightenment infrastructure' in order to properly develop capitalism. This means a greater focus upon the rule of law, independence of media and cultural institutions, and greater economic and political pluralism. The response of economist Meghnad Desai to Hutton's argument that there is one 'true' capitalism based on individualism, liberty and pluralism that China needs to adopt, is to make the point that 'capitalism ... has accommodated a variety of institutional arrangements and only in the most recent phase of globalization have we thought that an Anglo-Saxon style liberal democracy is its *sine qua non*' (Hutton and Desai, 2007). While the alignment of a capitalist market economy and Marxism-Leninism is certainly an unprecedented hybrid, the history of China since 1978 suggests caution about any simple equation between capitalist economies and Western political and legal institutions, or the institutional pre-conditions for the development of creative industries.

Australia and New Zealand

Both Australia and New Zealand took up the creative industries policy agenda soon after it was put forward in the United Kingdom, although they did so in significantly different ways. Indeed, some authors have identified the *Creative Nation* national cultural policy statement developed by the Keating Labor government in Australia in the early 1990s as providing a precursor for the UK creative industries model (Stevenson, 2000; Howkins, 2001). In Australia, the cultural policy agenda that was developed under Labor was largely shelved by the conservative parties when they gained power in 1996, but creative industries policies were adopted by Labor state governments, most notably in Queensland. In New Zealand, creative industries were promoted through the Growth and Innovation Framework announced in 2002 by the Labour government headed by Helen Clark, with creative industries identified as one of the three focal sectors of its growth and innovation strategy, alongside biotechnology and information and communications technologies (New Zealand Ministry for Economic Development (NZ MED), 2003).

The Keating Labor government's *Creative Nation: Commonwealth Cultural Policy*, released in 1994 (Department of Communications and the Arts (DoCA), 1994), made a significant contribution to the understanding of cultural sectors as generators of economic wealth, as well as the integration of arts and culture into wider policy debates. It emphasised the nation-building dimensions of a national cultural policy and the relationship of culture to citizenship, arguing that 'Culture ... concerns identity – the identity of the nation, communities, and individuals ... the ownership of a heritage and identity, and the means of self-expression and creativity, are essential human needs and essential to the needs of society' (DoCA, 1994: 5). At the same time, it made a strong case for the economic utility of cultural policy, particularly in a globalising, post-industrial economy:

> This cultural policy is also an economic policy. Culture creates wealth ... [and] adds value, it makes an essential contribution to innovation, marketing and design. It is a badge of our industry. The level of our creativity substantially determines our ability to adapt to new economic imperatives. It is a valuable export in itself and an essential accompaniment to the export of other commodities. It attracts tourism and students. It is essential to our economic success. (DoCA, 1994: 7)

Stevenson (2000) and Craik (2007) observe that the momentum of cultural policy in Australia was reversed under the Liberal-National Party government headed by John Howard, which governed from 1996 to 2007. In the 2000s, the dynamic of creative industries policy development in Australia was with state and local governments rather than the national government. The state of Queensland was a leader in this respect, with creative industries identified as a central plank of a 'Smart State' agenda, promoting value-adding knowledge-intensive industries as a way of leavening the state's historic reliance upon agriculture, mining and tourism as the foundations of economic growth. A report by the Department for State Development and Industry, entitled Creativity is Big Business (DSDI, 2003), sought to identify strategies to develop globally competitive creative industries in Queensland. It developed a six-fold typology of the creative industries in the state:

- Advertising, Graphic Design and Marketing;
- Architecture, Visual Arts and Design;
- Film, Television and Entertainment Software;
- Music Composition and Publishing;
- Performing Arts;
- Writing, Publishing and Print Media.

Interestingly, this study found that Writing, Publishing and Print Media was the largest creative industries sector in Queensland. This was despite the bulk of public policy being directed either towards encouraging 'offshore' film and television production by foreign investors (on 'offshore' film and TV production, see Miller et al., 2001; Flew, 2007), or on events and festivals that promote the creative and performing arts. It also identified problems in getting growth in the creative industries outside the affluent metropolitan region of South-East Queensland, incorporating Brisbane, the Gold Coast and the Sunshine Coast.

New Zealand enthusiastically adopted creative industries strategies in the early 2000s. The 2001 Growth and Innovation Framework, the centrepiece of economic strategy for the second term of Helen Clark's Labour government, identified creative industries alongside biotechnology and information and communications technologies as one of the three focal sectors that New Zealand would need to develop as part of promoting a 'growth culture' in the global knowledge economy, and creative industries were identified as contributing 3.1 per cent of New Zealand's GDP in 2001 (New Zealand Institute for Economic Research (NZIER), 2002; NZ MED, 2003). The centrepiece of New Zealand creative industries as a growth sector in the 2000s has been screen production. The phenomenal success of the *Lord of the Rings* trilogy, produced in New Zealand by NZ director Peter Jackson, has acted as a major catalyst for high-budget Hollywood films to be partly or wholly produced in New Zealand, including *King Kong*, *The Chronicles of Narnia: The Lion, the Witch and the Wardrobe*, *The World's Fastest Indian* and *The Last Samurai*. In addition, television series such as *Hercules* and *Xena: Warrior Princess* were produced in New Zealand. The impact of such productions, and particularly the impact of *Lord of the Rings*, was seen in New Zealand screen production investment trends between 1994 and 2005, where the value of screen productions trebled, from $NZ151 million in 1994 to $NZ572 million in 2001. At the same time, the resultant volatility arising from reliance upon foreign investment was seen in screen investment falling back to $NZ250 million in 2004 as the 'Lord of the Rings effect' worked its way out of the production system (Screen Production and Development Association (SPADA), 2004). More recently, major rallies took place in Wellington around concerns that production of *The Hobbit*, being produced by Jackson, would relocate out of New Zealand due to industrial concerns.

Creative Industries in Developing Countries: UNESCO and UNCTAD Perspectives

The United Nations has been playing an increasingly significant role in creative industries policy development at an international level, particularly through the United Nations Educational, Scientific and Cultural Organisation (UNESCO) and the United Nations Commission on Trade, Aid and Development (UNCTAD). UNESCO has had a remit in questions of cultural development and trade since the UN's inception in 1946, with its remit being 'to advance, through the educational and scientific and cultural relations of the peoples of the world, the objectives of international peace and of the common welfare of mankind' (UNESCO, 2004: 5). From the 1970s onwards, UNESCO more explicitly linked culture to development, particularly in the debates about inequalities in global communication that were linked to the New World Information and Communication Order (NWICO) proposals of the 1970s, and associated demands for cultural policy to be linked to 'endogenous development' pathways for developing newly independent nations that would promote political independence and economic empowerment (UNESCO, 2004; cf. Mattelart, 1994; Roach, 1997; Flew, 2007).

In recent years, UNESCO has promoted the principle of cultural diversity, through preserving diversity between nations through a Convention on Cultural Diversity, providing a legally binding instrument giving signatory states the option of taking measures to protect and enhance cultural diversity, while at the same time recognising and promoting cultural diversity within nations (e.g. recognising the cultural rights of indigenous or minority populations). In 2005, 146 member states endorsed the United Nations Convention on the Protection and Promotion of the Diversity of Cultural Expressions (UNESCO, 2005), which affirms the sovereign right of signatory nations to 'formulate and implement their cultural policies and to adopt measures to protect and promote the diversity of cultural expressions and to strengthen international co-operation to achieve the purposes of this Convention' (UNESCO, 2005: Article 5).

In 2009, UNESCO published its updated Framework for Cultural Statistics (UNESCO, 2009). This was the first major update of the Framework since it was first developed in 1986, and it aims to 'enable the measurement of a wide range of cultural expressions irrespective of the particular economic and social mode of its production', and to 'allow for the production of internationally comparable data' (UNESCO, 2009: 9). The full detail of the UNESCO Framework is outlined in Chapter Four, but it aims to respond to a variety of developments since 1986 that include: the growing importance attached to the contribution of culture to economic and social development; the convergence of previously discrete sectors associated with digital technologies; the impact of globalisation and the dramatic growth in international cultural trade; the importance attached to cultural policy from the framework of industry and economic development; and the need for more accurate mapping of the cultural sectors and their interrelationships. UNESCO has preferred to refer to the cultural industries rather than the creative industries, although it has begun to refer to both the cultural and creative industries. UNESCO has defined the cultural industries as 'industries which combine the creation, production and commercialization of creative contents which are intangible and cultural in nature', and 'generally include printing, publishing and multimedia, audiovisual, phonographic and cinematographic productions as well as crafts and design' (UNESCO, 2006). The creative industries include the cultural industries as well as 'those [industries] in which the product or service contains a substantial element of artistic or creative endeavour and include activities such as architecture and advertising' (UNESCO, 2006).

Figure 2.1 shows the extent to which exports of cultural goods grew over the period from 1994 to 2002, with the most rapid rates of growth being in low-income and middle-income countries. At the same time, Figure 2.2 shows that while the trade position of middle-income countries improved over the 1994–2002 period, while that of high-income countries deteriorated in relevant terms, this is counter-balanced by a significant deterioration in the cultural trade balance of low-income countries.

While UNESCO has been concerned with questions of access, development and inequality in the cultural sector, UNCTAD has more explicitly championed the role of creative industries as a new engine of economic growth in developing countries. The High-Level Panel on Creative Industries convened by UNESCO in São Paulo, Brazil in 2004 observed that:

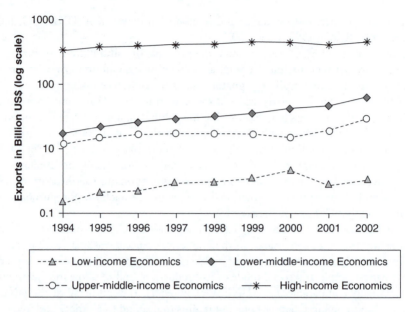

Figure 2.1   Total Export Value of Core Cultural Products, 1994–2002

Source: UNESCO, 2006.

Creative cultural assets and rich cultural resources found in abundance in all developing countries, based on inexhaustible human creativity and intangible assets, could be transformed into economic value and a source of economic development through the formation of coherent integrated sectoral policies that include a rapprochement between culture and trade policies … The age of globalisation offers new opportunities for developing countries in this area while at the same time containing potential threats to cultural diversity and creativity … a balance [must] be sought between achieving national cultural objectives and achieving international trade policy objectives. (UNCTAD, 2004: Summary prepared by UNCTAD Secretariat)

The UNCTAD definition of creative industries rejects the distinction between core cultural industries and other industries and sectors, preferring instead to identify nine interconnected sectors that operate across the sectors of heritage, the arts, media and 'functional creations', around the following broad definition of the creative industries:

- The cycles of creation, production and distribution of goods and services that use creativity and intellectual capital as primary inputs;
- A set of knowledge-based activities, focused on but not limited to the arts, potentially generating revenues from trade and intellectual property rights;
- Tangible products and intangible intellectual or artistic services with creative content, economic value and market objectives;

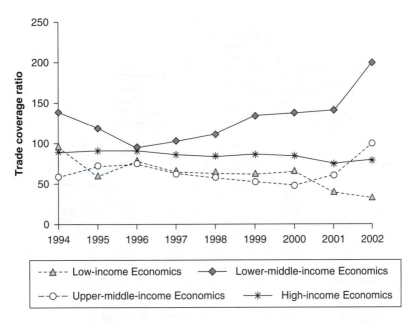

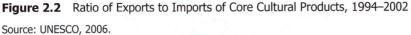

Figure 2.2 Ratio of Exports to Imports of Core Cultural Products, 1994–2002

Source: UNESCO, 2006.

- At the cross-roads among the artisan, services and industrial sectors; and
- Comprising a new dynamic sector in world trade (UNCTAD, 2008: 13).

UNCTAD has argued that the creative industries present opportunities for developing countries to harness distinctive resources of creativity and use creative industries policies to 'increase their shares of world trade and to "leap-frog" into new areas of wealth creation' (UNCTAD, 2004: 3). Noting that creative industries have been estimated to account for more than 7 per cent of the world's gross domestic product and are forecast to grow by 10 per cent annually, UNCTAD (2004: 5) identified a series of mutually reinforcing relationships between globalisation and the growth of creative industries including:

- Deregulation of national cultural and media policy frameworks, which promotes cultural trade, particularly in the audiovisual sectors;
- Increasing affluence, which promotes creative industries in terms of demand (growth in demand for discretionary goods and services with high cultural content) and supply (younger people in particular identifying these industries as attractive places to work for both monetary and non-monetary reasons);
- Technological change, which has transformed production and distribution platforms for content, with profound effects on the value chain of many creative industries as they have become increasingly digital;

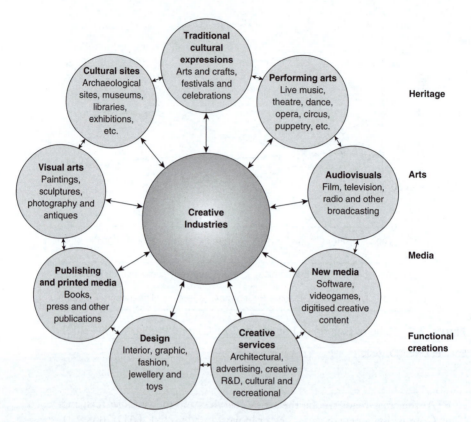

Figure 2.3 UNCTAD Model of the Creative Industries

Source: UNCTAD, 2008: 14.

- Rise of the service economy, which generates new demand for creative industries output in design, advertising and marketing, as well as generating greater returns for intangible investments in human capital;
- Expanding international trade, with global exports of services quadrupling between 1980 and 2002, from about $US400 billion to $US1.6 trillion, and with a slight increase in the share of exports of services from developing countries.

Developing countries are for the most part marginal players in these sectors, due to a mix of domestic policy factors and inequalities in global cultural trade. Barrowclough and Kozul-Wright (2008) observed that the risks to developing countries from not participating in global trade in creative industries are compounded for three further reasons. First, skills developed in the creative industries are often transferable to other sectors and contexts (e.g. skills associated with cultural entrepreneurship or digital animation), so the lack of opportunities to develop a creative industries workforce will impact upon the ability to participate in other high-value-adding product and service industries. Second, the declining costs and increased availability of cultural goods and services enabled by digital technologies means that more and more people in developing countries are consuming a wider range of these products, and they will consume imported materials in the absence of available local content of comparable quality. Third, the growing availability of Western cultural goods and services could promote greater global cultural homogenisation and narrow the potential for local cultures to exercise 'voice' through production and distribution opportunities of their own, risking cultural backlash that could in turn have significant political ramifications.

In its overview of the creative economy and its implications for developing nations, UNCTAD (2008) identified the following as key domestic policy issues:

1 Enhanced access to information and communication technologies (ICTs);
2 Availability of seed funding for small-scale cultural entrepreneurs who may lack access to standardised credit instruments;
3 Cultural agencies and ministries working in a more flexible and integrated way with other public sector agencies, particularly those engaged with industry development and technology;
4 Combating piracy and developing collection agencies to provide revenue streams for artists;
5 Developing creative clusters that can bring together small-scale cultural producers and enable them to pool resources and share infrastructure.

Barrowclough and Kozul-Wright also present a checklist of policies that developing countries can pursue in order to more effectively develop their creative industries sectors and participate more equitably in global markets. They note that policies will differ for countries with a larger population base, and hence are able to develop strong national supply capacities before venturing globally, to smaller countries that cannot achieve the same economies of scale. They also observe that countries speaking a global language (particularly English) will face a different mixture of threats (low price imports from market leaders) and opportunities (new markets for exports) from those speaking languages that are largely not used outside their national borders. Nonetheless, they present the following as the main areas requiring policy intervention in developing countries to promote the creative industries:

1 Investment in human capital (education, skills and training) with a focus on developing creative capacities as well as generic skills;
2 Facilitate transition to digital in all phases of the value chain to lower production costs and increase access to global markets;
3 Realign copyright and intellectual property rights to promote more fairly the rights of original creators, and strengthen national copyright and licensing agencies;
4 Provide incentives and build capabilities (both monetary and non-monetary) to promote innovation and creativity;
5 Facilitate access to finance for new and small producers and ensure access to capital for creative industries participants;
6 Adopt strategic trade policies, including measures to boost co-productions;

7 Provide incubators and business support to SMEs and new entrants, and assist them with access to global distribution networks;

8 Promote dynamism and creative clusters in cities to benefit from linkages and knowledge spillovers;

9 Promote creative industries products internationally to reduce information failures and introduce domestic producers to global consumers;

10 Explore strategies to link with independents' production and distribution structures in more advanced economies. (Barrowclough and Kozul-Wright, 2008: 27–28).

While such recommendations are valuable, they remain premised upon the classic developmental model, in that they propose that policies be adopted that best enable modernisation and 'catch-up' with the Western nations (Sparks, 2007: 38–55; Melkote, 2010). In the case of creative industries policies, as was noted in Chapter One, this has characteristically been premised upon strong protection of copyright and intellectual property rights (IPRs). In many of the countries that are now rising to prominence in the global creative economy, such as Brazil, China, India and South Africa, past experiences of dealing with the global IP regime have been unfavourable or – as in China's case in particular – a very complex and ambiguous relationship to IPR has continued to prevail in spite of considerable legislative reform (Tian, 2007: 229–253). It may well be the case that the creative communities in these countries seek different models for the management of IPRs from those developed through the World Intellectual Property Organization (WIPO) and other international institutional fora. There are salutary reminders here that we must not presume that the global creative economy of the 21st century is going to follow the paths laid down in the twentieth century, particularly if it is being accompanied by a power shift from the Euro-American axis to countries and regions that until very recently were identified as being part of the developing world.

Endnote

1 In 2008, the European Union had 27 member states. They were: Austria, Belgium, Bulgaria, Cyprus, the Czech Republic, Denmark, Estonia, Finland, France, Germany, Greece, Hungary, Ireland, Italy, Latvia, Lithuania, Luxembourg, Malta, the Netherlands, Poland, Portugal, Romania, Slovakia, Slovenia, Spain, Sweden and the United Kingdom. Twelve of these states were admitted to membership in 2004 (the Czech Republic, Cyprus, Estonia, Latvia, Lithuania, Hungary, Malta, Poland, Slovenia and Slovakia), and Bulgaria and Romania were admitted to the EU in 2007. Iceland, Liechtenstein and Norway are not EU members, but are a part of the European Economic Area, while Switzerland maintains participation with EU member states through a series of bilateral treaties. There are numerous difficulties with equating Europe with the European Union, and with comparing statistics over time as the membership base has changed. Nonetheless, this study draws primarily upon statistics and policy developed for the EU as a whole.

3 From Culture Industries to Cultural Economy

The use and applicability of the terms 'cultural industries' and 'creative industries' has been the subject of considerable debate since the DCMS in Britain introduced the concept of creative industries into policy discourse in the late 1990s. For some writers, the concept of creative industries provides a broader, more inclusive and more contemporary understanding of the field, and has superseded the concept of cultural industries. Others have argued that the term 'creative' has too broad and imprecise a remit, and dilutes the significance of the cultural dimension to these industries, artificially linking them to the ICT sectors and, in some instances, the sciences. As we have seen in the previous two chapters, another approach has been to differentiate 'cultural industries' from 'creative industries' on the basis of the former having a more direct relationship to the arts as traditionally defined, whereas the latter make use of creative inputs to produce outputs that are associated with other sectors of the economy. Such an approach is found in European Union definitions of the cultural and creative industries, as well as those used by UNESCO. In other contexts, such as those of East Asian countries, Australia and New Zealand, as well as UNCTAD, this definitional distinction has not been considered as important.

The term cultural industries has both a theoretical and a descriptive lineage. The concept has its origins in the ideological critique of art and culture under industrial capitalism associated with the neo-Marxist theorists of the 'Frankfurt School' such as Theodor Adorno, Max Horkheimer and Herbert Marcuse. As elements of this critique continue to have resonance in contemporary debates surrounding the creative industries, it will be considered in more detail below. At a more descriptive level, UNESCO has been drawing upon the concept of cultural industries and their role in national development since the late 1960s, and the gathering of cultural statistics has been a central plank of UNESCO's Charter; it has come to be of increasing importance in recent years as the relationship between culture and economic and social development has been explored in more depth (UNESCO, 2004, 2006, 2009).

UNESCO has defined cultural industries as 'those industries that combine the creation, production and commercialization of contents which are intangible and cultural in nature … [and] their contents are typically protected by copyright and can take the form of a good or service' (UNESCO, 2006). Cultural economists have tended to be less concerned with whether they are referring to cultural or creative industries as with understanding the distinctive industrial dynamics of cultural goods and services. Towse (2003b) defined cultural industries as those which 'mass-produce goods and services with sufficient artistic content to be considered creative and culturally significant. The essential features are industrial-scale production combined with cultural content' (Towse, 2003b: 170). In her more recent work, Towse dropped the distinction between cultural and creative industries altogether, referring instead to creative industries that are based in cultural markets (Towse, 2010). In a similar vein, Caves (2000) identified the creative industries as 'supplying goods and services that we broadly associate with cultural, artistic, or … entertainment value' (Caves, 2000: 1). A certain degree of elusiveness as to what is considered 'artistic' or 'cultural' is not considered unique to these sectors for economists, for as Throsby notes:

> Any self-respecting university course or textbook on industry economics spends some time at the outset discussing the difficulties of defining an industry – i.e. whether the concept of industry can be delineated according to groupings of producers, product classifications, factors of production, types of consumers, location, etc. (Throsby, 2001: 112)

By contrast, the distinction has been considered highly important for those approaching the question from cultural studies or critical humanities perspectives. Cunningham (2002) and Hartley (2005) have been among the most notable proponents of arguments that developments in the wider economy and society require that the concept of creative industries supersede that of the cultural industries. Hartley proposed that creative industries marked a bringing together of the creative and performing arts with the mass media and communications industries in a digital knowledge economy context where consumers are increasingly not only the drivers of content, but also – through user-generated online content – its co-creators. In this context, Hartley states that 'there is an argument for re-purposing the very idea of "creativity" to bring it into closer contact with the realities of contemporary commercial democracies. "Art" needs to be understood as something intrinsic, not opposed, to the productive capacities of a contemporary, global, mediated, technology-supported economy' (Hartley, 2005: 8–9). Cunningham (2002, 2005) argued that 'the concept of creative industries is trying to chart an historical shift from subsidized "public arts" and broadcast era media, towards new and broader applications of creativity … creative industries can lay claim to being significant elements of the new economy in and of themselves' (Cunningham, 2002: 58–59). He proposed that the term creative industries is more useful because:

- It recognises and 'mainstreams' the economic value of the arts and media by recognising the value of creativity inputs in the digitized 'new' economy;
- It identifies and works productively with the degree of convergence that has occurred within and between the arts, media and design sectors;
- It incorporates the spectrum of commercial and non-commercial arts, media and design activities by focusing on generically creative content rather than output-based or policy-driven industry silos. (Cunningham, 2005: 284)

Cunningham differentiates the creative industries model from that of the cultural industries according to five criteria. First, it was argued that while the nation-state and national cultural policy had been the locus of cultural industries policies, creative industries operate at the intersection of globalised market dynamics and local industry clusters and specialist resources. Second, creative industries have developed in tandem with digitisation and convergence, whereas cultural industries typically developed in industry silos. Third, while much of the applied work on cultural industries has involved the application of neo-classical economics through the specialist field of cultural economics, creative industries were often discussed in terms of 'new economy' dynamics and new tendencies in growth and innovation economics (Flew, 2003). Fourth, while cultural industries discourse often involved a re-badging of industries otherwise referred to as arts or media industries, the creative industries model draws upon new thinking about the relationship between large-scale enterprises and the plethora of surrounding small-to-medium enterprises (SMEs) who are frequently the drivers of innovation (cf. Scott, 2005, 2006). Finally, cultural industries policies were focused on already established sectors such as the arts and broadcast media, whereas creative industries policies were particularly interested in the emergent industries at the intersection of arts, design, media and digital technologies (Mitchell et al., 2003).

As was noted in Chapter One, a number of analysts have dissented from the proposition that there has been a transition from cultural to creative industries. Hesmondhalgh and Pratt (2005) find the concept of creativity to be too vague and all-inclusive to act as a definitional substitute for culture, while others such as Miller (2004, 2009b), Garnham (2005), Galloway and Dunlop (2007), Ross (2007) and O'Connor (2007, 2009) find the creative industries push to be too market-driven, and question its underlying assumptions about a transition within global capitalism towards a 'new economy' and an 'information society'. While attempts have been made to differentiate between these terms on the basis of their outputs and the object of analysis, with other terms such as content industries, copyright industries and digital content industries being thrown into the mix (Hartley, 2005: 30), the main intellectual debate has been around whether to prefer the term cultural industries or creative industries.

In this chapter, I will propose that while there are significant differences of perspective surrounding these terminological debates that can have important analytical and policy implications, both the cultural industries and creative industries academic literature draw upon a common pool of insights derived from fields such as political economy, institutional economics, cultural studies, cultural economy research, cultural economic geography, and the sociology of culture. As an analytical starting point, it is important to reflect upon the intellectual genesis of the term 'culture industry' in the work of the Frankfurt School, and the ways in which critiques of this analysis have acted as a catalyst to critical work on the cultural and creative industries that have developed alongside more pragmatic, policy-driven approaches.

From Culture Industry to Cultural and Creative Industries

Preferences for the term cultural industries or creative industries can be intellectually traced back to the work of Theodor Adorno and Max Horkheimer on the culture industry. Adorno and Horkheimer were German critical-Marxist philosophers who were associated with the

Institute for Social Research at the University of Frankfurt, until the rise of the Nazis to power in 1933 forced them to leave Germany and to reconstitute the Institute in the United States, at Columbia University. This group of authors, which also included Erich Fromm, Walter Benjamin and Herbert Marcuse, collectively came to be known as the Frankfurt School. The most famous work of Adorno and Horkheimer on the culture industry, 'The Culture Industry: Enlightenment as Mass Deception', was first published in 1947, and written when they were in exile in the United States (Adorno and Horkheimer, 1979).

Adorno and Horkheimer presented the gloomy prognosis that the once autonomous sphere of culture – art, aesthetics, music, literature, etc. – had become fully integrated into the dynamics of capitalist domination in the form of the culture industry. Drawing an analogy between European Fascism and capitalist democracies, it was argued that the production of culture had become industrialised under monopoly capitalism, and the commodification of all forms of culture had led to sameness and uniformity, under the guise of greater consumer choice based upon minor differences. Adorno and Horkheimer referred to this as 'the achievement of standardization and mass production, sacrificing whatever involved a distinction between the logic of the work and that of the social system' (Adorno and Horkheimer, 1979: 350). What appears as greater consumer choice and cultural freedom for the masses is thus their complete integration into the machinery of mass culture, where 'something is provided for all so that none may escape' (Adorno and Horkheimer, 1979: 351). The culture industry in turn functions as a powerful ideological and propaganda instrument, utilising the new technologies of mass communication and the techniques of mass production to impose ideological control on the mass population as cultural consumers:

> Under monopoly all mass culture is identical, and the lines of its artificial framework begin to show through … Movies and radio no longer pretend to be art. The truth that they are just business is made into an ideology in order to justify the rubbish that they deliberately produce. (Adorno and Horkheimer, 1979: 349)

Adorno and Horkheimer presented culture in advanced capitalist societies in terms of 'the overall standardised character of cultural production, and the way in which the culture industry seek to incorporate producer and consumer, artist and audience, into this process' (Negus, 2006: 198–199). O'Connor has observed that Adorno in particular was focused not simply upon the commodification of culture but upon 'the organization of cultural commodity production on a mass industrial scale … [where] the complex play between art as commodity and as autonomous form collapsed as the independent artist gave way to the culture factory' (O'Connor, 2007: 12).

The various critiques of Adorno and Horkheimer's *Kulturkritik* of the culture industry provide the foundations for understanding the strands of research that inform contemporary theoretical understandings of the creative industries. First, it has been argued that Adorno and Horkheimer presented a one-sided understanding of the cultural commodity, neglecting the extent to which cultural producers need to meet human needs for meaning and enjoyment – what is referred to as the use-value of a commodity – in order to realise profits on these commodities, or their exchange-value. The political economist Nicholas Garnham argued that 'the real weakness of the Frankfurt School's original position was not their failure to realise the importance of the base or the economic, but insufficiently to take account of the economically contradictory nature of the process ... and thus to see the industrialisation of culture as unproblematic and irreversible' (Garnham, 1990: 28). Second, the assumption was questioned that cultural commodities produced under the capitalist framework of mass production and distribution therefore successfully transmit dominant capitalist ideologies. Garnham observed that 'because capital controls the means of cultural production in the sense that the production and exchange of cultural commodities becomes the dominant form of cultural relationship, it does not follow that these cultural commodities will necessarily support, either in their explicit content or in their mode of cultural appropriation, the dominant ideology' (Garnham, 1990: 34).

Third, authors such as Miège (1989) and Ryan (1992) pointed to the complexities of cultural production and distribution, observing that there was not a singular logic to the 'culture industry', but rather complex and distinctive dynamics associated with different cultural industries. Miège argued that there were important differences in how commodities were sold in publishing industries as compared to broadcasting industries, for example, and that these in turn differed from those industries associated with public performance. A similar point is made about Adorno and Horkheimer's universal conception of the cultural commodity, where 'the mere existence of an industrial form of production lead them to lump together jazz and comic strips, radio and cinema' (Mattelart and Piemme, 1982: 53). Fourth, Mattelart and Piemme detected in their work a 'nostalgia for a cultural experience untainted by technology' (Mattelart and Piemme, 1982: 53), arguing that their critique of aesthetics under capitalism is underpinned by a distrust of reproducible cultural forms delivered by mass communications technologies (cf. Miège, 1989: 9–12). Finally, their understanding of the subsumption of creative labour to capital has been critiqued as a-historical, counter-posing a once heroic era of artistic autonomy to the enslavement of contemporary cultural production. By contrasts, Williams (1981) and Ryan (1992) argued that the era of market professional and corporate professional cultural production has in practice afforded different degrees of creative autonomy to different types of creative cultural producers, so there is no simple process of the once independent artist being sucked into the maws of the 'culture factory'.

One may ask what is the purpose of raking over debates about dated and, many would argue, discredited ways of thinking about cultural markets and cultural production? Aside from historical significance, there is also the important point that a version of culture industry thinking has informed arts and cultural policy as it developed in the second half of the twentieth century, and that creative industries constitutes an intervention into those policy debates. While Adorno and Horkheimer were hardly names known to most people, and certainly not to most arts and culture ministries, the underlying kernel of their thesis – that mass culture and commercial markets led to a debased form of culture – was certainly an underlying influence on the development of national arts and cultural policies. In his critique of this tradition, Garnham summarised the main tenets of this argument as being:

Public intervention, in the form of subsidy, is justified on the grounds: (1) the culture possesses inherent values, of life enhancement or whatever, which are fundamentally opposed to and in danger of damage by commercial forces; (2) that the need for these values is universal, uncontaminated by questions of class, gender or ethnic origin; and (3) that the market cannot satisfy this need ... The result of this cultural policy-making tradition has been to marginalize public intervention in the cultural sphere and to make it purely reactive to processes which it cannot grasp or attempt to control. (Garnham, 1990: 154)

In work undertaken for UNESCO, Augustin Girard was observing a similar paradox: the explosion in production of and demand for cultural products of all kinds, and the increased marginalisation of traditional forms of cultural policy, focused upon traditional art forms and cultural institutions. Like Garnham, Girard concluded that 'far more is being done to democratize and decentralize culture with the industrial products available on the market than with the "products" subsidized by the public authorities' (Girard, 1982: 25). The turn towards cultural industries, then, was marked by a turn towards a more descriptive and less moralistic account of large-scale cultural production, distribution and consumption in capitalist societies, informed less by what Girard referred to as 'the aesthetic point of view' (Girard, 1982: 33), and more by a strategic approach designed to inform policy makers of where and how to intervene in the operations of these industries for goals which may be technical, economic or political as well as cultural. The turn away from a monolithic and pessimistic model of 'culture industry' towards a more descriptive, pluralistic and positive assessment of the cultural and creative industries was thus marked by 'a conceptual shift ... to a more empirically based understanding of the complex structure and variable dynamics at work in the production of culture' (O'Connor, 2007: 22).

Political Economy

Many of the original critical commentaries on the cultural industries came from authors working within the political economy approach to media and communications. Vincent Mosco has defined political economy as 'the study of social relations, particularly power relations, that mutually constitute the production, distribution, and consumption of resources' (Mosco, 2009: 24). Of these social relations, class relations are seen as being of particular importance; Garnham (1995) argued that 'political economy sees class – namely, the structure of access to the means of production and the structure of distribution of the economic surplus – as the key to the structure of domination' (Garnham, 1995: 70). Boyd-Barrett has observed that political economy has a 'broadly "critical" signification', focusing on 'macro-questions of media ownership and control ... and other factors that bring together media industries with other media and other industries, and with political, economic and social elites (Boyd-Barrett, 1995: 186). Overviews of political economy (Wasko, 2004; Murdock and Golding, 2005; Mosco, 2009) identify core elements of the political economy approach as being:

1 An insistence upon linking media and communications research to study of the social totality, or the interconnection between systems of economic, political, coercive and symbolic power as they are related to the media and cultural spheres;
2 The need for a historical perspective, or the "'slow but perceptible rhythms" that characterize the gradually unfolding history of economic formations and systems of rule' (Murdock and Golding, 2005: 64);
3 Concern with relations between the commercial and government sectors, and trends over time towards the 'commodification of cultural life' (Murdock and Golding, 2005: 64); and
4 An emphasis upon moral philosophy, or the relationship between media, communications and cultural policies and wider normative principles, such as public intervention to ensure 'that people have access to a range of cultural and communicative resources that support participation' (Murdock and Golding, 2005: 65), and an associated desire to link academic research to campaigns to transform media policies, institutions and practices.

In his overview of political economy approaches to cultural industries, David Hesmondhalgh (2007a) has argued that work in this field has evolved in two directions. The first, which he associates with North American writers such as Herbert Schiller, Noam Chomsky, Edward Herman and Robert McChesney, has been primarily focused upon the concentration of wealth and power in the cultural and media industries, and its links to broader system of corporate control and political power. The second, which he terms the cultural industries approach, was more specifically developed in Europe by authors such as Miège (1989), Garnham (1990) and Ryan (1992), and has more of a focus upon industry dynamics and the risks, complexities and contradiction associated with cultural production in capitalist economies. Hesmondhalgh argues that the second approach provides a stronger basis on which to understand features of the cultural industries such as:

- The management of risk that derives from high production costs and low reproduction costs for cultural commodities, and the unpredictability of demand that arises from how 'audiences use cultural commodities in highly volatile and unpredictable ways, often in order to express that they are different from other people' (Hesmondhalgh, 2007a: 19);
- Strategies to manage and minimise risk, including development of a repertoire of cultural products, promotion, marketing and publicity strategies, strategies to artificially generate scarcity such as copyright, and the ways in which cultural commodities are formatted, through genre, the star system and serialisation;
- The differing degrees of creative autonomy that creative personnel (artists, musicians, screenwriters and directors, journalists, authors, etc.) may have in relation to the production of creative work that takes the form of cultural commodities. In particular, what Hesmondhalgh terms the 'management of symbolic creativity' may give considerable autonomy to the individuals and teams responsible for production, while using the variety of risk management strategies identified above to manage distribution in ways designed to maximise market share and profitability;

- Contradictions that nonetheless remain between 'the "fundamentally irrational;" process of symbolic creativity ... [and] the calculating, accumulative logic of modern capitalism' (Hesmondhalgh, 2007a: 306) that continue to be central to questions of power, conflict and change in the cultural industries.

A final point to be noted about the political economy approach is that it prefers the term cultural industries to that of creative industries. This is reflective in part of scepticism about the policy agendas of 'New Labour' in Britain (e.g. Garnham, 2005) and a view of the concept of creative industries as 'effectively abandoning the notion of critique' (Miller, 2004: 56). Hesmondhalgh believes that replacing cultural industries with creative industries as a concept can fail to 'emphasise the downsides of the marketisation and commodification of culture ... [or] consider the ways that capitalist markets systematically (although not in any predefined way) produce inequalities of access and outcome' (Hesmondhalgh, 2007a: 149).

Cultural Studies

Cultural studies is a sprawling intellectual enterprise that has over the last 40 years generated a huge body of academic work, and is difficult to adequately summarise. Grossberg et al. define cultural studies as 'an interdisciplinary field ... committed to the study of the entire range of a society's arts, beliefs, institutions, and communicative practices' (Grossberg et al., 1992: 4). Hartley (2003) and During (1993) help to clarify such a sweeping definition further by noting that cultural studies has characteristically been concerned with contemporary culture in modern industrial societies, and the experience of people and communities in this industrialised society and mediated culture, being drawn towards anthropological approaches to culture as part of everyday life. It has been particularly engaged with questions of power and its relationship to culture and social relations and institutions, and Bennett argued that work in cultural studies is 'characterised by an interdisciplinary concern with the functioning of cultural practices and institutions in the contexts of relations of power of different kinds' (Bennett, 1998: 27). This has entailed understanding culture in its relationship to other fields of power and social organisation, such as the economy and the political sphere, as well as other academic disciplines, in order to better analyse what Stuart Hall referred to as relations of articulation, in terms of both how they construct social relations and individual subjectivities. Cultural studies research has been particularly attentive to popular culture generally, and to the media in particular, which Hall identified as having 'established a decisive and fundamental leadership in the cultural sphere' (Hall, 1977: 340). Cultural studies has also been associated with an ethics of political engagement, where 'practitioners see cultural studies not simply as a chronicle of cultural change but as an intervention in it, and see themselves not simply as scholars providing an account but as politically engaged practitioners' (Grossberg et al., 1992: 5).

John Hartley (2003, 2004, 2005) has argued that creative industries marks a continuity in themes developed from cultural studies. Hartley proposed that cultural studies has been differentiated from political economy in its insistence that 'culture might be investigated as a cause rather than an effect of economic circumstances and political outcome' (Hartley, 2003: 92). It thus has a particular interest in understanding the forms of culture (or, following semiotic analysis, its texts) and what people do with them – particularly the texts of popular culture – in their everyday lives and in the formation of consciousness and identity, whether as readers, audiences, users or however they are positioned in relation to these cultural texts. Hartley (2004) argued that in late twentieth-century and early 21st century societies there has been a shift in what he terms the value chain of meaning, from authority lying with the author as in pre-modern times (or, in religious texts, to God as the ultimate 'author'), to the text or the 'thing itself' in modernity (as seen in modernist literary criticism, scientific semiotics or empiricism social science), to audiences or readers as 'consumers-citizens', as mass literacy and the uptake of media technologies gives individuals new interpretative capacities and the power as consumers to more decisively influence cultural markets and cultural production.

From this perspective, the rise of the creative industries to economic and policy prominence is linked to five wider trends (Hartley, 2005):

1 The growing links between the creative arts, as a locus of creative activity, with large-scale media and cultural industries, with their focus on national or global distributional scale, in the context of technological convergence;
2 The joining-up of identities found with the modern 'consumer-citizen', a product of the joint development of industrial capitalism and liberal democracy (cf. Livingstone et al., 2007);
3 The shift in the economic base of post-industrial capitalism from the processing of things (large-scale manufacturing) to the processing of information and the delivery of services, and the growing economic premium attached to the commercialisation of ideas into new products and services;
4 The capacity of new digital media technologies to enable user-created content that can be distributed on a large scale through the Internet, thereby newly empowering users, and shifting the base of media technologies from read-only (mass communications) to read-and-write, where users become content co-creators with industry, or what Bruns (2008) has termed produsers;
5 Shifts in public policy that identify new sources of global competitive advantage in the creative economy, and therefore seek to overcome historic divides between arts policy (focused on public subsidy), media policy (focused on ownership and content regulation), and information policy (focused on information technology infrastructure), around the opportunities for wealth creation and export arising from the creative industries sector.

Henry Jenkins has also argued from a cultural studies perspective for the need to understand new media and media convergence from the perspective of its users and participatory culture. His 2006 book *Convergence Culture: When Old and New Media Collide* (Jenkins, 2006) was based around the relationship between three concepts: media convergence; participatory culture; and collective intelligence. It understood media convergence as 'the flow of content across multiple media platforms' (Jenkins, 2006: 2), seeing this not so much as a consequence of the merging of media forms through digital technologies, but rather as involving a new level of engagement with media by its users, as 'consumers are encouraged to seek out new information and make connections among dispersed media content' (Jenkins, 2006: 3). The concept of participatory culture drew attention to the transformation of media communication in the early 21st century from a system of mass communication, based around one-to-many message transmission and a structural separation between the producers and consumers of media, to one where both now constitute 'participants who interact with each other according to a new set of rules that none of us fully understands' (Jenkins, 2006: 3). This has been occurring in digital media environments through multi-player online game cultures, online video sites such as *YouTube*, and media practices such as blogging and citizen journalism, as well as in 'old' media such as broadcast television, with the explicit engagement of audiences as participants in the story-telling practices of 'reality' television. Collective intelligence referred to the power of networked communities in developing knowledge systems that are not only greater than the sum of their individual parts, but which grow, evolve and collectively learn through ongoing interaction. Wikipedia is a leading example of the interaction between convergence culture and collective intelligence, as it is both collectively and collaboratively authored, with all of its users having the capacity to comment on, contribute to, revise or question its content.

Jenkins' work is grounded in a cultural-studies-based approach to new media that tends to be optimistic about its potential, and seeks to adopt the perspective of its users or con-sumers. Like Hartley, Jenkins argues that there is instead a cyclical relationship between audience demand for more complex media forms, the growing textual sophistication of media producers, and more interactive new media technologies, which is producing more complex forms of popular culture that engage the brain more systematically. Importantly, Jenkins' work consistently stresses that it is the 'work' performed by media users with new media technologies, rather than innate properties of the technologies themselves, that are the primary drivers of such transformations.

Cultural Economic Geography

Perspectives from cultural and economic geography have been important in developing an understanding of the creative industries, particularly in identifying the significance of geographical clustering, the formation of global production networks, and the significance of cities and regions in the context of economic globalisation. In their overview of the rise of cultural economic geography, James et al. (2008) distinguished five distinct but related factors associated with this emergent hybrid discipline.

The first arose out of the transformation of economic geography from the 1970s onwards. Economic geography was strongly shaped in the 1970s and 1980s by Marxist political economy, and the 'Marxist turn' in economic geography involved the development of a 'thoroughgoing historical geography of the capitalist mode of production' (Scott, 2003: 25), with particular reference points including capital accumulation, the labour process, economic crisis, and the spatial mapping of class relations. David Harvey (1982, 1989) was one of the more famous of many Marxist geographers working this terrain (for a summary, see Swyngedouw, 2003). By the 1990s, Marxism was being challenged by the 'cultural turn' associated with post-structuralist theories, which questioned implicit hierarchies of thought in the dominant forms of critical geography (Gibson-Graham, 2003; Anderson, 2008). In particular, they questioned the discursive construction of 'the economy' in such analyses, and what it prioritised and what it downplayed. For example, taking the category of 'labour', is paid wage-labour more significant than domestic labour? Is the fact of labouring more 'real' than the ways in which it is understood and approached in labour market theories, management discourses, or policy-related definitions of work that impact upon welfare policies? Associated with the 'cultural turn' in economic geography was greater interest in consumption. Rather than being seen as the subordinate category to the dominant driver that was production, consumption 'has come to represent the site on which culture and economy most dramatically converge' (Slater, 2003: 149), and the traditional silence of economists about the formation of consumer preferences was now rejected; consideration was being given to questions of status, meaning and identity attached to particular commodities, with these questions being inherently cultural in their nature.

A second driver of cultural economic geography has been greater attention being given to the particular ways in which culture and economy interlock, such as the relationship between markets and production as spatially grounded economic practices, and the lived experience of people within such economic spaces. This turn towards cultural economy studies (du Gay and Pryke, 2002; Amin and Thrift, 2004) will be reviewed in more detail later in this chapter. Third, the cultural constitution of economic practice has been linked to a growing awareness that 'cultural' factors can mark significant sources of regional differentiation, local entrepreneurship and competitive advantage in globalised economies, as seen in the debates surrounding clusters and learning regions (Cooke and Lazzeretti, 2008), as well as considerations of the cultural geography of economic production. Gertler (2003) has pointed to three 'big ideas' that have given increasing significance to a cultural economic geography of production. First, the reorganisation of corporate production models away from vertical integration and towards 'flexible specialisation' and global production networks has drawn attention to both the economic advantage of geographical proximity between producers, suppliers, distributors, specialist workers and service providers, or the phenomenon known as spatial agglomeration or clustering. Second, shifts in innovation models away from linear 'ideas-push' approaches (ideas are developed in research and development labs, and then applied in the market by firms), towards models that derive their strength from interaction between suppliers, producers and users (Dodgson et al., 2002), have focused attention on the importance of such clustering to innovation, and the question of how and why a propensity for innovation becomes embedded in particular regional cultures, through what Storper (1997) refers to as untraded interdependencies. Finally, the concept of path dependency in technology development and design (Arthur, 2009), combined with the significance of increasing returns to scale in economic theory (Krugman, 2003), has drawn attention to the cumulative advantages that can accrue to regions from achieving early leadership in particular industries. Gertler noted that 'once a region establishes itself as an early success in a particular set of production activities, its chances of continued growth are very good indeed' (Gertler, 2003: 135). In order to achieve cumulative growth over time, there are typically a supportive set of accompanying social, institutional and cultural factors at play within a particular region; at the same time, these socio-cultural and institutional factors may also present difficulties in reversing regional decline.

A fourth factor promoting cultural economic geography has been the rise of actor-network theory. James et al. observe that networks feature in this new literature in three ways: the mapping of network ties among economic agents, as in much of the regional innovation literature noted above; the rise of network governance as a hybrid form of inter-institutional relationships that combine elements of market relations, formal law and informal associational relations (Thompson, 2003; Pratt, 2005); and post-structuralist inspired work that explores 'the heterogeneous interactions, translations, associations and mediations between human and non-human actors through which economic networks are (re) constructed' (James et al., 2008: 11). The latter set of approaches has been particularly significant in focusing attention upon the performative and discursive dimensions of what Nigel Thrift (2005) has referred to as soft capitalism, and the ways in which it is engaged in new business management practices.

Finally, growing interest among academics and policy makers in the creative industries has intensified interest in locational decisions surrounding these industries, and the relationship between the attributes of the industries (their propensity for project work, networking, unpredictability of demand, need for continuous novelty and innovation, etc.), and those of the urban environments in which they are primarily located. The work of Allen Scott has played a vital role in understanding the cultural-economic dynamics of contemporary creative industries. Scott's work on the cultural economy of cities (Scott, 2000, 2008b) identified five major features of the creative industries that promote both network organisation and clustering and agglomeration in particular cities and regions:

1 The importance of specific forms of labour input, which possess specialist tacit knowledge and whose skills can be acquired on a flexible, just-in-time basis;
2 The organisation of production in dense networks of small-to-medium-sized enterprises (SMEs) that are strongly dependent upon each other for the provision of specialised inputs and services;
3 Employment relations that are frequently characterised by intermittent, project-based work, which promotes co-location of industries and workers in particular areas in order to reduce transaction costs and search costs;
4 Indirect, synergistic benefits that result from the co-existence of many people and enterprises engaged in interrelated activities, such as the enhanced capacity to match individual creativity to market opportunity;
5 The development of associated services and institutional infrastructure such as specialist intermediaries (e.g. entertainment lawyers) and a supportive public policy environment.

Scott identified Hollywood – or, more accurately, the region of southern California based around Los Angeles – as the exemplar of locational clustering and agglomeration in the global media and entertainment industries. The break-up of the Hollywood studio system after World War II saw the externalisation of a range of in-house activities, leading to a more diffuse organisational system of production, characterised by project-based work and the intensification of clustering of firms in industries and activities related to film and television production in greater Los Angeles, as 'the relations between firms cannot be planned over extended periods of time so that inter-firm contacts need to be constantly programmed and reprogrammed' (Scott, 2005: 7). At the same time, the instability of these networks – perhaps paradoxically – reinforces the durability of the localised production system, with the result that Hollywood remained a magnet for creative people from around the world, and, as a result, 'new aptitudes flow continuously ... from outside, thus helping to enlarge production capacities and to refresh pools of talent' (Scott, 2005: 7). Hollywood is thus not only an attractor to those seeking to apply their skills in film and television (actors, director, scriptwriters, etc.), but also to a related set of adjunct and associated industries, ranging from fashion to marketing, and digital visual effects to restaurants and catering. Moreover, successful creative industries clusters such as Hollywood 'accumulate place-specific cultural associations as the symbologies embedded in goods and services produced in the same area are absorbed into the local urban landscape' (Scott, 2005: 7). Whether it is the touristy perceptions of Hollywood as the 'home of the stars', or the more dystopian landscapes of films such as *The Terminator* and *Blade Runner*, the association of Hollywood with cinema impacts upon the shape of the city, its global cultural connotations, its self-image, and its attractiveness as a destination for creative workers of various kinds.

Cultural economy geography raises important questions about the durability and transferability of creative industries models from one place to another. On the one hand, it provides correctives to the automatic association of economic globalisation with a 'race to the bottom', as globally mobile multinational capital plays off one place against another in order to drive down wages, working conditions and environmental standards. Storper (1997) has argued that while the 'off-shoring' of work to low-wage economies, runaway production and a more polarised new international division of labour – what he refers to as de-territorialised economic development – is one possible scenario arising from economic globalisation, it exists alongside what he refers to as territorialised economic development, or 'economic activity that is dependent on territorially specific resources' (Storper, 1997: 170). Territorialised production is that where products and services are not standardised, quality is prioritised by consumers and not only price, and produc-tion processes rely upon both specialist labour inputs and untraded interdependencies, or 'conventions, informal rules, and habits that coordinate economic actors under condi-tions of uncertainty ... [and] constitute region-specific assets' (Storper, 1997: 4–5). At the same time, concepts from critical economic geography such as uneven development serve as reminders of the limits of replication of models derived from success stories elsewhere, to be 'the new Hollywood' or the 'next Silicon Valley', in an environment of 'heightened inter-place competition' (Harvey, 1989: 295), and where already successful cities and regions possess considerable advantages in global competition based upon place competitiveness.

Cultural and Institutional Economics

The creative industries concept is often associated, favourably or otherwise, with the greater application of economic discourses and methodologies to the study of the arts and culture. Australian cultural policy writer Jo Caust (2003) captured this concern when she argued that:

> When it became increasingly difficult in the early eighties to successfully 'argue the arts' to government purely on the basis of the community welfare model, bureaucrats, practitioners and academics began the shift towards using a language that described the arts as an industry and developed the economic/cultural industry model. This led to the use of the terms 'cultural industries' in Australia or in the United Kingdom, 'creative industries' to describe all activities connected with the arts, as well as sectors far removed. (Caust, 2003: 54)

It can be seen as indicative of a wider discontent with the role played by economics in contemporary cultural debates. Much of this literature is associated with the critique of neo-liberalism, which is discussed in detail in Chapter Seven. The view has been widespread in both the cultural fields and the critical humanities that 'the influence of the dismal science of economics on media and cultural policy has been profound' (Hesmondhalgh, 2007a: 30). This has in turn generated an urgency to arguments that a critical deconstruction of economics as a discipline is required in order, as cultural studies author Lawrence Grossberg has put it, to 'do economics better than the economists' (Grossberg, 2006: 21).

When such critics are referring to economics, it is typically what is known as *neo-classical economics*, or what constitutes textbook microeconomics in undergraduate business and commerce courses around the world. Hesmondhalgh (2007a: 30) refers to neoclassical economics as being 'not concerned with determining human needs and rights, nor with intervening in questions of social justice', but rather with 'how human wants might be most efficiently satisfied', and which 'equates the well-being of people with their ability to maximize their satisfactions'. Miller et al. (2001) refer to the 'neo-classical vision of Hollywood' as 'bourgeois economics' which:

> asserts that the supposedly neutral mechanism of market competition exchanges materials at costs that ensure the most efficient people are producing, and their customers are content. This model may occasionally describe life in some fruit and vegetable markets today. But as a historical account, it is of no value: the rhythms of supply and demand, operating unfettered by states, religions, unions, superstition and fashion, have never existed as such. (Miller et al., 2001: 48)

The dominant view of economics from the perspective of critical cultural studies is of a discipline with a singular dominant set of priorities, which are narrowly focused and lack realism. The next step, which emerges with the critique of neo-liberalism, is to argue that such economics effectively functions as an ideology, serving dominant economic interests through the mystification of social reality. Hesmondhalgh refers to the manner in which 'mainstream economics has helped to fuel a neo-liberal approach to culture ... Underpinning the neo-liberal approach to culture is the idea, derived from neoclassical theory, that "free", unregulated competition will produce efficient markets ... [and that] the production of efficient markets should be the primary goal of public policy' (Hesmondhalgh, 2007a: 31).

I have argued elsewhere that this presents far too crude and one-dimensional account of dominant strands of economic knowledge and the degree of intellectual heterogeneity in the discipline, and that these authors are engaging with a straw figure, drawing upon the textbook representation of undergraduate economics as a stand-in for the economic discipline as a whole (Flew, 2009d).[1] Such a caricatured account of economics also has the potential to lose sight of the extent to which there have been shifts in the dominant forms of economic discourse used towards culture between the 1990s and 2000s. Traditionally, the dominant economic approach to the arts and media has been that of cultural economics – sometimes also referred to as the economics of the arts – that used neoclassical welfare economics to answer questions primarily related to the costs and benefits of various forms of public subsidy. As authors such as Throsby (2001) and Towse (2010) have observed, rationales for government support for the arts and culture have typically revolved around the following five sets of arguments, which are drawn from cultural economics:

1 Public good arguments: public support for the arts generates generalised community benefits over and above measurable direct consumption impacts. These include community education, contributions to cultural identity, their role as a stimulus to further cultural production and creative activity, and inter-generational transfer of cultural wealth and heritage.
2 Externalities arguments: public support for the arts generates positive 'spillover' benefits, which range from direct employment benefits to the indirect 'multiplier' benefits that result from consumption of cultural goods and services that would not otherwise be available, such as tourism and recreation.
3 Option demand arguments: even among those taxpayers who do not consume publicly supported arts and culture, ensuring the provision of these cultural products and services gives them an 'existence value' should they choose to consume them in the future.
4 Market distortion arguments: there may be insufficient information or excessive uncertainty to generate a socially optimal level of private investment in some forms of cultural production, and government support can correct such market distortions.
5 Merit goods arguments: some forms of cultural good possess an intrinsic value that justifies public support for supply over and above those levels that the market would support.

Following influential studies such as Myerscough (1988), there was a fashion in the 1990s for what have been termed arts impact or arts multiplier studies, that sought to demonstrate the positive outcomes to the wider economy deriving from government support for the arts and culture. This emerged as a very pragmatic response in the arts sector to the perceived need for measurable benefits from public expenditure that could convince public policy makers, particularly sceptics in economics departments such as Treasury and Finance.

A series of economic impact models were developed that pointed to direct and indirect economic benefits of cultural expenditure including:

1 Immediate consumption impacts, e.g. the amount spent on tickets to attend an art exhibition, performance or festival, and the jobs that it creates;
2 Intermediate 'multiplier' impacts, e.g. the spending by those who consume cultural goods and services on ancillary goods and services, such as restaurant meals or taxi rides associated with the visit, or provision of catering for those involved in making a film on location, or hotel bookings by tourists attending an event;
3 Long-run growth impacts, e.g. increases in property values arising from the 'buzz' of a vibrant cultural environment or the prestige associated with hosting major cultural events or housing major cultural institutions (Seaman, 2000).

Economists have identified several problems with these arguments. The most notable is that they typically ignore the concept of opportunity cost, or the options that are foregone when a decision is made to spend public funds on one activity rather than another. The fact that public spending on the arts and culture has positive multiplier or spillover effects does not resolve the question of whether the same money may generate more benefits if spent on something else, whether it is more hospital beds, new schools, highways or nuclear weapons (Seaman, 2000; Towse, 2010: 283–286). There is inevitably an implicit preference for arts expenditure in such arguments that arise, as Throsby (2001) correctly notes, from the perception that forms of cultural value exist in the goods, services and activities themselves that warrant their support whether or not they are also economically beneficial. There is also the danger, noted by Court (1994), of management capture, where the current beneficiaries of public subsidy – particular clusters of arts managers, artists and patrons – use these arguments to defend the arts funding *status quo* and marginalise critics. At any rate, whatever the merits attached to public support for the arts and culture in its own terms, economic impact statements did not constitute arguments that economists accepted as a suitable use of the tools of their discipline.

Cultural economics models based on applied neoclassical welfare economics implicitly accept that these sectors are a net cost to the economy overall and, almost in spite of themselves, primarily focus upon those cultural activities and sectors that are the largest recipients of public funding support. This can in turn further the perception that the arts sectors are not net creators of economic value, and that the case for public subsidy arises from the absence of commercial value attached to such activities. A different approach can be found in new institutional economics as applied to the creative industries by Richard Caves (2000). Caves notes that whereas 'economists … have mainly focused on public subsidy for the elite performing arts', the ambit of economic argument can be extended to 'the "creative" industries supplying goods and services that we broadly associate with cultural, artistic or … entertainment value', and can include 'book and magazine publishing, the creative arts (painting, sculpture), the performing arts (theatre, opera, concerts, dance), sound recordings, cinema and TV films … fashion and toys and games' (Caves, 2000: 1). Caves explores the characteristics through which 'creative goods and services, their processes of production, and the preferences and tastes of creative artists differ in substantial and systematic (if not universal) ways from their counterparts in the rest of the economy where creativity plays a lesser (if not negligible) role' (Caves, 2000: 2).

On the question of what makes the creative industries different, Caves identifies seven core elements:

1 Considerable uncertainty about the likely demand for creative product, due to the fact that creative products are 'experience goods', where buyers lack information prior to consumption, and where the satisfaction derived is largely subjective and intangible;

2 The importance of non-economic motivations for creative producers in pursuing their work and creative activity, but also their reliance upon the performance of more 'humdrum' activities (e.g. accounting, marketing and legal services) in order for such activities to be economically successful;

3 The frequently collective nature of creative production, and the need to develop and maintain creative teams with diverse skills, who often also possess diverse interests and expectations about the final product;

4 The almost infinite variety of creative products available, both within particular formats (e.g. DVDs at a rental store), and between formats;

5 Vertically differentiated skills, or what Caves terms the 'A list/B list' phenomenon, which leads to substantial pay differentials (the 'star system') and the ways in which producers or other content aggregators rank and assess creative personnel;

6 The need to co-ordinate diverse creative activities within a relatively short and often finite time frame;

7 The durability of many cultural products, and the capacity of their producers to continue to extract economic rents such as copyright and royalties payments long after the period of production.

If these are unique features of the creative industries, Caves' key insight lies in his application of the theory of contract and the economics of institutions to these questions. What these seven characteristics point to, for Caves, is major risk and uncertainty about the economic outcomes of creative activities. This uncertainty and risk, and the need to spread risk and provide insurance to creative producers, has provided one reason for public funding for some creative activities. In commercial terms, risk and uncertainty are also managed through contracts, whereby the various parties involved in the production and distribution of a creative product seek to manage risk and diversify rewards, based upon the skills and capacities they bring to the project and the need to ensure mutual obligation to meet commitments. The ongoing management of risks, contracts and creative production processes is a factor that leads to industrial organisation in the creative industries, in forms such as publishing, recording, broadcasting and film companies for commissioning production and managing distribution; guilds, unions, and legal arrangements for protecting creative producers; and intermediaries such as agents for managing the more commercial elements of a career in creative practice.

In emphasising the role of contracts and networks in the formation of 'loose teams' in the creative industries, Caves points to a way in which the economic logics of these sectors are becoming more generalised. This trend has also been observed by Lash and Urry (1994) in their analysis of how cultural industries provided a template for post-Fordist manufacturing, and Rifkin's (2000) analysis of the 'Hollywood model' as the team-based production prototype of 21st century 'cultural capitalism'. This notion of the creative industries as 'canaries in the coal mine' for the 21st century innovation-led economy has been further developed from the perspective of new institutional or evolutionary economics by Potts (2007), Potts et al. (2008) and Cunningham and Potts (2009). These authors argue that the cultural economics approach outlined above is flawed both in terms of the logic and consistency of its arts advocacy claims, but also in its acceptance of common wisdom that 'the arts were a perpetual economic basket case of productivity deficits, and market failure that rendered them effectively permanent wards of the public purse' (Potts, 2007: 2), which was in turn reflective on their exclusive focus upon the publicly supported elite arts. If, however, we extend the concept outwards to consider sectors such as digital content, games and interactive media – as creative industries policy has explicitly sought to do – it is argued that these industries are at the core of contemporary innovation systems. In the relationship between creativity and innovation and its application in the form of new and innovative product, services, design and processes, it is argued, the creative industries sectors 'do not just facilitate the origination of novelty, but also work to facilitate the adoption and adaptation of new technologies – through design and advertising, for example – along with the embedding of new technologies and their ongoing maintenance' (Potts 2007: 8). The 'surprising' implication of this work – and the marker of how far the economic discourse has moved from the 1990s to the present – is that as the cultural sectors and creative industries are founded around dynamic, open, self-organising networks, they come to be at the centre of what Benkler (2006) terms the networked information economy, rather than being the 'worthy' recipients of public subsidy out of economic wealth generated primarily by the industrial economy. Creative industries instead appear as important enablers to the economy as a whole, providers of intermediate inputs to other industry sectors, and as sites for experimentation and the search for novelty, as part of wider innovation trends in the economy:

> Although these shifts are occurring in all industries, the leading sectors are in the creative industries – film, TV, computer games, e-business, mobile phones ... This is because we now live in a world where everything is connected and where innovation is the key to survival. The creative digital sectors are the canaries in the mine ... the first signs of the wave that is moving through all industries. (Hearn and Pace, 2006: 55)

Production of Culture/Cultural Economy

An important perspective on the creative industries has been provided from a series of researchers working within a framework that may be termed the production of culture or cultural economy approaches. The origins of the production of culture approach can be found in the work of Richard Peterson (1976) on the occupational and organisational factors that shaped the relationship between cultural producers and markets in fields such as popular music, and the work of Howard Becker (1982) on 'art worlds' as the point of intersection between artists, art markets, art institutions and arts discourse and criticism that filters and shapes what artistic and creative works become the most prominent and successful (cf. Hesmondhalgh, 2007a: 35–36). More recently, the term is associated with applied research into the creative industries undertaken by authors such as Andy Pratt (Pratt, 2004a, 2004b) which seeks to integrate analyses of cultural production, distribution and consumption with an emphasis upon the spatial dimensions of the interaction between economy and culture 'to fashion an account of the situated nature of economic action and the ways in which this articulated to place … and to cultural production' (Pratt, 2004b: 118). It has often had a policy orientation, although in doing so this work has often been critical of dominant creative industries policy approaches.

Work on the production of culture draws attention to the questions of breadth and depth involved in analysing the creative industries, as discussed in Chapter One. In the work involved in revising the UNESCO Framework for Cultural Statistics, it was noted that any attempt to generate statistically meaningful and policy relevant data for these sectors confronts the breadth question, or which industries are included in the definition of creative industries, and the depth question, or what are the range of activities that need to be undertaken to produce a cultural output and what are the relationships between these activities? The breadth question was explored in Chapter One with particular reference to creative industries debates in the United Kingdom, but it intersects with the depth question in so far as the production of cultural or creative inputs rest upon a range of non-cultural or non-creative activities associated with manufacture and distribution, and that the circulation and consumption of creative products is itself embedded in a wider institutional infrastructure that includes activities such as exhibition, archiving, education and interpretation.

In moving to develop a revised Framework that recognised the expanded economic and social significance of culture, enabled current available data to be used, and would allow for international comparative assessments, UNESCO understood culture as operating across six direct domains and two related domains (UNESCO, 2009: 22–32). The direct domains were:

1 Cultural and natural heritage: museums, archaeological and historical places, cultural landscapes, natural heritage;
2 Performance and celebration: performing arts, music, and festivals, fairs and feasts;
3 Visual arts and crafts: fine arts, photography, crafts;
4 Books and print media: books, newspapers and magazines, other printed matter, virtual publishing, libraries, book fairs;
5 Audiovisual and interactive media: film and video, television and radio, Internet TV and podcasting, video games;
6 Design and creative services: fashion design, graphic design, interior design, landscape design, architectural services, advertising services.

In addition, there were two related domains:

1 Tourism, hospitality and accommodation;
2 Sports and recreation, including amusement parks, theme parks and gambling.

All of these domains possess what are referred to as transversal domains that include:

- Intangible cultural heritage: oral traditions and expressions, ritual, languages, social practices;
- Education and training: specialist pedagogical and other learning activities that support the development, understanding and reception of culture, including vocational training (e.g. art and dance schools, film and digital media production courses) and critique (e.g. art history, literary critique, media and cultural studies);
- Archiving and preserving: the conservation, collection and management of particular sites and repositories of cultural forms (material and immaterial) for the purpose of preservation, exhibition and re-use (e.g. preservation of historic sites and buildings, picture libraries, sound recordings, digital archives);
- Equipment and supporting materials.

The concept of a culture cycle was developed by UNESCO (2009: 19–21) to capture the process of value creation within and across these domains, and includes:

1 Creation: the origination and authoring of ideas and content;
2 Production: the making of cultural works, whether as one-off productions (e.g. crafts, paintings, sculptures) or as mass reproducible cultural forms (e.g. books, movies, TV programmes), as well as the manufacture of goods required for the production of cultural works (e.g. musical instruments, printing materials);
3 Dissemination: the distribution of generally mass reproducible cultural products to consumer and exhibitors (e.g. film and video distribution, retailing of music and computer games);
4 Exhibition/reception: provisions of live and/or unmediated experiences to audiences through granting or selling restricted access to consume/participate in often time-based cultural activities (e.g. play, concerts, museum and gallery exhibitions, festivals);
5 Consumption/participation: the activities of audiences and participants in consuming cultural products and taking part in cultural activities and experiences (e.g. book reading, dancing, watching movies and TV programmes, listening to radio, visiting museums and galleries).

The culture cycle emphasises how 'culture can be viewed as resulting from a cognate set of processes', as well as how, as a result, 'policy makers must work with the knowledge that any intervention may have wider repercussions within the whole cycle' (UNESCO, 2009: 19, 21). Importantly, the Framework was revised between its draft stage and final stage to change this process from one of a culture production chain that was linear, to a network form that draws

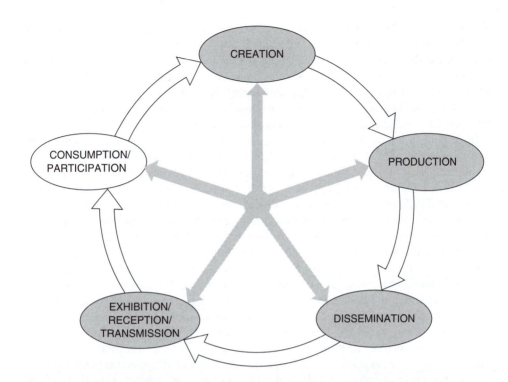

Figure 3.1 UNESCO Model of Culture Cycle

Source: UNESCO, 2009: 20.

attention to 'the interconnections across these activities, including the feedback processes by which activities (consumption) inspire the creation of new cultural products and artefacts' (UNESCO, 2009: 20). Moreover, it is acknowledged that new digital media technologies may in fact merge some of these functions, as seen with the ways in which people can now create, distribute and consume video simultaneously through *YouTube* (Burgess and Green, 2009). The concept of the culture cycle makes explicit the extent to which the production and distribution of culture is becoming less and less the exclusive preserve of unique communities of artists as content creators, and how it is increasingly the case that consumption drives cultural production as well as production shaping cultural consumption (Hartley, 2004).

The production of culture perspective also provides vital insights into the spatial dimensions of cultural production and consumption, and the scope and limitations of creative industries policy initiatives to develop particular locations as leading cultural sites. The resilience of Hollywood as a film and television industry production cluster, outlined by Scott (2005), means not only that its high volume of audiovisual productions acts as a magnet attracting creative people to southern California, such as actors, scriptwriters, producers and digital effects production houses, but also that archiving institutions such as the American

Film Institute (AFI) locate there, and that universities such as the University of California, Los Angeles (UCLA) attract the most talented film and television students and scholars from around the world. On the other hand, as Coe and Johns (2004) observe, alternative film and television production sites, such as Vancouver in British Columbia, Canada, and Manchester, England, face challenges in developing and maintaining vibrant sectors due to their reliance in the 'political economy of networks' upon Los Angeles and London respectively for finance, decision-making, distribution and exhibition.

In Britain, an important question for creative industries policy is whether there can be sectoral diversification of production and distribution activities outside London to the benefit of the rest of the UK economy. Pratt identified that London accounted for 24 per cent of all cultural employment in the UK in 1991 (Pratt, 1997) and 24.5 per cent of cultural employment in England in 2000 (Pratt, 2004a), and that the focus on national indicators of creative industries' economic performance left open the question of whether there was scope to develop these sectors across the regions of England, Scotland, Wales and Northern Ireland, given the dominance of London over distribution, exhibition and decision-making. Attempting to do this requires specific attention to what Jeffcutt (2004) refers to as the 'creative industries ecosystem' of particular cities and regions in order to best target policy initiatives, although as Hesmondhalgh and Pratt (2005) observe, this does come up against the increasingly multinational nature of economic organisation of creative industries at the national and global scales. The danger involved in ignoring local structures of cultural production are those described by Jeffcutt as 'a policy of late "me too" – an economic region that, from a situation of unexplored disadvantage, desires to imitate the economy of elsewhere in the vain hope that its success will also arrive once a copy … is established locally' (Jeffcutt, 2004: 79).

This interest in the dynamics of the production of culture is not associated with cultural economics in its traditional sense, but rather with the work arising out of cultural and economic geography, institutional economics, cultural studies and political economy, which points to the growing culturalisation of the economy, or what is also referred to as *cultural economy* (du Gay and Pryke, 2002; Amin and Thrift, 2004). In this literature, one of the difficulties in attempting to define the creative industries is the fact that the capitalist economy more generally is acquiring characteristics and features historically associated with the cultural sectors. Lash and Urry (1994) argued that contemporary capitalism was marked by a growing degree of reflexive accumulation, marked by a new degree of aesthetic reflexivity in the spheres of both production and consumption, as capitalist production became increasingly design-intensive and oriented towards niche consumer markets. In a similar vein, Scott (2004) observed that the line between 'symbolic' and 'material' goods is increasingly difficult to sustain, as 'One of the peculiarities of modern capitalism is that the cultural economy continues to expand … as an expression of the incursions of sign-value into ever-widening spheres of productive activity as firms seek to intensify the design content and styling of their outputs in the endless search for competitive advantage' (Scott, 2004: 462–463). In this literature, a pervasive question arises as to whether economic relations have become more 'cultural' over time, or whether there is a greater awareness among theorists of intersections between cultural and economic factors. As Don Slater has observed:

There is the constant danger of confusing new movements within thought (the new understanding that culture and economy cannot be theorized separately) from new empirical developments. Is it the case that culture is actually more central to economic process than it was before? We need to develop more adequate theories of the sociology of economic life rather than proclaim epochal social revolutions that are merely the artefact of the inadequate theories and theoretical division of labour we have inherited. (Slater, 2002: 76)

Du Gay and Pryke (2002) have usefully broken down the question of whether there has been a culturalisation of economic life into three component elements. First, there are arguments that the management of culture is now the central element of improving organisational performance. Business management literature has increasingly focused upon culture as the key variable in organisational performance, and the need for successful organisations to develop shared symbolic systems that link performative activity to wider systems of meaning both within and outside of the organisation (Clegg et al., 2005). Second, the growth of creative industries is linked to the rise of service industries more generally, and the increasingly important component of services to all areas of economic production. Giarini (2002) has observed that the pure cost of production or manufacturing of goods rarely accounts for more than 20 per cent of the final price, and that 70–80 per cent of the cost is attributable to service and delivery functions undertaken before manufacturing (research and development, financing), during manufacturing (quality control, safety), selling (logistics, distribution networks), during product and system utilisation (maintenance, leasing), and after product and system utilisation (waste management, recycling). Growth in the 'services component' of all industries has placed renewed attention upon those market transactions where 'the interpersonal links, the attachments, are inscribed in the service relation itself' (du Gay and Pryke, 2002: 3). Finally, there is the question of whether consumption practices have become more reflexive, and greater attention is attached by a wider section of the population to the status attributes of goods and services, as linked to brand identity, design, fashion, etc. While there has been much discussion of standardisation in the service industries, Callon et al. (2004) have argued that the rise of the services sector is better understood as emblematic of what they term the *economy of qualities*, where the satisfaction consumers seek from particular products and services is increasingly particular and reflexive, as 'the economy of goods gives way to the economy of relations' (Callon et al., 2004: 75). They argue that one of the features of what is sometimes referred to as the 'new economy' is that consumers are themselves increasingly invited to participate in the processes through which one type of product is differentiated from a seemingly similar one on the basis of its perceived 'qualities', but that the qualities do not exist independently of the judgements made by multiple agents, including consumers as well as producers, advertisers, marketers, regulators, etc.

The field of cultural economy research is growing. New academic journals, such as the *Journal of Cultural Economy*, have emerged. The aim of this journal is described as being to understand 'the role played by various forms of material cultural practice in the organisation of the economy and the social, and of the relations between them' (*Journal of Cultural Economy*, Aims & Scope). I would argue that one limitation with these projects as currently constituted, however, is a lack of engagement with relevant thinking in economics, due in part to a caricatured understanding of the field, but also due to a tendency to think of economists as the ideological foes of researchers in cultural studies and the critical humanities. Creative industries research, as it evolves, will be one arena where we can expect growing collaborative work around questions of cultural economy, particularly as they are emerging in new fields such as actor-network theories, cultural economic geography, and the new institutional economics. It can be argued that this growing interdisciplinarity can be seen as a corollary of a growing culturalisation of the economy, which runs much deeper and along a much wider and deeper range of tributaries than claims that the cultural field is being captured by neoclassical and neo-liberal economists.

Endnote

1   If we take the annual awarding of a Nobel Prize for Economics as one of the clearest and most public indicators of where the mainstream of the economics discipline is situated, it can be noted that a significant number of Nobel Prizes have been awarded to economists who have been identified critics of established orthodoxies in the field, including Amartya Sen (1998 Nobel Prize winner), Joseph Stiglitz (2001), George Akerlof (2001), Paul Krugman (2008) and Elinor Ostrom (2009). It must also be noted that perhaps the most famous economist of the twentieth century, John Maynard Keynes, was perhaps the founder of cultural economics in its current form, reflecting his role as the founding chair of the Council for the Encouragement of Music and the Arts (CEMA), which would become the Arts Council of Great Britain (Flew, 2010). For those whom critics identify as neo-liberals, Keynes has always been a major intellectual foe. For a recent critique of elements of neoclassical economics from within the discipline, see Quiggan (2010).

4 Products, Services, Production and Creative Work

Having reviewed the development of creative industries as a policy discourse and its theoretical and conceptual underpinnings, the next two chapters will consider the economic dynamics of creative industries. In this chapter, we will consider some of the features of production processes, products and services, and the nature of labour markets that enable us to speak of these sectors in a collective sense as being the creative industries. At the same time, this analysis will draw attention to some of the differences that exist among these sectors which require close attention in order to recognise that there are divergences among those industries that preclude a one-size-fits-all response at either a policy or an analytical level. This will allow for consideration in the next chapter of the differential impacts of technology, location, international trade and public policy on these industries.

It was noted in Chapter One that the original DCMS classification of the British creative industries was a list-based approach. This had the advantage from a policy point of view of identifying relevant communities of interest, bringing together the arts, media and ICT sectors, and producing data that could demonstrate the value of these industries to the British economy, in a context where traditional industry statistical measurements appeared to have understated the size and significance of these sectors. It left some recurring problems, however, such as presenting a seemingly heterogeneous set of industries as possessing an underlying commonality around creativity as a primary driver, and conflating industries with very different economic dynamics and relations between market forces and state support. It was also seen as being based around concepts – individual creativity and intellectual property – that were either too loose to be a means of differentiating one set of activities from another, as in the case of creativity, or, through identifying the outputs of the creative industries in terms of intellectual property, generating policy outcomes that may be problematic for the application of creativity itself (Flew, 2005a). The list-based approach also invariably drew attention to the question of boundaries – which industries were in and which were out. The British DCMS list included antiques and crafts, but excluded the GLAM (Galleries, Libraries, Archives and Museum) sectors, as well as sport, tourism and significant parts of the entertainment industries.

There are two further aspects of the boundary question that need further elaboration: the creative elements of cultural products with increasingly complex global production value chains, and the more generalised application of creativity in a much wider range of products and services as a value-adding element. In relation to the first, one of the manufacturing industries which has been most dramatically transformed by economic globalisation has been the textile, clothing and footwear (TCF) industries. Clothing manufacture has largely migrated from the advanced industrial nations of Europe, North America, Australia and New Zealand, to the lower-wage developing nations of Asia (especially China), the Middle East and North Africa (MENA) and Latin America. While clothing and textiles are considered to be manufacturing industries, where there remain considerable cost advantages to large-scale production and where globalisation has generated powerful imperatives to relocate production in order to reduce costs, the process of designing fashionable clothes is an activity that is distinct in the value chain to their manufacture. It is in the area of fashion design where particular metropolitan centres (New York, Paris, London, Tokyo, Milan and a small number of others) have sought to maintain global ascendancy, with design occurring independently of the clothing manufacture. Successful fashion design requires design skills, of course, but it also requires something more intangible, which can be referred to as creativity, that is then linked to particular individuals and brands (Santagana, 2004). At the demand end, the social nature of consumption, and the importance of fashion as a driver of conspicuous consumption, invidious distinction and social emulation, ensures that questions of fashion overlay debates about the utility of clothing. Whether conspicuous consumption, invidious distinction and social emulation drives are increasing over time is an open question, but the rise of mass media and celebrity culture have certainly given new momentum to such trends, first identified by Thorstein Veblen when he was writing in the late nineteenth century (Carter, 2003; Marshall, 2006; Hartley and Montgomery, 2009). Creative industries arise at the distinction here between design and manufacture, although there is always the potential for arbitrariness in such distinctions, as they co-exist within the same TCF value chain.[1]

Design as a Creative Industry

Design has consistently been identified as being at the core of the creative industries, along with the arts, media and information technology. In their report for the US National Research Council of the National Academies, Mitchell et al. observed that: 'Innovative design is often situated precisely at the intersection of technologically and culturally creative practices. On the one hand, designers are frequently avid to exploit technological advances and to explore their human potential. On the other, they typically have close intellectual alliances with visual and other artists' (Mitchell et al., 2003: 8).

The Cox Review of Creativity in Business (HM Treasury, 2006) saw the application of creativity through innovative design as being at the core of maintaining the competitiveness of British industry, as globalisation eroded traditional sources of competitive advantage. It understood design as providing the link between the generation of new ideas (creativity) and the application of new ideas as new products and services (innovation), as 'it shapes

Table 4.1 Design Disciplines and Resulting Specialisations

Primary Disciplines	Alternate names or terms used in the industry and education at present	Specialisations of the primary disciplines	Other specialisations which use the primary area of training
Industrial Design	Product Design	Furniture Design, Textile Design (construction and finish of fabrics), Fashion Design (design of apparel for manufacture), Jewellery Design (design of jewellery for batch or mass production	Exhibition and Display Design, Digital Animation Design, Digital Game Design
Interior Design	Interior Architecture, Spatial Design	Commercial Interior Design, Residential Interior Design, Retail Design, TV, Film & Theatre Set	Exhibition and Display Design, Furniture Design
Graphic Design	Visual Communication	Web Design, Multimedia Design, Digital Animation Design, Exhibition and Display Design, Digital Game Design	Textile Design (printed textiles)

Source: DIA, 2010.

ideas to become practical and attractive propositions for users or customers. Design may be described as creativity deployed to a specific end' (HM Treasury, 2006: 2). Singapore has given design a central place in its creative industries strategy, establishing the Design Singapore Council and identifying design as an activity that 'changes and improves lives, inspires creativity and new forms of expression [and] also enhances business competitiveness in today's crowded marketplace' (Design Singapore Council, 2010).

Design as an activity occurs across a range of industries, and it has only been very recently that people have spoken of a design industry. The Design Institute of Australia (DIA) classifies the design professions as shown in Table 4.1.

As Table 4.1 indicates, design works across manufacturing, services and digital media. While Fashion Design is classified here as a form of Industrial Design, it is commonly located within the creative industries space, along with the Visual Communications sectors, such as Graphic Design, Web Design, Digital Animation Design and Digital Game Design.

Design exemplifies the creative industries' concept of commercial applications of creativity. The Design Institute of Australia describes a designer as one who applies rational

(Continued)

(Continued)

creativity to a business product, process or service, and who 'can be said to be both technician and artist', as they 'develop solutions to commercial needs that require the balancing of technical, commercial, human and aesthetic requirements' (Design Institute of Australia, 2010). The value that design adds to a business product or service is often barely tangible, but can be a distinctive source of competitive advantage. Products that exemplify good design principles can become market leaders and maintain brand leadership even as lower cost alternatives become available. Ten years after its introduction, the Apple iPod still accounted for 70 per cent of global sales of portable media players, even though a plethora of cheaper alternatives were on the market; a significant part of this was due to its design leadership, combining simplicity, functionality and style.

The scope to generate leadership through design varies across firms and industries. The Swedish Industrial Design Foundation refers to a four-step 'design ladder', from design being a marginal component of product development, to design as styling of the final physical form, to design as a method applied to product development, to design as innovation, where designers are involved in all stages of a business development process (SIDF, 2010). The most difficult element of design to capture is that associated with aesthetics and subjective or creative processes that 'relates to fashion, human behaviour, emotion and cultural influences such as the cultural meaning of symbols' (DIA, 2010). The capacity to generate design excellence, however, is increasingly valued around the world, and points to the fusion of creative thinking and business innovation that is central to twenty-first-century creative industries.

The other issue that arises is the value of distinguishing the creative industries in an environment where applications of creativity are of increasing importance throughout the economy. Part of the interest in the DCMS definition was that it seemed to give policy weight to a set of trends that had been observed by sociologists and cultural theorists for a number of years, particularly the relationship between the turn towards more flexible, small-batch systems of production – what has also been termed post-Fordism – and a growing reflexivity in personal consumption, whereby people were increasingly using commodities to construct a personal identity (Lash and Urry, 1987; Murray, 1989). Bilton and Leary proposed that the creative industries 'produce "symbolic goods" (ideas, experiences, images) where value is dependent upon the end user (viewer, audience, reader, consumer) decoding and finding value within these meanings' (Bilton and Leary, 2002: 50). The growing 'semiotisation of consumption' (Lash and Urry, 1994: 61) or the 'aestheticisation of everyday life' (Featherstone, 1991) were arguably turning the traditional 'culture industry' thesis on its head: rather than cultural production becoming more like large-scale manufacturing, it was proposed that 'ordinary manufacturing is becoming more and more like the production of culture' (Lash and Urry, 1994: 123). In particular Lash and Urry argued that capitalism was increasingly driven by the production of 'newness' through design and other forms of product innovation rather than the reproduction and steady refinement of established commodities. For Allen Scott (2004) the line between 'symbolic' and 'material' goods was becoming more difficult to sustain since:

> One of the peculiarities of modern capitalism is that the cultural economy continues to expand … as an expression of the incursions of sign-value into ever-widening spheres of productive activity as firms seek to intensify the design content and styling of their outputs in the endless search for competitive advantage. (Scott, 2004: 462–463)

Nonetheless, the DCMS focus on creative inputs and intellectual property outputs generated as many questions as it resolved at both ends of the equation. The blurring of lines between the cultural and the economic, or the symbolic and the material, raises the question of what is a non-creative industry or activity, and whether claims about the distinctiveness of creative industries can continue to be made if creativity is becoming increasingly important to competitive survival (Pratt, 2005)? If the application of fashion design to clothing marks out a creative industry space, could the same claim be made for the interior design of a BMW car, or the cabin design of a QANTAS aircraft? The literature on creativity makes it difficult to demarcate industries on the basis of its application, both because it tends to be noticed *ex post* – we typically recognise it only when it is applied successfully – and because there is a striving to apply creativity more effectively across all branches of economic production.[2]

At the same time, there are a number of authors who have expressed the concern that the creative industries net has already been cast too widely from a policy point of view, obscuring core cultural policy questions as they pertain to the publicly-supported arts in particular, by meshing it in with policy discourses pertaining to media convergence and the 'information society' (Garnham, 2005; Galloway and Dunlop, 2007; O'Connor, 2009). It was noted in Chapter One that while Howkins (2001) may be technically right in questioning the demarcation between the arts and sciences found in restricting definitions of the creative industries to some IP-generating activities while excluding others, the policy implications of an all-inclusive definition were likely to become particularly unwieldy. The 'concentric circles' approach adopted by The Work Foundation (2007) and the European Union, which distinguishes between the cultural and creative industries on the basis of the extent to which particular goods and services are 'vehicles for symbolic messages to those who consume them' (Throsby, 2008a: 219), is representative of such an approach, distinguishing 'core' cultural industries from more commercially oriented creative industries such as advertising, architecture, design and software.

This chapter will draw upon the approach developed by the National Endowment for Science, Technology and the Arts (NESTA) (2006), Higgs et al. (2007) and Higgs et al. (2008) in moving beyond individual industries – the list-based approach – to developing more workable taxonomies of creative industries sectors by the types of outputs they produce. There is invariably a degree of arbitrariness in such taxonomies, but this also exists with the list-based approach, and moving beyond the flat terrain of lists to broad taxonomies enables a better handle to be gained on the dynamics of broad sectors and practices within which particular firms and industries are located. For example, it can be recognised that the issues facing books, newspapers and magazines are not synonymous, but a category such as publishing and print media does identify commonalities in terms of the form of output, the medium being used, and the technological changes it faces (e.g. the impact of digitisation in all of its forms on practices of reading and writing).

It also represents my considerable scepticism as to whether taxonomies based on the perceived intrinsic value of some cultural products, or the question of whether some are 'more than simply utilitarian, insofar as they serve in addition some larger communicative purpose' (Throsby, 2008a: 219) is a sustainable distinction from either a policy or an intellectual point of view. From a policy point of view, its most obvious implication – and arguably the reason for its attractiveness – is that it re-establishes the distinctiveness of arts policy, and particularly the intrinsic value of those arts sectors primarily reliant upon public sector support. As a result, it has a natural constituency of support among those in major cultural institutions and in the broadly defined arts community. But this is also precisely its weakness. In Australia, Westbury and Eltham have argued that 'the logic of many [publicly] funded arts organisations is poorly equipped to respond to the plethora of new artists, art forms, audiences, genres, and subcultures emerging in a rapidly changing cultural dynamic' (Westbury and Eltham, 2010: 42). Even critics of creative industries, such as Hesmondhalgh, nonetheless acknowledge that one important contribution of the term has been to 'draw attention to relationships between commercial and non-commercial sectors of cultural production' (Hesmondhalgh, 2009: 247). In his exhaustive account of questions of cultural value, John Frow concluded that 'there is no longer a stable hierarchy of value ... running from "high" to "low" culture' (Frow, 1995: 1). John Holden has systematically presented the case for a need to now think of the arts and the media, high and popular culture, and commercial and publicly supported culture together:

> Under the old model, politics could confine cultural policy to a very narrow field, and hence it had a very low value in the pecking order of governments. In the old model, popular culture could be left to its own devices. You might want to put some limits on the content of books and films, and censor them, you might want to licence the playing of live music in pubs, but popular culture could more or less get on with it. As for the arts, so-called high culture, well there you might want to argue that as a matter of national status you should have a gallery and an opera house, but you would conceive of culture as essentially peripheral, a leisure pursuit, an ornament to society, something to be afforded and indulged in once the hard business of the day was done ... But under the new model of culture ... cultural policy is no longer confined to a small budget line and a narrow set of questions about art. On the contrary, if we understand culture ... as a networked activity, where funded, home-made and commercial culture are deeply interconnected – then we can start to appreciate the wider value of culture in and to society. (Holden, 2009: 449–450)

A Sectoral Taxonomy of the Creative Industries

In Chapter One, we considered both the 'concentric circles' model of distinguishing cultural and creative industries proposed by The Work Foundation (2007), and the multi-sectoral model developed by NESTA (2006). The NESTA study proposed a four-fold classification

Table 4.2 Creative Sectors by Type of Product

Group	Industry examples
Creative originals producers	Visual arts and crafts, antiques, designer-making, writing, photography
Creative content producers	Film, broadcasting (TV and radio), publishing, recorded music, interactive media (games, Web, mobile)
Creative experience providers	Performing arts, museums, galleries and libraries, live music, heritage and tourism
Creative service providers	Advertising, architecture, graphic design, public relations, promotion (e.g. agents), production facilities

Source: NESTA 2006: 55.

of the creative industries based around sectors that have sufficient commonalities in terms of the business models, value chains, market structures and final products to warrant a common approach for the purposes of policy development.

Within these four categories of creative industries, a distinction can be made between simple cultural goods and complex cultural goods. The economist Richard Caves (2000) makes this distinction between producing/supplying simple creative goods and complex creative goods, and it is central to differentiating the complexity of contract relations within these sectors. Simple creative goods are those where 'one artist deals with a single firm that promotes and distributes their creative work' (Caves, 2000: 19). Caves identifies four elements that shape the supply of simple creative goods:

1 Endemic oversupply of creative talent relative to market opportunity, and the processes through which one aims to get ahead of a very large pack, such as professional training, getting noticed by relevant 'gatekeepers', and getting work published, exhibited or distributed;
2 The role played by cultural intermediaries such as dealers and agents in providing exposure to the artist's creative work, and its distribution through relevant channels;
3 The one-to-one contracts that are developed between individual artists (e.g. visual artists, writers, musicians) and distributors, which provide a revenue stream in the form of royalties based upon sales of the creative product;
4 The tendency for highly unequal distribution of income derived from creative work in these sectors (what Caves refers to as the 'A list/B list' phenomenon (Caves, 2000: 7–8)), and the large number of artists who either supplement their income through other forms of work or pursue their creative work more as an intermittent hobby than as a full-time career.

Caves draws a contrast with complex creative goods, which require complex teams and have time-dependent production schedules, where there are multiple contracts in existence, and where businesses face a recurring question of whether to employ people through individual one-off contracts or to acquire creative talent through long-term contracts, in-house production or industrial organisation. The term complex cultural goods is not primarily based upon the nature of the creative product itself – films typically cost more to produce than music, but you can have high-budget ('high concept') music and low-budget films – but rather on the complexity of the contractual arrangements associated with large creative teams and time-dependent production schedules. Associated with such complex teams is the tendency towards industrial organisation (large corporations, industrialised production processes, workers organised into guilds and unions, etc.) to ensure ongoing production of a sufficient quality to go to market, so that distributors have a product catalogue or repertoire that enables them to balance successful and less commercially successful individual products ('hits and misses').

Using the typology of simple and complex cultural goods, and mapping it on to the classificatory schema developed by NESTA, we find that what we have referred to as the creative originals sector broadly corresponds to the supply of simple cultural goods, and that the creative content sector broadly corresponds to individuals and firms engaged with the production of complex cultural goods. The latter are also synonymous with what Hesmondhalgh refers to as the core cultural industries, that 'deal primarily with the industrial production and circulation of texts', and into this catagory he includes film, broadcasting, Internet content, music, print and electronic publishing, digital games and advertising (Hesmondhalgh, 2007a: 12–13). Yet what is also apparent is that different elements of a creative activity can sit within different segments of the creative industries. In the case of music, the actual musical output may entail the production of a simple cultural good, but its distribution is large scale and a part of the creative content sector; moreover, live music events are a part of the sector based around creative experience services, and the musicians will draw upon creative service providers for the organisation of concerts, marketing of products, design and art work for albums, promotion and publicity, etc. Similarly, the act of writing a book is typically akin to the production of a simple cultural good, but these books are mostly distributed by large publishers, and authors may both engage agents and publicists and participate in creative experience events such as writers' festivals, as well as having their work made available at museums, galleries, libraries, etc.[3] Fashion design may be a simple cultural good, but sits within a wider nexus of creative content production (large-scale distribution), creative service provision (publicity and promotion), and creative experience services (fashion shows, events, etc.).

What is apparent is that value chain analysis is required in order to address what Pratt (2005) refers to as the depth question in creative industries research, or understanding cultural production as a multi-layered process that goes through different institutional and contractual arrangements, organisational forms, and modes of market and non-market relationships. The 2009 UNESCO Draft Framework for Cultural Statistics identified four elements (excluding consumption/participation, which will be returned to below) in the culture cycle discussed in Chapter Three:

1 Creation/origination;
2 Production/manufacture;
3 Distribution/dissemination;
4 Exhibition/reception.

The relationship between these stages will vary across creative industries types, but there is a characteristic creative industries model that is known as the 'hourglass' structure, with a large and dispersed number of content creators/originators and a small number of highly concentrated and often multinational distributors. The 'hourglass' structure has been understood by political economists such as Garnham (1990) and Hesmondhalgh (2007a) as being the defining organisational characteristic of production relations in these industries, and is described by Pratt (2008: 46) as involving 'domination by a handful of major international corporation, and sitting below them are many thousands of "companies" – these companies are very small … micro-enterprises comprising self-employed and two or three person businesses. There is a "missing middle" of small- and medium-sized enterprises, which leads to some challenges in terms of coordination'.

Finally, how do these understandings of creative industries sectoral types, production processes and cultural production cycles map on to the domains that have been developed as a way of clustering the *ad hoc* industry lists that were provided in the first iteration of creative industries policy discourse and academic research? The framework developed by

Table 4.3 Creative Industries Sectors by Type of Product

	Creative originals	Creative content	Creative experiences	Creative services
Advertising, Graphic Design and Marketing				Application of time and IP to other businesses
Architecture, Visual Arts and Design	Visual arts and crafts			
Film, Broadcast Media and Entertainment Software		Complex cultural goods with valuable IP		
Music Composition, Publishing and Performance	Music creation – simple cultural goods	Distribution of music through labels and agents	Live performances	
Performing Arts			Live performances – complex cultural goods	
Writing, Publishing and Print Media	Writing – simple cultural goods	Distribution of books and other works through publishers	Writers' festivals	

the Department of State Development and Industry (DSDI) (2003), Higgs et al. (2007) and Higgs et al. (2008) proposes six domains of creative industries activity: Advertising, Graphic Design and Marketing; Architecture, Visual Arts and Design; Film, Television and Entertainment Software; Music Composition, Publishing and Performance; Performing Arts; and Writing, Publishing and Print Media. Applying Caves' framework of simple and complex cultural goods, and the typology of creative originals, creative content, creative experiences and creative services, we find that there is a good match of three of these domains to the NESTA sectors:

- Film, Broadcast Media and Entertainment Software as creative content sectors, with high up-front costs, complex production processes, large-scale distribution, and valuable intellectual property (IP) embodied in the final product;
- Performing Arts (theatre, dance and opera) as creative experience sectors, with complex production processes and income contingent upon access to consumers in a particular time and place;
- Advertising, Graphic Design and Marketing as creative services sectors, which earn revenue by devoting time and applying IP to other businesses and organisations.

The complex and variegated nature of the cultural production cycle is most apparent in the domains of Music Composition, Publishing and Performance, and Writing, Publishing

Table 4.4 Classification of the Creative Industries

	Creative originals	Creative content	Creative experience	Creative services	Simple cultural goods	Complex cultural goods
Advertising				✓		
Architecture				✓		
Broadcast Media (TV and Radio)		✓				✓
Design (incl. Fashion)				✓		
Film and Video		✓				✓
Interactive Media (Web, Games, Mobile)		✓				✓
Museums, Galleries and Heritage			✓			
Music	✓	✓	✓		✓	
Visual Arts (incl. Crafts)	✓				✓	
Writing, Publishing and Print Media	✓	✓	✓		✓	

and Print Media, which involve activities across the dimensions of production of creative originals, large-scale distribution of content with potentially valuable IP, and a strong link between promotion, publicity and creative experiences. From this analysis, it is argued that the category of Architecture, Visual Arts and Design needs to be disaggregated, as the dynamics of the visual arts and crafts (creative originals, simple cultural goods, typically small-scale distribution) need to be separated from the architecture and design industries, which are more clearly commercial and client-driven enterprises that are congregated in the area of creative services.

For the remainder of this chapter and Chapter Five, we will understand the creative industries as a sector based around the ten industries identified by UNCTAD (2008) as those most commonly included in national cultural statistics, locating them within the four fields identified by NESTA (2006) and, where applicable, as producing simple or complex cultural goods as defined by Caves (2000).

Identifying the Creative Industries Workforce: The Creative Trident Approach

One of the difficulties that arises in making claims about the size and significance of the creative industries is that there has not until recently been an agreed methodology for determining the number of people working in these industries, and there has been a systematic tendency to underestimate the number of people working in creative industries occupations. The major issue is that there are two ways in which data derived from sources such as censuses and the Standard Industrial Classification (SIC) data can be used to measure the creative industries workforce. The first starts from the industries themselves, counting the number of people employed in creative industries. The second starts from occupational data, and counts the number of people working in creative occupations. The first counts the number of people engaged in non-creative occupations but working for creative industries firms (e.g. a sales person at a video store, a ticket seller at a theatre, or an accountant for a performing arts company), but misses those who are engaged in creative occupations but not working in the creative industries (e.g. a web designer employed by a bank, or a musician employed as a teacher). Both approaches understate the actual number of people engaged in creative industries employment, while producing different figures.

Major work has been undertaken on this by the Australian Research Council Centre of Excellence for Creative Industries and Innovation (CCI), based at the Queensland University of Technology, who have developed the Creative Trident approach in order to resolve this dilemma (Higgs et al., 2007; Higgs and Cunningham, 2008; Higgs et al., 2008). The nature of the problem, and the solution provided by the Creative Trident, can be illustrated using Australian Bureau of Statistics (ABS) data. From the 2001 data, the number of people employed in creative industries was 299,916 people, of whom 134,450 (44.8%)

(Continued)

(Continued)

were employed in creative occupations. The number employed in creative occupations was 271,467, of whom 137,017 (50.5%) were employed in other industries. Putting these two sets of figures together in the Creative Trident, there were 436,933 people in the sector, of whom:

- 134,450 were employed in creative occupations in the creative industries (Specialists);
- 137,017 were employed in other industries (Embedded Creatives);
- 165,466 were employed in business and support occupations in creative industries, who are often responsible for managing, accounting for, and technically supporting creative activity.

The figures are shown in Table 4.5.

Table 4.5 Creative Trident – Employment in Australian Creative Industries, 2001

Australian Census 2001 Employment	Employment within Creative Industries	Employment within Other Industries	Total Creatives	Embedded Proportion
Employment of People in 89 Specialist Creative Occupations	134,450	137,017	271,467	50.5%
Business and Support Workers	165,466		165,466	
Total Creative Industry	299,916	137,017	436,933	35.7%
Creative Occupation Proportion	44.8%		62.1%	

Source: Higgs et al., 2007: 10.

Importantly, the Creative Trident methodology finds that creative industries and occupations accounted for 5.4 per cent of the total Australian workforce in 2001, whereas earlier studies that focused solely upon the industries or occupations would find that the sector accounted for somewhere between 3.4 per cent and 3.7 per cent of the workforce. While more recent studies (Centre for International Economics, 2009) have modified these figures slightly downwards to 4.8 per cent in 2006, it nonetheless points to an industry sector that is among Australia's ten largest industries, and whose contribution to the economy is considerably higher than estimates from earlier studies from the 1990s, when major national cultural policies were being developed (DoCA, 1994). The CCI Creative Trident methodology has been applied to UK creative industries data by Higgs et al. (2008), who found that creative employment had grown by four times the total UK employment level over the 1981–2006 period, now accounting for 7 per cent of the UK workforce in 2006, as compared to 3.9 per cent in 1981 and 4.8 per cent in 1991 (Higgs et al., 2008: 5).

Table 4.6   Long-run Growth Rates in UK Creative Employment, 1981–2006

Mode	Census 1981	1991	2001	20-Year Average Growth	LFS 2006	25-Year Average Growth
Specialist	157,020	285,460	552,170	6.5%	699,931	6.2%
Support	288,850	313,440	690,641	4.5%	585,111	2.9%
Creative Industries	445,870	598,900	1,242,811	5.3%	1,285,042	4.3%
Embedded	457,130	524,750	645,067	1.7%	698,244	1.7%
Creative Occupations	614,150	810,210	1,197,237	3.4%	1,398,175	3.3%
Creative Employment	903,000	1,123,650	1,887,878	3.8%	1,983,286	3.2%
UK Workforce	22,866,100	23,452,230	26,575,780	0.8%	28,165,612	0.8%
Embedded Share of Creative Employment	51%	47%	34%		35%	
Creative Employment as Share of UK Workforce	3.9%	4.8%	7.1%		7.0%	

Source: Higgs et al., 2008: 6.
(NB: LFS stands for Labour Force Survey).

The Creative Trident methodology provides a level of rigour to calculating levels of the creative industries workforce, allowing for both comparisons over time and comparisons between countries. It can be extended to enable comparisons of average incomes in each of the creative industries sectors, the ratio of specialist to embedded creatives across each occupational groupings, industry growth rates over time, levels of income variation within the creative industries, and between the creative industries and industry as a whole. For example, the CCI study of Australian creative industries found that, contrary to received wisdom that creative industries workers earn lower incomes than other workers as a trade-off for greater enjoyment of creative work, average incomes were above the national average in all sectors except one (Music and Performing Arts), and were 77 per cent above average incomes for the Australian workforce in the Software Development and Interactive Content industries and 31 per cent above the average for all industries in 2001 (Higgs et al., 2007: 20). Using this data in another way, it found that 33 per cent of the creative industries workforce earned incomes above $A1000 per week in 2001, as opposed to 18 per cent for Australian workers as a whole.

While recognising the advance provided by Creative Trident methodology for understanding the size, significance and longer-term trends in the creative industries workforce, there remain a number of distinctive challenges for measuring this workforce that differ from those of other industries. The Centre for International Economics (CIE, 2009: 20–21) has identified these as including:

(Continued)

(Continued)

- The extent to which creative industries employment is 'hidden' in other industries, such as education (over 50 per cent of those in Music and Performing Arts occupations in Australia are 'embedded' in other industries, of which education is the largest).
- A high number of people working in the creative industries are doing so in a volunteer or unpaid capacity. It was estimated that 60 per cent of those working in arts activities in Australia were doing so in an unpaid capacity (CIE, 2009: 20).
- Many people in these sectors have more than one occupation, and pursue their creative industries activity as a second job. Higgs et al. found that in the UK, while only 3.7 per cent of the workforce had more than one job, 39.5 per cent of those in Music and Performing Arts had more than one job, as well as 8.5 per cent of those in Publishing (Higgs et al., 2008: 65).
- The creative industries have a long time line, and people may identify as working in creative occupations even if their actual participation is more sporadic.
- There are high levels of self-employment in the creative industries. While 13 per cent of all working in the UK were self-employed in 2006, and 14 per cent of professionals were self-employed, 33 per cent of those in creative occupations were self-employed, including 82 per cent of those in Music and Performing Arts and 47 per cent of those in Film, Radio, TV and Photography (Higgs et al., 2008: 93).
- Industry and occupational classifications are often changing quickly, particularly in those industries associated with digital content, where distinctions between 'creative' and other activities can shift quickly.
- Many of the fastest-growing activities related to the creative industries are being pursued on a non-paid, non-market basis, and the motivations for activities in this fast-growing 'social economy' remain an ongoing challenge to recognise their value and significance (Benkler, 2006; Quiggan and Potts, 2008).

Financing Creativity

The significance of differentiating the creative industries on a sectoral basis becomes apparent when we consider the variable significance of finance to different creative industries sectors. As Williams (1981) and Lee (1993) observed, there is a stage in cultural production that precedes the bringing together of creative talent, capital and technology, achieved through acquiring the financial resources by which they can be applied to cultural production. The significance of this 'moment' is substantially greater the more complex the process of cultural production of a particular good or service is. The importance of finance is highest in what have been referred to as the creative content industries, such as film, broadcasting and games, where the opportunities to realise creative talent in the absence of securing financial support to produce at an accepted industry standard level of product quality are limited, as is the ability, to distribute creative work in commercial markets on a large scale. Janet Wasko captured this point succinctly when she observed: 'Contrary to popular belief, Hollywood films do not begin when the camera starts rolling, but involve a somewhat lengthy and complex development and pre-production phase during which an idea is turned into a script and preparations are made for actual production followed by post-production' (Wasko, 2003: 15). Even for those forms of cultural production that are less complex in their application of capital, equipment and technology to the creative process, such as writing, music and the visual arts, the finance question arises in the difference between being able to produce any creative work and being able to produce and distribute successful creative work (measured through sales, profits, prestige, awards, etc.).[4]

The centrality of finance to the creative industries arises for three reasons. First, there is the pervasiveness of high fixed costs in the creative industries. The production, distribution and exhibition of creative works are dependent upon the existence and maintenance of a cultural infrastructure that can rarely be supported through the returns on individual creative products. The network of theatres, galleries, exhibition spaces, performance venues, museums, libraries, etc. through which creative work is performed or exhibited typically requires funding from sources other than the receipts or returns from a single performance or exhibition. Second, there is the role played by what have been referred to as cultural intermediaries (Bourdieu, 1984; Davis and Scase, 2000; Negus, 2002) and creative managers, who 'act as brokers or mediators between, on the one hand, the interests of owners and executives, who have to be primarily interested in profit (or, at the very least, prestige), and those of creative personnel, who will want to achieve success and/or build their reputation by producing original, innovative and/or accomplished works' (Hesmondhalgh, 2007a: 64). Creative industries typically have a complex and changeable relationship between creative and managerial functions, and in many cases these functions can be combined in a particular individual, as in the case of the commissioning editor in the book publishing industry, and producer/manager in the music industry. Finally, markets for cultural products are characteristically scalable, meaning that the costs associated with expanding geographical reach grow at an increasing rate as one moves from local to national markets, and from national to international markets. This is particularly the case in media markets, which are very often dual product markets, where the one good – the aggregated media content product – is competing for both consumer time, attention and expenditure and for advertising revenue. The advantages that accrue to large-scale distributors in dealing with national and international advertising markets are substantial, and it is difficult for small-scale distributors, let alone cultural producers directly selling their own creative work, to compete effectively in these markets.

The creative industries have a distinctive industrial profile that accentuates the complexity of financing issues in these sectors, which is the phenomenon of the 'missing middle'. The Banking on Culture study undertaken for the European Union (Hackett et al., 2000) found that cultural employment in EU member states tended to conform to an 'hourglass' structure, with jobs concentrated either among a small number of large public and private organisations in that industry, or highly dispersed among a plethora of small-to-medium enterprises (SMEs) and individual small traders, including volunteers and those registered as unemployed. It found a notable lack of medium-sized enterprises, as there are strong pressures towards concentration of ownership and funding at the top end of the creative industries, particularly in the creative content sectors producing complex cultural goods through quasi-industrial processes, such as film, broadcasting and games, while more and more people are offering their creative talents to markets at the bottom end, as noted by Caves (2000).

Many cultural policy debates that focus on the relative merits of public ownership and subsidy versus private ownership and the commercial market miss an important point: they are typically referring to the largest enterprises in these industries. For SMEs, sole traders and micro-businesses, a more basic problem of lack of access to finance exists, since the lack of any physical assets – which makes these sectors comparatively easy for individuals and small firms to enter – also acts as an obstacle to accessing commercial credit, since most assets are intellectual property-based (commercialisable creative products), and these are hard to value and secure against. UNCTAD has identified access to investment finance as a particular problem for creative industries entrepreneurs in developing countries as 'many skills and professions related to the creative economy are not recognized as business categories in legal terms. Because of this, many small creative industries do not have access to credit facilities or to the loans and investments that would make their businesses more viable' (UNCTAD, 2008: 178).

The Creative Industries 'Hourglass' Industry Structure

The tendency for the creative industries to take an 'hourglass' shape, with concentration of employment and market share among a small number of large firms at one end, and a large congregation of SMEs, sole traders and micro-businesses at the other, means that they have the characteristics of both oligopolistic and highly competitive market structures. Industries such as film, broadcasting, book publishing and recorded music possess elements of oligopoly, with a small number of distributors dominating the market and being able to maintain dominance, due to high fixed costs for new entrants, and economies of scale and scope in production and – especially – distribution. At the same time, there is also extreme competitiveness in many of these industries, particularly among those who broker resources for creative production. Storper and Christopherson (1987) traced the rise of flexible specialisation in the Hollywood film industry, and the extent to which a degree of 'vertical disintegration' occurred between the major film studios and independent production houses – while further vertical integration occurred between film and broadcast television. Toynbee (2000) noted the continuing significance of independent production in the popular music industry, relating it to longstanding distrust among musicians of the major recording labels, and the capacity to bring performers and audiences together in 'proto-markets' through small, independent labels.

There are two core principles of markets for cultural products and services that play a particularly important role in shaping market structure and behaviour. The first is that most cultural products fail to achieve commercial success, and there is a substantial degree of randomness and unpredictability to what cultural products are ultimately successful. De Vany (2004) has estimated that only one in ten Hollywood movies return a profit. It is estimated that 80 per cent of revenues from sales of online music singles come from 52,000 tracks, or 4 per cent of the 13 million tracks available (Foster, 2008). The combination of a high failure rate and the uncertainty of demand – what film producer William Goldman famously termed the 'nobody knows' principle – means that the cultural business is a highly risky one, with this risk accentuated by the relatively short promotional life that each product has compared to the more familiar product life cycle for other goods and services (Grant and Wood, 2004: 55).

The second feature of the market for cultural products and services is that successful cultural products can produce returns far in excess of those of most other commodities. This is in part because of the very low costs of reproduction of most cultural products, meaning that the ratio of variable cost to fixed costs – including the development costs of the 'first copy' – are typically extremely low. It also reflects the existence of durable rents for successful cultural products, or their capacity to generate sales, and hence copyright payments, long after their original moment of production. Business success in the creative industries, therefore, is premised upon higher risk/return ratios than those that characterise most other industries, so that 'the big hits [which] are extremely profitable … compensate for the inevitably high number of misses that come about as a result of the volatile and unpredictable nature of demand' (Hesmondhalgh, 2007a: 21).

Among the strategies that are used to manage the uncertainty of demand and the resulting volatility of industry revenues are:

1   Development of a repertoire or catalogue, or deliberate overproduction of the number of titles available so that the ability to spread risk through diversification of available products is increased;
2   Development of content taxonomies, such as formats and genres, that better align creative output with audience expectations and demographics and hence can generate more predictable demand, e.g. 'horror film', 'romance novel', 'police TV drama', 'game show', 'hip hop album';
3   The marketing of celebrity and the star system, whereby the likelihood of a particular cultural product being commercially successful is enhanced by its association with a particular individual (an actor, writer, producer, performer, etc.) who already has high public recognition and a track record of commercially successful cultural products;
4   Heavy use of advertising and marketing to generate 'buzz' for cultural products and hence increase audience share (Caves, 2000). While many industries use advertising, marketing and promotion to generate new demand, the extent to which cultural products are experience goods, whose qualities, as experienced by the consumer, are highly subjective and difficult to know prior to the decision to consume, the importance of advertising, marketing and promotion in inducing the consumption decision is a particularly vital one.

All of these means of managing endemic uncertainty in the creative industries tend to promote industry concentration as they raise the costs of entry, raise overall production costs, and encourage creative talent to cluster around established industry leaders. Wasko (2003) has observed that the average cost of producing and marketing a Hollywood film increased by 300 per cent between 1985 and 2002. What is most striking about this figure is that while the average production costs increased by 250 per cent during this period (from US$16.8 million in 1985 to US$58.8 million in 2002), the average marketing costs increased by 488 per cent over the same period, from $5.2 million in 1985 to $30.6 million in 2002, or an increase from 23.6 per cent to 34.2 per cent of total costs (Wasko, 2003: 33). While the rising production costs are indicative of barriers to entry associated with economies of scale in production, the latter also point to massive economies of scope, and are reminders of Garnham's observation that 'It is cultural distribution, not cultural production, that is the key locus of power and profit' (Garnham, 1990: 161–162, emphasis in original).

This focus on distribution as the locus of power and profit provides a second way in which we can understand the hourglass structure of the creative industries. In addition to the relatively small number of people employed in medium-sized firms, as compared to large corporations and public institutions or in SMEs, micro-businesses or as sole traders, there is also an hourglass shape in the relationship between production, distribution and consumption. There are a large number of creative producers and a potentially infinite number of consumers of creative products, but a degree of artificial scarcity arises from concentration of control at the point of distribution, which better aligns production and distribution costs to the capacity to realise profits from the sale of cultural commodities (Garnham, 1990: 39–40, 160–161; Hesmondhalgh, 2007a: 20–24). How this distribution bottleneck operates in practice across different sectors of the creative industries, and whether there are factors that are opening up this bottleneck, which has historically been most apparent in those sectors associated with complex cultural goods and the mass communications industries (film, print media, radio and television) will be considered in more detail in later chapters.

Creative Labour and Cultural Production

The complexities of cultural production are overlaid by the distinctive features of creative labour, and the market environments that exist for creative workers. A number of writers have been posing the question of whether creative workers, long considered anomalous in terms of conventional labour market theories, have now come to be in the advance guard of wider changes in the economy and society. Among such analyses are Richard Florida's claims about the rise of the 'creative class' (2002, 2007, 2008); theories of the 'brave new world of work' and the 'risk society' theorised by sociologists such as Zygmunt Bauman and Ulrich Beck (Bauman, 2000; Beck, 2000); and critiques of precarious labour as a condition of globally networked capitalism developed in various Marxist and post-Marxist analyses (Hardt and Negri, 2000, 2005; Terranova, 2004; Neilsen and Rossiter, 2005; Rossiter, 2006; Ross, 2008, 2009). The capacity to be creative is something that is highly regarded. It is seen as being a part of what makes us human, and a creative society is seen as something worth aspiring to (see e.g. Howkins, 2005). From such an angle, it would appear that creativity, like culture, is something that you cannot have too much of. There is also ample evidence that the ability to pursue creative work is highly sought after. The continuing high demand for fine arts programmes in universities and colleges is one indicator of this, and McRobbie (1999) documented the boom in courses such as fashion that offer young people the opportunity to establish a business

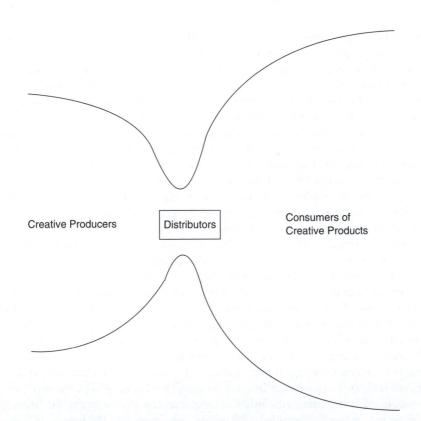

Creative Producers   Distributors   Consumers of
Creative Products

Figure 4.1 The Distribution 'Bottleneck' in the Creative Industries

out of aspects of popular culture that they are deeply immersed in. Authors such as Daniel Pink proposed that 'the MFA (Master of Fine Arts) is the new MBA (Master of Business Administration' (Pink, 2006), and management theorists were paying increasing attention to the 'soft skills' generated in the arts, such as reflexivity, intuition, valuing intrinsic motivations, presentation skills, and an ability to work in collaborative teams, as well as the question of 'emotional literacy' (McWilliam and Hatcher, 2004). A 'New Humanism' emerged in higher education discourse that sought to align traditional humanist concerns for generalisable critical skills and an enquiring mind with the development of self-management skills, in an environment of pervasive uncertainty and disruptive change, available to all graduates through the embedding of generic skills and capabilities (Flew, 2004b). Critics of such trends observed how creative workers were being championed as 'paradigms of entrepreneurial selfhood … [and] the apple of the policy maker's eye … [as] creativity is viewed as a wonder stuff for transforming workplaces into powerhouses of value' (Ross, 2008: 32), while neo-Marxists extended this into a wider critique of 21st century capitalism as being based around a 'social factory', paralleling the industrial factory that was at the forefront of Marx's outlining of the evolutionary dynamics of class exploitation in *Capital* (Harney, 2010).

The relationship between creative labour and cultural production will be considered here from four angles. First, there is the question of whether creative work is inherently attractive, and the longstanding tensions between creative work and bureaucratic forms of work organisation. Second, consideration will be given to how creative industries have been articulated to a discourse of entrepreneurship, presenting the possibility of harnessing creative capacities in the pursuit of a portfolio career, which has proved highly appealing in sectors such as music, fashion and new media industries, but also in the more traditional arts. Third, work that has been undertaken on arts and media labour markets draws attention to structural features of employment in these sectors that point to significant downsides to being engaged in creative labour. Finally, the concept of precarious labour will be critically evaluated in terms of its relevance to an understanding of creative labour and cultural work.

In relation to the arts, there has long been the question of whether creativity has particular ends, or whether the ends–means dichotomy misunderstands the drivers of artistic creation. While contemporary discussions of creativity have sought to distance themselves from claims that it is uniquely associated with the arts, and that creative self-expression can also occur in business, the sciences and information technology (e.g. Howkins, 2001; Mitchell et al., 2003), it has certainly been in relation to the arts that claims about the uniqueness and intensity of creativity as arising from the free play of the imagination have been strongest. Charles Taylor has noted that in European societies from the nineteenth century onwards 'artistic creation becomes the paradigm mode in which people can come to self-definition' (Taylor, 1991: 62). Raymond Williams saw the rise of the 'Romantic Artist' concept in nineteenth-century Europe as a reaction to emergent industrial capitalist society, that looked to naturalism and experience as alternative sources of 'imaginative truth' (Williams, 1958). Creativity thus came to be positioned as the humanistic 'other' to instrumental reason, whereby 'the free, wakeful play of the imagination ... provided a life-enhancing presence in the process of being that would provide the appropriate balance to a secularised, utilitarian society, a force that would break the cold, clinical fetters of rationalism and instrumental approaches to knowledge' (Negus and Pickering, 2004: 7). Angela McRobbie has observed that such tensions between creativity and practicality were inscribed in the history of British art and design schools from their inception, between those such as the artist and socialist John Ruskin, who believed that 'all ideas of reference to definite business should be abandoned in such schools', and utilitarian reformers such as Henry Cole, who pursued more practical links between art and design on the one hand and on the other manufacturing and teacher training (McRobbie, 1998: 17–18).

The economist Richard Caves has observed that 'In creative activities ... the creator (artist, performer, author) cares vitally about the originality displayed, the technical prowess demonstrated, the resolution and harmony achieved in the creative act', and that 'while these concerns with artistic achievement bear some relationship to consumers' ultimate reception of the product, the relationship need not be close' (Caves, 2000: 4). At the same time, the realisation of creative goals is very much contingent upon the support of those who perform more mundane or humdrum tasks. This means, for example, that organisations can inhibit creativity, but they can also provide the framework for its effective realisation as new ideas that are useful or valuable to others. In other words, 'creatives' need the suits', or creative inputs also sit alongside more 'humdrum' contributions (Caves, 2000; Bilton, 2007). Bilton illustrates this with the example of the French football (soccer) team of the 1990s, with the playmaker Eric Cantona describing his team-mate Didier Deschamps as 'merely a water-carrier'. While this sounds like Cantona was insulting Deschamps, there is another way of reading it, which was that the ability of a player such as Cantona to demonstrate genius on the field rested upon the solid contributions of the French team's defenders, of whom Deschamps was the leader. Without a strong defence, creative playmakers such as Cantona, Diego Maradona or Lionel Messi, would have less opportunity to display their skills. Bilton observes that, in a similar way:

> Creativity in the commercial creative industries is represented through the branding and packaging of individual talent and the personality cult fostered around stars and celebrities. Yet behind the scenes, a more realistic unit of analysis for creative processes and product is the team or the partnership. At the core of the creative team is the double-act of the genius and the water-carrier. Creative thinking, like football, depends upon a union of contrasting abilities and styles of thinking or playing. (Bilton, 2007: 19)

Davis and Scase (2000) have observed three features of the creative process that make its relationship to organisations complex:

1 Autonomy: individuals engaged in creative processes need to be given considerable scope to exercise independent judgement on how tasks are to be undertaken and organisational goals are to be achieved.
2 Non-conformity: since the nature of the creative process is that there is no single path to the realisation of goals, individuals engaged in it are often non-conformist in their patterns of work, personal dress codes, forms of communication, etc.
3 Indeterminacy: the goals of the organisation are frequently emergent and arise through the creative process, rather than being set in advance of the process, as is more characteristic of problem-solving approaches.

What this exposes is the difficulty of meshing the nurturing of creativity with bureaucratic forms of organisation. Davis and Scase discuss various ways in which media organisations have sought to manage the relationship between promotion of creative processes and the achievement of organisational goals through strategic management, including: separating the 'creative' divisions from other parts of the organisation; the selective absorption of key creative roles into the management structure; the breaking up of large bureaucracies into smaller semi-autonomous work teams; and greater use of short-term contracts or freelance relationships between independent creative producers and large distributors (publishers, broadcasters, etc.). All of these strategies have possessed problems, and the trend over time away from formal control over work practices and creative processes towards soft control, through contractual and market relations rather than internal organisational processes (Davis and Scase, 2000: 75–77, 101–102), has raised the question of the rise of insecurity and 'precarity' among creative workers.

This familiar script of creative talent failing to mesh with bureaucratic management began to morph from the late 1990s into something more optimistic and positive. It was connected to the rise of new economy discourses, which saw the generation of new ideas rather than productivity improvements as the primary generators of wealth and corporate profitability (Stiroh, 1999; Flew, 2003). Richard Florida referred to a historic reconciliation between the Protestant work ethic and the bohemian ethic into the creative ethos, and that 'the rise of the Creative Economy is drawing the spheres of innovation (technological creativity), business (economic creativity) and culture (artistic and cultural creativity) into one another, in more intimate and more powerful combinations than ever' (Florida, 2002: 201). Underpinning this was an idea that everyone needed to engage with the twenty-first-century creative economy as workers, teachers, citizens and consumers. Erica McWilliam argued in relation to the role of education in the 21st century that:

> New technology and modes of production make it possible for everyone – indeed they require everyone – to be active co-creators of value for themselves and others, not just passive consumers at the end of a supply-and-demand chain … If our young people can learn to cross borders of all types – disciplinary borders, geographical borders, relational borders – they are more likely to be successful in the world of 21st century work. They will have the mental and cultural agility needed to work as 'creatives'. (McWilliam, 2008: 29)

Boltanski and Chiapello (2005) have referred to this as a 'new spirit of capitalism', arguing that the artistic critique of capitalism – as a system that is alienating of human potential as a consequence of being hierarchical, formalist and bureaucratic – had been incorporated into managerial discourses, which promised a new world of work that could enable greater autonomy, employee initiative and personal creativity in a less hierarchical, more networked environment.

Studies of the labour markets for artists and creative workers suggest that the turn towards more creative workplaces, and labour generally becoming more like creative labour, is not something to be unequivocally welcomed. Menger (1999) observed a paradox with artistic labour markets when compared to labour markets more generally. The theory of dual labour markets identifies a distinction in modern capitalist economies between 'primary' labour markets, where jobs are characterised by high wages, job security, worker autonomy over decision-making, and opportunities for career advancement through internal promotion and workplace training, and 'secondary' labour markets, characterised by low pay, job insecurity, and work that is often menial and/or repetitive (Bulow and Summers, 1986). Why these two labour markets remain distinct is a result of, on the one hand, larger firms being more willing and able to offer employees a premium in order to retain and motivate them, and, on the other, workers in the secondary labour market typically having fewer skills and lower average levels of education. What Menger identified is that most employment in the artistic and cultural sectors tends to be based upon short-term, contingent contracts, and have the characteristics of secondary labour markets, but, paradoxically, those working in these sectors are among the most educated and highly trained workers in the whole economy. In seeking to address this paradox, which manifests itself in comparatively low wages and a chronic oversupply of artistic and creative labour, three possibilities have suggested themselves to Menger and others (e.g. Throsby, 1992; Towse, 1996; Caves, 2000; Hesmondhalgh, 2007a):

1 The possibility that the intrinsic motivators for those pursuing artistic and creative careers are such that they are willing to forego monetary gains in order to achieve personal satisfaction and peer group recognition that derives from creative 'inner drives' (the 'art for art's sake' proposition).

2 The highly skewed and seemingly random distribution of incomes and other rewards (e.g. awards, celebrity status) that accrues to the 'A-list' in the arts and cultural sectors promotes what economists term 'risk-loving' behaviour, where participants respond to endemic uncertainty by over-investing in their skills in these sectors relative to the probability of their personal success.

3 The mix of monetary and non-monetary rewards is complex, and artistic and creative careers can offer substantial non-monetary rewards due to the personally challenging and non-routine nature of creative work. As Menger describes it, 'self-actualisation through work, which makes artistic activity so attractive, occurs only if the outcome is unpredictable ... [and] the possibilities of personal invention are wide open' (Menger, 1999: 558).

For critics such as McRobbie (2005), Ross (2008), Hesmondhalgh (2008) and Miller (2009b), this combination of 'Fame Academy' artistic and creative ideals and seemingly endless workplace flexibility generates employment conditions that are rife for exploitation. McRobbie argued that the 'utopian thread embedded in this wholehearted attempt to make over the world of work into something closer to a life of enthusiasm and enjoyment' rubs up against 'a marked absence of workplace politics in terms of democratic procedures, equal opportunities [and] anti-discrimination policies ... maybe there can be no workplace politics when there is no workplace' (McRobbie, 2005: 380). This would point to a second issue for consideration, which is the strong propensity towards entrepreneurship in the creative industries. Taking the fashion and digital media industries as their case studies, Neff et al. (2005) observed that 'this entrepreneurial work force is risk-taking rather than risk-averse and willing to accept more flexibility in both jobs and careers', and that whether or not they establish their own businesses (and many do), they 'share a more explicit, individualized, profit-oriented risk ... that aligns them both economically and culturally with firm founders and employers in a "winner-take-all" society' (Neff et al., 2005: 309, 310). Their willingness to internalise risk, and to view endemic uncertainty as desirable, relates to the perception that they are in 'cool' jobs in 'hot' industries, where the scope for autonomy, creativity and personal self-fulfilment is mixed with the appeal of celebrity, the visibility of their work and the sense that they 'own' the product – it bears the signature of their personal labour, creativity and skill. For Neff et al., the rise of entrepreneurial labour in such 'cool' creative industries jobs had three implications. First, they identified a strong alignment between the values of these professionals and the ways in which these industries are projected in the media and through their own public relations activities. Second, the pull of creative industries work promoted a 'postmodern work ethic' where flexibility is actively sought and the individualisation of risk is taken as a given, in ways that were not characteristic of more unionised workforces in more traditional industries. Finally, they expressed concern that as 'culturally desirable jobs bring, paradoxically, lowered expectations of economic stability' (Neff et al., 2005: 331), this marks a triumph of values associated with enterprise culture and individualism over those such as social justice and collective solidarity.

Precarious Labour?

Concerns about dystopian elements of creative labour and its manifestations in the working lives of artists and cultural workers has developed over the 2000s into a larger critique of the nature of precarious labour in contemporary capitalism. The roots of the concept, taken from the French term *precarité*, are many and varied: Neilsen and Rossiter (2005) take it to refer to:

> All possible shapes of unsure, not guaranteed, flexible exploitation: from illegalised, sea-sonal and temporary employment to homework, flex- and temp-work to subcontrac-tors, freelancers or so-called self-employed persons … its reference also extends beyond the world of work to encompass other aspects of intersubjective life, including housing, debt, and the ability to build affective social relations. (Neilsen and Rossiter, 2005)

Ross (2008) understands its significance in relation to creative industries as arising from a combination of how 'the precariousness of work in these fields … reflects the infiltration of non-standard employment from low-wage service sectors … Capital-owners have won lavish returns from casualisation – subcontracting, outsourcing and other models of flexploitation – and increasingly expect the same in higher-skill sectors of the economy' (Ross, 2008: 34). Harney (2010) associates the concept with a wider set of claims about the experience of precarity providing resources for new political alliances, noting 'a new understanding of this labour as deriving from the artistic life but bred with the precarious life, the migrant life [and] life in the reserve army of labour at the sharp end of responsibility for survival, a responsibility for reproduction almost entirely abdicated by state and capital' (Harney, 2010: 432).

Precarious labour is clearly a concept that has caught the imagination of critical theo-rists worldwide, pointing as it does to the post-industrial, services and information-based economy as a kind of social factory, where the tentacles of capitalist exploitation are to be found not only in the workplace, but also in neo-liberal subjectivities passionately motived to engage in affective labour leading to the exploitation of the self (see Harney, 2010, for a review of the literature). At the same time, two problems present themselves with the concept. The first problem is that it is too all-inclusive. From a perspective that is other-wise sympathetic to this line of critique of the creative industries, Hesmondhalgh (2007b) observed that the concept draws on the one hand upon theories concerning the rise of immaterial labour, or 'labour that produces an immaterial good, such as a service, a cultural product, knowledge, or communication' (Hardt and Negri, 2000: 290), and on the other hand upon the generalisation of conditions of work associated either with artistic labour markets or with the secondary labour market. From this starting point, it presents the case for a sort of common cause between cultural and informational workers on the one hand – and intellectuals and others involved with the education and reproduction of this work-force – and the full range of marginalised workers operating at the edges of the secondary labour market as cleaners, construction workers, domestic labourers, etc. on the other hand, around a shared experience of precarity. The result, for Hesmondhalgh, is that 'too many different kinds of work are being lumped together in the same category … [and] this may well undermine the coherence of the critique being presented' (Hesmondhalgh, 2007b: 62).

In his work on this new workforce, found at its most intense in global centres of the creative economy such as Los Angeles and London, Scott (2008b) observed the rise of jobs character-ised by the rise of a workforce that typically has high levels of formal qualifications (human capital) as well as well-honed networking and other intangible skills. Such workers are engaged in 'industries whose final outputs are permeated with high levels of aesthetic and semiotic content … where such matters as fashion, meaning, entertainment value, look and feel, are decisive factors in shaping consumers' choices', and where 'heavy doses of the human touch are required for the purposes of management, research, information gathering and synthesis, communication, interpersonal exchange, design … feeling, and symbolic content' (Scott, 2008b: 67–68). These exist alongside a large number of lower-tier jobs that are both less well paid and less personally satisfying, which include sweatshop-type manufacturing as well as lower-level service jobs, domestic work, facilities maintenance, and other related jobs. As Scott observed, 'in the more advanced countries, a high proportion of the labour force in this segment of the production system is made up of immigrants (many of them undocumented) from developing parts of the world. Large numbers of these immigrants form a polyglot underclass with at best a marginal social and political presence in their host environments' (Scott, 2008b: 68). The common element between the two types of work environments, which forms the basis for generalising the concept of precarious labour to both, is that:

> Both strata are subject to much labour market instability. Workers of all types face increasingly frequent bouts of unemployment, and are more and more likely to be caught up in temporary, part-time, and freelance modes of labour. Along with these shifts in the structure of the employment relation has gone what some analysts iden-tify as a declining sense of allegiance among workers to any single employer. (Scott, 2008b: 67)

On the other hand, the circumstances that workers in these segments face in the context of such instability are profoundly different. It remains the case that possession of a tertiary degree qualification is a significant source of variation across every relevant labour market category: wages, unemployment levels, time spent out of work, etc. In their international survey of tertiary education and labour markets, Machin and McNally (2007) found that in all OECD countries except two (Spain and New Zealand) there was an increase in the wage differential between those with tertiary qualifications and those without during the 1990s and 2000s, in spite of the fact that the numbers engaged in tertiary education increased considerably in all OECD countries over this period. In West Germany, the wage differential between tertiary educated and non-tertiary educated workers increased by a massive 19 per cent. In the UK, which has been the most studied nation on this question, there were big increases in the 1980s and 1990s that slowed in the 2000s, but the differential remained at 62 per cent in 2003 (Machin and McNally, 2007: 43). Unemployment rates for university graduates are also substantially lower, being almost half of those for people without tertiary degrees in Australia, the USA and the UK (Machin and McNally, 2007: 46–48). The fact that the wage premium has generally increased, rather than declined, suggests that labour markets are not becoming more precarious for those with tertiary qualifications, if this is measured in terms of wages, levels of income over time, and rates of unemployment. In other words, there has not been an immiserisation of the highly educated, in either relative or absolute terms. This aggregate data does not tell us about trends in individual fields of study, or types of institution, so it may be possible that greater precarity is experienced by those in newer, less prestigious universities or in arts and humanities degrees, but this would return us to questions about the quality of different institutions, learning styles, and the market value of different degrees and how they change over time. The main finding is that the extension of a precarious labour framework to those with university degrees is not supported by the available evidence.

The absence of empirical work found in the application of the category of precarious labour, as well as the difficulties involved in empirically identifying the creative workforce, has meant that work too often tends to engage in proof through a kind of auto-ethnography, whereby activists and intellectuals can proclaim themselves to be cultural producers and immaterial labourers working under conditions of precarity. Hesmondhalgh has argued that 'assertions are often made about the nature of sociability and subjectivity amongst "immaterial workers" under conditions of "precarity", but there is little explanation of what forms these subjectivities take in everyday life, through actual instances, or through hearing the voices of a range of "immaterial workers" … we are simply meant to take it on trust that these workers' subjectivities are how they are purported to be' (Hesmondhalgh, 2007b: 63). In the worst case scenario, this leads to a complete neglect of 'the need to talk to anyone else involved in very different forms of cultural production or "immaterial work" in order to make assertions about the subjectivities of cultural producers or immaterial workers as a whole' (Hesmondhalgh, 2007b: 63).

One author who has undertaken detailed empirical work on such trends has been Andrew Ross, and in his 2009 essay 'On Digital Labor' – presented to the Internet as Playground and Factory conference hosted by the Institute for Distributed Creativity in New York – he presented an argument that the digitisation of the media, entertainment and creative industries has been associated with the displacing of skilled labour with unpaid labour, estimating that at least 150,000 jobs have been lost in the US publishing industries alone through 'work … simply being transferred into the interstices of the amateur/user economy that prevails on the web' (Ross, 2009). Yet one is struck in such accounts by questions about whether this can all be sheeted back to free labour and amateur content, as Ross seems to do. Much as consumption is sometimes derided as a bourgeois category by Marxist critics (e.g. Miller, 2004), one factor that lies behind the precarity of employment in some of the leading-edge digital media industries, such as games, is the rapidity of shifts in consumer demand and consumer preferences in these industries. It is striking how absent considerations of consumer demand are from accounts of precarious labour, as if a focus on consumer demand would be synonymous with a wholesale endorsement of theories of consumer sovereignty and a neglect of production and labour.

Moreover, claims about a wholesale shift of media production from paid labour to free labour are simply not convincing. Ross's preferred example of reality TV programmes rests upon the continued ability of such shows to attract audiences, and evidence in the late 2000s has been that the worldwide reality TV boom is waning. To take another example, for all of the talk about how citizen journalism and blogging would put journalists out of work by enabling the crowdsourcing of news production, user contributions remain utterly at the margins of almost all major mainstream news organisations, and newer web-based competitors have invariably faced the question at a certain level of development of whether to hire ongoing staff and develop viable business models or go under due to the inability to secure ongoing advertising revenue for the content available (Flew, 2009b; Flew and Wilson, 2010). The bigger changes have been in the work practices of journalists, including the way they interact with online media contributors, not the replacement of journalists by unpaid contributors (Fortunati and Deuze, 2010; Singer, 2010).

Finally, there is the question of whether the vast conceptual apparatus of precarious labour has been constructed where the more established yet prosaic propositions associated with theories of unemployment would have sufficed. Theories of unemployment typically distinguish between frictional, structural and cyclical unemployment. Frictional unemployment involves jobs routinely lost (and created) as demand, investment and profits shift between firms, industries and sectors; it could only be eliminated by displacing the market mechanism from modern economies altogether, although the role of the state in minimising the costs of such unemployment is significant and highly variable between sectors. Structural unemployment refers to more longstanding patterns of job loss, and is more likely to be what Ross is describing in the US publishing industries, arising from larger shifts in technologies, consumer preferences and production processes: it too is a recurring feature of capitalist economies, and not the specific outcome of digitisation or the emergence of user-created media content. Finally, cyclical unemployment relates to the overall state of aggregate demand in individual capitalist economies, and the global economic crisis of the late 2000s triggered a Keynesian response to this in a number of countries, with various public works programmes, tax cuts, etc. introduced to respond to sagging private sector demand and investment. It is worth noting in this regard Pratt's (2009a) observations that the creative industries actually did reasonably well in the face of the 2008–2010 recession in the UK economy, and that more needs to be done on how these cultural sectors are themselves moving to the centre of contemporary capitalism, rather than being the outgrowths of a speculative and predatory mode of financial capitalism. While the cautionary notes about the downsides of cultural labour and the creative workforce are well noted, and can be identified from literature associated with artistic labour markets and empirical work being undertaken on the creative workforce, the concept of precarious labour would appear to add little as it currently stands to our knowledge of such processes.

Endnotes

1 There is also the important question, considered in the Cox Review in the UK (HM Treasury, 2006) of whether developing countries will develop their design industries to the point where design along with manufacture is relocated to countries, such as China.

2 An analogous issue exists in the growing difficulties in differentiating manufacturing and services. In his 1999 Presidential Address to the American Economic Association, Robert Fogel identified problems associated with measuring output in the services sector as an area where 'the economics profession is lagging behind the economy' (Fogel, 1999: 8).

3 There is also the relationship of journalism to writing, and to the creative industries generally, to be considered. Journalism has characteristically been organised in highly industrialised forms, with relatively small numbers of large employers and workplaces with established news production practices, stable career paths, and typically unionised workforces. The professional ideology of journalism was one of objectivity, and creativity was discouraged from the mainstream of journalistic culture, instead pursued by columnists or in niche publications (Zelizer, 2004). The range of forces transforming journalism over the last decade in particular are beyond the scope of this book to review in detail, but virtually every core principle and practice of journalism, particularly in its print forms, has been under profound challenge over the 2000s, due to a mix of technological factors, shifts in the revenue base, new competition from non-traditional news sources, and the expectations of readers to be more engaged in the production of and commentary on news stories (Deuze, 2007: 141–170; Curran, 2010; OECD, 2010). Responses to such developments, frequently experienced as a decline in the numbers employed in newsrooms, loss of control over content, and a growing fuzziness of work definitions and who is a journalist, have included 'networked journalism' (Beckett, 2008; Singer, 2010) and 'innovation journalism' (Nordfors, 2009). As what Fortunati and Deuze (2010) refer to as 'atypical' journalism and news management become the norm, it may be the case that journalism is thought of less as a quasi-industrial practice and more as a creative practice.

4 Music is notable for there being examples of both simple and complex cultural production. The live performance of an orchestra is notably a complex co-ordination activity, whereas a live show by a local rock band may be relatively straightforward to organise; a similar spectrum exists in terms of costs of recording music. One feature of commercial popular music is that the artists are often able to engage in more complex forms of cultural production as they become more commercially successful. The studio time and budgets available to The Beatles for albums such as *Sergeant Pepper's Lonely Hearts Club Band* (1967) and *Abbey Road* (1969) as compared to their earlier work is a famous example of this.

5 Consumption, Markets, Technology and Cultural Trade

A starting point for thinking about cultural markets and the creative industries is to consider how consumption has been understood, both historically and analytically, and the ways in which the relationship between culture and consumption has been interpreted. Human societies have always engaged in consumption, but consumption in its contemporary sense is associated with what has been termed consumer society, which is in turn linked to the rise of capitalism and modernity. Historical work has suggested that consumer society is by no means simply a phenomenon that emerged in the twentieth century. The economic historian Ann Bermingham has argued that 'one of the most extraordinary aspects of mass consumption since the seventeenth century ... is the fact that consumption has been the primary means through which individuals have participated in culture and transformed it', while McKendrick, Brewer and Plumb observed that 'There was a consumer revolution in eighteenth-century England [where] more men and women than ever before in human history enjoyed the experience of acquiring material possessions' (quoted in Storey, 1999: 3).

As we conceive of consumer society, three further issues arise. The first is that this marks a historical moment of beginning to think about mass behaviour, or activities engaged in by very large number of individuals, possibly in a collective form. This leads to various analyses – often highly critical – of mass culture and mass society, which from the mid-nineteenth century onwards would increasingly be linked to mass media, mass communications and popular culture more generally (Bennett, 1982; Thompson, 1991, 1995; Strinati, 2004). Second, consumption comes to be less associated with the products of one's own labour, and more involving the buying and consuming of products and services provided by others. In other words, what is consumed increasingly takes the form of commodities, bought and sold in a commercial market place through the medium of monetary exchange. Finally, larger economic logics of production and consumption become increasingly and more tightly interlocked. As the eighteenth-century political economist and moral philosopher Adam Smith put it:

> Consumption is the sole end and purpose of all production and the interest of the producer ought to be attended to, only in so far as it may be necessary for promoting that of the consumer. The maxim is so perfectly self-evident, that it would be absurd to attempt to prove it. (Quoted in Appleby, 2003: 36)

A central contribution to understanding consumption was made by Karl Marx is his analysis of the commodity-form in capitalist economies. Commodities are the form that products take in societies where production is organised for exchange rather than for direct personal use. Marx held commodities to possess two forms of value: use value, or the capacity of the product to satisfy some form of human need or want; and exchange value, or the capacity of the commodity to command a price, and therefore to be exchangeable for other commodities. Understood in this way, commodities have existed for as long as markets, as political economists such as Adam Smith also observed. But Marx distinguished between societies where there was what he termed simple commodity production and those where capitalist commodity production had more fully evolved. In capitalist economies, for Marx, the purpose of production is not simply exchange but profit, and the fundamental drivers of the economic system revolved around the exploitation of labour by capital to realise surplus-value, the continuous expansion of markets, and the accumulation of capital through these processes (Marx, 1976 [1867]; cf. Harvey, 1982; Lee, 1993). In this socio-economic order, consumption is increasingly driven by the imperatives of capitalist production, which 'involves a broadening of the sphere of consumption … [and] implies a growing manipulation of the consumer by capitalist firms, in the production, distribution and publicity spheres' (Mandel, 1983: 93). Contemporary interpretations of Marx argue that 'consumerism, that is the active ideology that the meaning of life is to be found in buying things and pre-packaged experiences … has become the major ideology that legitimates modern capitalism' (Bocock, 1993: 50, 51). While the proposition that consumerism is the primary source of alienation in capitalist societies is not necessarily a Marxist one – Marx's own theory stressed the alienation of social labour from the collective products of their work, and the Christian case against coveting material goods certainly predated socialist ideas – it has become an increasingly pervasive claim about the nature of contemporary capitalism and how it incorporates individuals into dominant ideologies while failing to adequately meet human needs.[1]

While much attention has been given to Marx's theory of exchange value and its relationship to theories of value in political economy more generally (e.g. Dobb, 1973), Jean Baudrillard has persuasively argued that the weakness of Marx's political economy of the commodity form arises from its account of use value (Baudrillard, 1988). Baudrillard argued that whereas exchange value is presented as something that emerges in concrete social and historical circumstances, use value is conceived in terms of an a-historical anthropology of human needs, as something that exists independently of the social context in which it arises. Drawing an equivalence between the system of economic exchange as analysed by Marx and the system of symbolic exchange as developed in semiotics, Baudrillard points to a homology between the exchange value/use value couplet in the commodity form, and the signifier/signified relationship in semiotics. He argued that, just as there is no universal conception of the signified that exists independently of the signifier, or that objects can be understood independently of their regimes of representation, there is no foundational concept of use value that exists independently of what he termed the political economy of the sign, or the interaction between the commodity form and regimes of signification. In this way, as Lee has observed, Baudrillard broke ranks with those strands of Marxism which understood 'use value ... as the material basis of humanity's potential for self-advancement', which is denied or distorted under capitalism, but which can nonetheless provide 'the objective and stable foundations upon which some utopian system of production could be established' (Lee, 1993: 22). Baudrillard's critique of use value also opens up questions, that are somewhat foreclosed in Marxist political economy, about the relationship between commodities, culture and consumption. Lee has pointed out how:

> Baudrillard's ideas draw our attention to the complex manner in which commodities function as signs and symbols in the sphere of consumption, as well as their potential as regulating agents in the domain of culture. This represents the logic of 'sign-value', where, through advertising and marketing especially, commodities acquire certain cultural meanings. (Lee, 1993: 23)[2]

The reason for focusing upon Baudrillard's critique of Marx's theory of the commodity form is that it provides us with a valuable starting point for critiquing the line of thinking which views cultural consumption in terms of mass manipulation, and consumers as victims or dupes (Storey, 1999: 18–22; Aldridge, 2003: 19–23). As we have seen in Chapter Three, the critique of the culture industry developed by Adorno and Horkheimer, as well as Herbert Marcuse's later critique of advanced capitalist society, rested upon a distinction between 'the false needs for popular cultural goods which are imposed and met by the culture industry, and the true or real needs for freedom, happiness and utopia which are suppressed by the culture industry' (Strinati, 2004: 70). As the above analysis suggests, the ability to determine what 'true needs' are, and differentiating them from 'false needs', is an endlessly hazardous venture, highly prone to denunciations of mass popular culture from more lofty intellectual standpoints. Although critiques of this line of thinking are widespread in cultural studies and sociological literature, variants of the consumption-as-manipulation continue to emerge. These include the burgeoning literature on the McDonaldisation of society (Ritzer, 2006) and the Disneyfication of entertainment and culture (Bryman, 2004), arguments that consumerism is the ideology of global capitalism (Herman and McChesney, 1997; Sklair, 2002), and critiques of global media as agents of Americanisation and cultural imperialism (Schiller, 1991; Barber, 2000). Drawing upon anthropological accounts of consumption as well as historical work and critiques of economic theories, Daniel Miller has drawn attention to some of the prevalent myths surrounding consumption, including such ideas as: the existence of global brands produces cultural homogenisation; only large corporate producers can develop mass markets; cultural trends cannot be premised upon the autonomous behaviour of individuals, but only from top-down manipulation through advertising and marketing; mass consumption has been associated with a turn away from communal sociality and towards acquisitive individualism; and the rise of mass consumption represents a loss of authenticity (Miller, 1995: 21–27). Slater (2003) has also argued that arguments about economic globalisation that associate it with the spread of consumer culture tend to contain an implicit 'romanticisation of the pre-modern', and assume 'an opposition between pristine indigenous cultures existing before the intrusion of consumer culture, and their afterlife as commodity culture – a fall from grace' (Slater, 2003: 158).

Rejecting theories of consumption-as-manipulation is not the same as denying the importance of social factors in influencing consumption, or believing that every individual is an autonomous, sovereign consumer. On the contrary; it is only by getting away from either theories of mass manipulation on the one hand, and individual consumer sovereignty on the other, that full weight can be given to analysis of social and cultural forces that shape consumption decisions. Writing at the turn of the twentieth century, the American institutional economist Thorstein Veblen developed, in *The Theory of the Leisure Class* (Veblen, 1994 [1899]), a general theory of status-led consumption, where he argued that the display of wealth, or what has since come to be termed conspicuous consumption, had been as historically significant as its accumulation. He emphasised how status-driven consumption had been a major driver of social change, as the consumption patterns and habits of the wealthy had major 'trickle down' impacts upon all sections of society, who engaged in what Veblen termed pecuniary emulation to demonstrate how they had attained social standing (Mason, 1998: 50–60). Moreover, with the mechanisation of industrial production that would subsequently be termed 'Fordism' (Harvey, 1989; Lee, 1993), this status game could escalate, as more and more commodities could be made available to a wider section of the population. While Veblen's account was largely marginalised from conventional consumer demand theory, Mason (1998) has drawn attention to the dilemma that this has generated for mainstream economists. As the role played by interpersonal comparisons in driving individual consumption decisions is fundamental to shaping consumer demand, such behaviour is not confined to economic elites; as a result, Veblen's model captures better than conventional consumer demand theories the extent to which 'consumer goods of all types are today purchased not only for their practical use but also because of a real or imagined status which "visible consumption" subsequently bestows upon the buyer' (Mason, 1998: x).

Writing in early twentieth-century Berlin, the sociologist Georg Simmel was developing similar observations about the relationship between economic wealth and status-driven consumption, observing links between the role played by fashion as consumption, commodities as a source of economic status, and cities as incubators of status-driven consumption, as they spatially concentrated people of different classes and cultural backgrounds. Simmel argued that fashion was in contradiction to utilitarian consumption since:

> The essence of fashion consists of the fact that it should be exercised by only a part of a given group, the great majority of whom are merely on the road to adopting it. As soon as a fashion becomes universally adopted, that is, as soon as anything that was originally done only by a few has really come to be practiced by all … we no longer characterize it as fashion. (Simmel, 2003 [1902]: 238)

While Veblen and Simmel identify consumption as the social practice through which class differences are played out and made visible – what is known as the trickle down theory of consumption – other writers, such as anthropologists Mary Douglas and Baron Isherwood, have emphasised the role played by consumption as a form of social communication, and how 'consumption decisions become the vital source of the culture of the moment' (Douglas and Isherwood, 2000: 74). Indeed, consumption practices need not revolve around emulation and conformity to social norms; they may, as Michel de Certeau argued in his vision of everyday consumption practices, constitute tactics of public resistance to rationalised systems of economic production (de Certeau, 1984). Colin Campbell has observed that 'the fact that modern societies are characterised by multiple and diverse elite groups presents a problem concerning who exactly one is to emulate' (Campbell, 1983: 284).[3] In considering the role played by consumption as a driver of the creative industries, an important fault line that Pierre Bourdieu (1984) drew attention to was the one existing between economic capital and cultural capital. While economic capital is associated with possession of goods and services associated with wealth and status, cultural capital revolves around practices of distinction that may be linked to taste and aesthetics, but which operate in a cultural field whose definitional criteria, institutions, rules and practices are highly fluid and contested. At the same time, its patterns of inclusion and exclusion are no less real, and no less keenly felt, than those arising from inequalities of access to economic resources (Bourdieu, 1984; Webb et al., 2002). Indeed, a familiar comedic trope found in TV programmes such as Australia's *Kath and Kim* revolves around laughing at those who have acquired economic wealth, but lack the requisite cultural knowledge to know what are suitable forms of middle-class consumption (Turnbull, 2008).

Creative Industries Markets

The products and services of the creative industries and the consumption preferences of individuals are brought together in markets. The study of markets is characteristically the domain of economics, and so it is to economic theories that we turn to in the first instance in order to better understand creative industries markets. Yet what we can take from economics for understanding creative industries markets is less clear-cut than it may first appear. The first point to be noted is that two distinct sub-branches of economic theory have emerged: cultural economics and media economics. Cultural economics, as represented in Throsby (2001), Towse (2003), and in journals such as the *Journal of Cultural Economics*, has its origins in what was known as the economics of the arts. Towse (2003a: 1) observes that this has generated biases in the field towards the study of the creative and performing arts and publicly subsidised cultural forms – what is sometimes also referred to as 'high culture' – to the neglect of cultural institutions, cultural heritage, the mass media, and commercial culture more generally. It has also tended to give the field something of a defensive tone, arising from a combination of three observations:

1 Standard economic measures of value, such as the willingness of consumers to pay for something, are inadequate ways of assessing cultural value.
2 As a result, the allocation of resources exclusively or primarily though the price mechanism will fail to produce the socially desirable output of cultural goods and services, or distribute these resources in ways that are socially appropriate.
3 Cultural activities therefore require some form of public subsidy, and the role of cultural economists is to determine the appropriate levels and best means of providing these subsidies.

This combination of factors can sometimes lead to the curious situation whereby cultural economists see their primary role as being to protect the arts and culture from other economists (see e.g. Caust, 2003). It has also led to the obverse phenomenon of economists talking up the contribution of the arts and cultural sectors, through broader impacts such as the 'arts multiplier' effect (e.g. Myerscough, 1988). Both approaches tend to take the appropriate domain of cultural economics as largely constituting the arts, and both may be seen as working with a somewhat static definition of their field. They may be able to tell us about the appropriate level for public support for symphony orchestras, but offer little insight into, say, the recurring success of rock bands such as the Rolling Stones or AC/DC. This is not to make a value judgement about either form; it is to say, however, that both are a part of culture, yet cultural economics has traditionally had a lot to say about the former and little to say about the latter.

By contrast, media economics has emerged as an application of mainstream economic theory to the media. Influential texts in the field define media economics as 'the study of how media industries use scarce resources to produce content that is distributed among consumers in a society to satisfy various wants and needs' (Albarran, 1996: 5), and 'how media operators meet the informational and entertainment wants and needs of audiences, advertisers, and society with available resources' (Picard, 1989: 5). In these influential texts, media economics is essentially about the application of conventional neoclassical microeconomic theory, and to a lesser extent macroeconomic theory, to the media industries. Questions relating to culture and cultural value are bracketed off into second-order questions around government regulation of media industries, support for local content in industries such as film or television, and the role played by public broadcasters in the media landscape (e.g. BTCE, 1991). The idea that the products of the media industries are no less cultural goods and services than those of the creative and performing arts has tended to be a minority proposition in the field, even though media economists identify many instances of market failure in the media sectors (Withers, 2003).

The other feature of media economics is that it has tended to take economics to be synonymous with the neoclassical paradigm as it has developed from the 1870s onwards. In particular, it has adopted methodological individualism, the bracketing off of 'markets' and 'culture', and an understanding of the economic problem as how producers meet the needs and wants of consumers through the buying and selling of goods in the overarching context of scarce resources. This is despite the fact that, as leading cultural economists such as David Throsby observe:

> Despite its intellectual imperialism, neoclassical economics is in fact quite restrictive in its assumptions, highly constrained in its mechanics and ultimately limited in its explanatory power. It has been subject to a vigorous critique from both within and without the discipline. Furthermore, its supremacy can be challenged if a broader view of the discourse of economics is taken. In common with all great areas of intellectual endeavour, economics comprises not a single paradigm, but a number of schools of thought offering alternative or contestable ways of analyzing the functioning of the economy or the actions of individual economic agents. (Throsby, 2001: 2)

The critique of neoclassical economic models as applied to the media has been vigorously made over a number of years by theorists associated with the political economy of communication. Murdock and Golding (2005) contrast mainstream economics to critical political economy by arguing that 'mainstream economics sees "the economy" as a separate domain … In contrast, critical political economy is interested in the general interplay between economic organization and political, social and cultural life', and that '[w]hile mainstream economics focuses on sovereign individuals, critical political economy starts with sets of social relations and the play of power' (Murdock and Golding, 2005: 62). Vincent Mosco (2009) has critiqued mainstream media economics as 'limited to taking up incremental change within one given set of institutional relations', and argues, among other lines of critique, that 'it tends to ignore the relationship of power to wealth and thereby neglects the power of institutions to control markets' (Mosco, 2009: 62).

Working through this range of competing claims about media and cultural economics, I want to draw attention to four ways in which media and cultural economics enable us to get a better understanding of some of the key issues surrounding the nature of markets in the creative industries. The first concerns industry structure, and the insights that can be derived from industrial organisation theory into how the level of competition in different media and creative industries markets shapes the conduct of firms in that industry. Industrial organisation theory has made use of what is known as the structure–conduct–performance (SCP) model to determine how the number of firms in a market, the types of product they produce, and the extent of barriers to entry for new competitors shape a range of conduct and performance variables in that industry.

The structure–conduct–performance model is articulated to theories of market structure, which range from perfect competition, with multiple buyers and sellers and no capacity to control market prices or the entry of new competitors, to monopoly, where there is a single seller with substantial power over prices and market entry (Picard, 1989; Albarran, 1996, 2010). Between these two poles sit monopolistic competition and oligopoly, which typically characterise media industries. In such environments, control over both prices and the entry of new competitors is considerable but not absolute, and competition occurs as much through branding and product differentiation as it does through offering consumers lower prices or better products.

The important point that arises from industrial organisation theory is that most media and media-related industries are highly concentrated. In other words, a very small number of firms account for the majority of market share. Industry economists use what are known as concentration ratios to measure market concentration, such as the percentage of total market share accounted for by the four largest firms (CR4) and that accounted for by the eight largest firms (CR8). Using concentration ratio analysis, Albarran and Dimmick established that US media and media-related industries are characterised by oligopoly or monopolistic competition, with the broadcast television, advertising, publishing and recorded music industries having CR4 ratios of over 80 per cent (the four largest firms accounted for over 80 per cent to total market share), and all industries surveyed except for the newspaper and magazine industries having CR8 ratios of over 70 per cent (Albarran and Dimmick, 1996). According to the SCP model, we can expect this market structure to influence aspects of

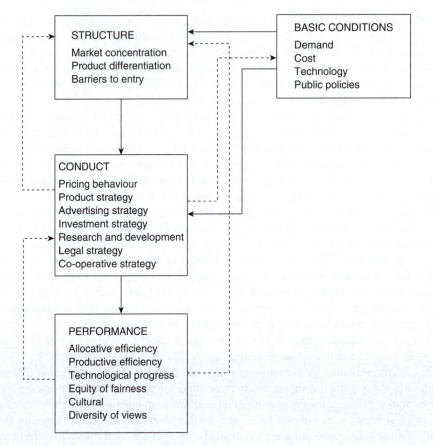

Figure 5.1 Industrial Organisation Framework

Source: Hoskins et al., 2004: 145.

market conduct (including pricing strategy, product development strategy, advertising and new product strategy, as well as the propensity to co-operate or compete), and this has further market performance implications that may warrant government regulation to deal with consequences of imperfectly competitive markets, such as over-investment in similar products and under-investment in others (e.g. specialist programmes and those of interest to minorities), or political power arising from the capacity to exercise market power (Picard, 1989: 94–99).

While industrial organisation theory provides a starting point to understanding media markets, and particularly the much-discussed question of whether there is greater concentration of media over time with the rise of media monopolies (e.g. Murdock, 1982; Bagdikian, 2004; Winseck, 2008), it has some limitations. One concerns the direction of causality. As Hoskins et al. observe, activity that is associated with market conduct, such as heavy advertising or predatory pricing, could constitute a barrier to entry, although it is not directly related to market structure (Hoskins et al., 2004: 152). More significantly, it only measures media concentration within industries, whereas the dominant strategies of the largest media corporations have been to operate across multiple industries, generating market advantages arising from supply-chain integration (e.g. ownership of both film studies and television networks), or what has been variously termed multiformity (Albarran and Dimmick, 1996) and synergistic expansion (Doyle, 2002; Wasko, 2003), whereby particular media content and products constitute a brand that can be exploited and cross-promoted across multiple revenue streams. Disney's Mickey Mouse was the first great synergistic media product, but we find its pervasive significance across everything from theme park rides to toys and other merchandise. The SCP model has also been criticised as being a static one, where as technological and industry changes can cause major shifts over time in the competitiveness of an industry. Hoskins et al. noted how the audience share of the big three commercial networks in the United States had fallen from 92 per cent in 1978 to 37 per cent in 2003; it is now estimated to be less than 15 per cent (Hoskins et al., 2004: 144). This was partly due to the role played by new entrants into the network television market, most notably the FOX network established in the mid 1980s, but was mostly due to the large-scale migration of US TV audiences from the broadcast networks to the more niche-oriented multichannel cable services. This in turn had a great impact upon market strategy in the television industry, as it established the profitability of specialist channels targeted at niche audiences.

A second important concept for understanding creative industries markets, particularly in the media industries, is that of dual product markets. Many media industries 'create one product but participate in two separate goods and services markets' (Picard, 1989: 17). In some instances, with broadcast radio and television being the obvious example, the media product is a public good, with no direct cost to consumers over and above having the receiver through which to access the product/service. In others, such as newspapers and magazines, the price to consumers does not cover production costs. In these instances, it is advertising that meets the costs of production, so that not only is content being produced for consumers but, in the famous observation of Canadian political economist Dallas Smythe (1995), audiences are being produced as markets for advertisers. The implications of advertising being such a central source of revenue for the media industries are many and varied. For Smythe, it meant that the media integrated the 'audience commodity' into the capitalist economic system, as 'the audience commodity is a non-durable producers' good which is bought and used in the marketing of the advertiser's product [and] the work which audience members perform for the advertiser to whom they have been sold is learning to buy goods and spend their income accordingly' (Smythe, 1995: 222).

It certainly means that the economic performance of media industries is inextricably linked to the economics of advertising. This means that the microeconomic level of media industries' structure and market performance is linked to the macroeconomic performance of the economy as a whole, as there is a strong correlation between advertising and business cycles. Advertising expenditure grows at a faster rate than economic growth in boom periods, and falls more quickly in periods of recession, as its primary variables tend to be company profits, consumer expenditure, and consumer confidence about future income (Doyle, 2002: 49). It has also meant that media industries have grown most quickly in advanced economies, and tend to constitute a higher share of total GDP in higher-income economies, as there is a strong positive correlation between advertising expenditure as a percentage of GDP and a country's overall GDP level (Doyle, 2002: 48).

While media industry performance and the overall health of the economy are therefore strongly connected through the influence of the advertising industry, it is not the case that advertising is equally important to all corporations. The largest commercial advertisers are typically in the fast-moving consumer goods sectors (groceries, packaged food and drink, personal items, fast food and other retailing), and in other sectors strongly oriented towards direct sales to households, such as electrical goods and motor vehicles; telecommunications and banking also feature prominently (Sinclair, 2010). Also, advertisers will engage in switching behaviour across media, as they seek to best target their message to the market segments they are seeking. The major development of the 2000s has been a shift towards online advertising, but this has been associated with incremental shifts in market share away from other media such as television, newspapers, radio and magazines, rather than a wholesale migration from 'old' to 'new' media (Flew, 2009a). From the point of view of advertisers, there are always questions about whether they are seeking mass audiences, such as those who watch prime-time television or major sporting events, and where the costs of slots is the highest, or whether they are seeking particular demographics or niche market segments, which may be more effectively targeted through more specialist media (e.g. magazines dedicated to weddings, or TV programs targeted at fishing enthusiasts).

The final point to be observed about creative industries markets is the significance of demand uncertainty. Contrary to the gloomy prognoses of consumption-as-manipulation, industry insiders tend to adhere to the no less gloomy conclusion of the famous Hollywood film producer Samuel Goldwyn that 'Nobody knows nothing' about what audiences want. Caves (2000) stressed profound demand uncertainty as one of the defining features of the creative industries, and he attributed it to the interaction between two sets of factors. The first is that the creative industries continually produce new creative products, and these are typically experience goods. This means that consumers are largely unaware of the product's qualities in advance of direct consumption. The second problem is that, because creative industries are about new product, there are high sunk costs in their production – most of the capital involved in the production needs to be invested in advance of knowledge about the product's appeal in the market. The problem is what is known as symmetrical ignorance – producers don't know what consumers want, and consumers don't know what is being offered to them in advance of consuming it – and despite the highly sophisticated forms of market testing that have been developed in large commercial creative industries such as film and television, it remains an endemic feature of these industries.

Endemic demand uncertainty and how those in the industry respond to it provide some important insights into how the creative industries as an economic-industrial system and its products as part of a textual-cultural system interact (Beilby and Beilby, 1994; Caves, 2000; Hesmondhalgh, 2007a). Among the range of strategies that are used to manage risk and therefore consumer demand in the creative industries are the following:

- Genre: cultural products are labelled in ways that provide audiences with an expectation of the kinds of pleasure they may derive from consumption, e.g. horror movie, situation comedy, hip-hop album, etc.
- Star system: the association of particular stars (actors, writers, musicians, etc.) to particular cultural products, associating that star's aura with the marketing of the particular product. Hesmondhalgh (2007a: 23) notes that, of the 126 movies that made more than $US100 million at the US box office in the 1990s, 41 of them starred one or more of seven actors: Tom Hanks, Julia Roberts, Robin Williams, Jim Carrey, Tom Cruise, Arnold Schwarzenegger and Bruce Willis.
- Reputation: well-known producers, directors, script writers, etc. may be seen as being able to attach particular qualities to a cultural product, e.g. a Steven Spielberg film.
- Imitation: a successful new cultural product usually attracts a series of imitators. For example, the reality television format surged in popularity in the 1990s and 2000s, as particular programme successes, such as *Survivor*, *Big Brother* or *The Apprentice*, generated a vast range of comparable or even copycat programmes that tapped into a seeming demand for 'real people' on the TV screen (Murray and Ouellette, 2004).
- Innovation: the capacity to generate 'buzz' around a cultural product that is not only generically new, but which can provide a whole new experience for its consumers, is a way of tapping into new sources of consumer demand. The arts, music and fashion have been seen as needing to continually generate innovation as part of their cycle of economic reproduction (Caves, 2000: 201–205).
- Critical opinion: endorsement of a cultural product by specialist critics (e.g. art critics, film reviewers, music journalists) can provide a 'gatekeeper' for consumers in decisions about what they will consume and how they will spend available leisure time; awards and prizes play a similar role (Caves, 2000: 190–200).
- Social networks: particularly as the Internet has developed, the scope for self-forming communities to develop their own means of critically evaluating cultural products, and sharing their opinions in these communities, has come to play an increasingly critical role in what Potts et al. (2008) term *social network markets* in the creative industries.

Culture, Needs and Wants

The anti-immigration, rural populist One Nation Party came up with many unconventional ideas during its brief moment of electoral prominence in Australia in the late 1990s. One of its more unique policy proposals was that government funding for the arts should be halved, and the money saved be used for low-interest loans to impoverished farmers. Why they felt it to be justified to take money away from the arts and give it to farmers was based on the

(Continued)

(Continued)

proposition that funding for the arts and culture was an indulgence when there were people in Australia's rural areas who, they argued, were unable to meet basic needs.

The One Nation Party's view could be seen as a particular interpretation of what is known as Maslow's hierarchy of needs. First proposed by the psychologist Abraham Maslow in 1943 (Maslow, 1943), it posits that there are five levels of human needs: physiological needs; safety needs; social needs; esteem needs; and self-actualisation needs. These are often presented as a pyramid of human needs, with physiological and needs at its base and self-actualisation needs of creativity and intellectual wholeness at its apex. What was being perceived, by One Nation and its followers was a bias in forms of cultural consumption associated with the subsidised arts towards urban, highly educated professionals and away from lower-income earners, the less educated, or those living in rural and regional areas. In their study of Australian cultural consumption, Bennett et al. (1999) found that in the field of what they termed subsidised culture (attendance of public musical performances, orchestral concerts, public lectures, chamber music concerts, ballet, opera, theatre and cultural festivals), professionals were 2.5 times more likely to attend than manual workers, and people living in inner-city areas were twice as likely to attend as those from rural areas (Bennett et al., 1999: 240).

Yet all of these claims draw upon a particularly narrow conception of culture as the publicly subsidised high arts. The meeting of needs across all levels of Maslow's hierarchy can be seen as cultural, from how food is prepared to satisfy hunger, to how property and familial relations are organised, to the exercise of intellect and creativity to better achieve the meeting of basic needs. Development theorists such as Manfred Max-Neef have argued that it is wrong to think of these in terms of a hierarchy; he instead proposes that they exist as a matrix of human needs, which different forms of social organisation and institutional arrangements may enable or inhibit to greater or lesser degrees (Max-Neef, 1992). One of the reasons why creative industries strategies have come to be of greater interest for developing nations is the possibility they open up for cultural activities that meet basic community needs, such as arts, crafts and music, also having the potential to be commodified and exported as income generators without a loss of artistic and cultural integrity (Barrowclough and Kozul-Wright, 2008; UNCTAD, 2008).

Technologies

Dramatic shifts in the dominant technologies of production and consumption are central to the economics of media and creative industries. Looking in the 2010s at the market concentration data developed in the recent past (e.g. Albarran and Dimmick, 1996), what is striking is the extent to which new technologies blew apart some of the key media industry oligopolies. It was inconceivable in the late 1990s that Apple would become the leading global player in the music market, but this is what occurred with the mass popularisation of the iPod and iTunes. Similarly, Google would never have featured in a discussion of the newspaper business a decade ago, but its capacity to aggregate and redistribute news content online through Google News sites fundamentally shifted the relationship on the Internet between news content and its associated 'masthead' provider, and the established newspaper businesses have been struggling to address the consequences of this (OECD, 2010).

Media economics has been a part of the problem here, since the neoclassical model has characteristically treated technology, like consumer preferences, as something formed outside the market system, an 'exogenous force' arising from the scientific world that then acts upon supply and demand relations. Yet there are many alternative economic theories that see a far closer and more symbiotic relationship between technological change and the capitalist market economy. Following Karl Marx's observation that 'The hand-mill gives you society with the feudal lord; the steam-mill, society with the industrial capitalist', the economic historian Robert Heilbroner proposed that capitalism is characterised by a 'soft' technological determinism where 'the prevailing level of technology imposes itself powerfully on the structural organization of the productive side of society' (Heilbroner, 2003: 398, 401). Heilbroner argued that large-scale industrial production required the development of a market system organised around the principle of private property in order to generate an institutional form, the modern corporation, that was 'capable of systematically guiding the inventive and innovative abilities of society to the problem of facilitating production' (Heilbroner, 2003: 402). The famous Austrian economist Joseph Schumpeter was critical of the neoclassical models prevailing in his day as failing to understand the importance of technological change to the underlying dynamics of capitalist economies:

> In capitalist reality as distinguished from its textbook picture, it is not the kind of [price] competition which counts but the competition from the new commodity, the new technology, the new source of supply, the new type of organization … competition which commands a decisive cost or quality advantage and which strikes not at the margins of the profits and the outputs of existing firms but at their foundations and their very lives. (Schumpeter, 1942: 84)

In the study of media in particular, a lack of attention to changes in technological form is particularly odd since, as Sandra Braman points out, 'The media in media studies are the technologies that mediate between those who make messages and those who receive them' (Braman, 2003: 123). While there have been media theorists who have placed technological form at the centre of their analysis, perhaps most famously the Canadian communications theorists Harold Innis and Marshall McLuhan, it has remained the case that while 'models of the communication process have long included the media … research [has] almost exclusively focused on message production and reception, with little attention to how messages got from here to there' (Braman, 2003: 123; cf. Meyrowitz, 1994 on Innis and McLuhan).

Braman has observed that 'the word technology has its roots in the Greek *techne*, referring to what both art and engineering have in common' (Braman, 2003: 124). She suggests that we can usefully distinguish three levels of making. First, there are the tools that can be made and used by individuals working alone to transform matter and process energy. All human societies have been tool-making societies, but tools can be distinguished from technologies, which are social in both their making and use, and require people to work together in complex and interrelated processes. It is in this sense that industrial society and intensified technological development can be seen as being connected and mutually reinforcing. Finally, we have what Braman refers to as *meta-technologies* or those complex technologies that 'can process an ever-expanding range of types of inputs and can produce an essentially infinite range of outputs' (Braman, 2003: 124). Electrical technologies can be seen as a meta-technology of the industrial era, and computing and digital media technologies have established a comparable paradigm-defining position in the current informational era (Castells, 1996: 16–18, 40–60). A similar three-part structuring of technology is developed by Lievrouw and Livingstone, who propose that rather than thinking about new media in terms of particular technical features or uses, we need a definition that incorporates social and cultural dimensions by framing mew media technologies around: (1) the artefacts or devices used to communicate or convey information; (2) the activities and practices in which people engage to communicate or share information; and (3) the social arrangements or organisational forms that develop around those devices or practices (Lievrouw and Livingstone, 2006: 2).

Lievrouw (2006) identifies the two major paradigms on the development of new media technologies as being diffusion of innovations theories and the social shaping of technology perspective. Diffusion of innovations was pioneered in communications research by Everett Rogers (2003), and 'describes how new ideas or practices are introduced and adopted in a social system, with a special focus on the communication relations and information flows that promote adoption' (Lievrouw, 2006: 250). A critical distinction needs to be made between invention, innovation and diffusion. The focus of these approaches is less on invention than on innovation, with a particular interest in why clusters of innovation emerge in particular sectors at particular times. For Schumpeter, these innovation clusters were associated with long cycles of economic growth; the stimulus to innovation, or the application of new inventions for the development of new products, processes and services, was the entrepreneurial opportunity offered by changing the structural conditions of markets to earn above-average profits (Ferguson, 1988: 80–82). Not all innovations have this impact; indeed, most do not. We therefore need to make a further distinction between types of innovation:

1 Incremental innovations, or day-to-day improvements in products, production processes, services and marketing activities;
2 Radical innovations, arising from more committed research and development activities, that generate transformations within an industry or production sector;
3 Innovations in technological systems, or what Braman referred to as meta-technologies, whose impact is experienced across multiple sectors;
4 Changes in the *techno-economic paradigm*, or the dominant technologies, production inputs, and scientific 'common sense' of an era (typically about 50 years). Christopher Freeman defined a techno-economic paradigm as 'a cluster of interrelated technical, organizational, and managerial innovations whose advantages are to be found not only in a new range of products and systems, but most of all in the dynamics of the relative cost structure of all possible inputs to production' (quoted in Castells, 1996: 60–61).

A critical implication of this analysis is that the majority of non-incremental innovations fail commercially. In order to better understand this, we need to consider the relationship between what Everett Rogers (2003) referred to as the diffusion of innovation curve, whereby enthusiasts and early adopters take to a new technology before it gains mass market acceptance, and the evolutionary development of the technology itself, whereby performance typically improves dramatically at some point in time after it is first introduced to market. This generates what Christensen (2003) referred to as the *innovator's dilemma*, where a radical innovation may be too innovative relative to the needs of the majority of users, but still possess sufficient 'bugs' and flaws to leave the early adopter community dissatisfied and generate negative publicity (Flew, 2008: 206–210). Radical innovations are therefore most likely to generate a receptive response in the context of major shifts in technological systems and dominant techno-economic paradigms.

The other major approach to analysing technologies is the social shaping of technology paradigm. The social shaping of technology paradigm focuses upon 'the socio-economic patterns embedded in both the content of technologies and the process of innovation' (Williams and Edge, 1996: 866), and critiques arguments that technology shapes society, identifying these as examples of technological determinism. Again, the focus here is not so much on invention as it is on adoption, but these approaches tend to point to the role of powerful institutions such as corporations, the military and governments as key agents determining the trajectory of technological developments (MacKenzie and Wacjman, 1999). They also focus upon the sociology of knowledge, and particularly upon how 'scientists' own beliefs, opportunities and relationships are as important in the establishment of scientific facts or truths as the natural phenomena that they study' (Lievrouw, 2006: 249). Raymond Williams' account of the development of television is one of the most famous applications of a social shaping of technology approach to media (Williams, 1990), while Brian Winston (1998) has undertaken a broader historical account of the development of media technologies based upon a social shaping of technology approach.

International Trade in Creative Goods and Services

The creative industries have been identified as a major source of growth in international trade. UNCTAD has estimated that the value of world exports of creative industries goods and services was US$424.4 billion in 2005, accounting for 3.4 per cent of world trade. Of this, creative goods exports accounted for US$335.5 billion, with an annual growth rate of 6.1 per cent over a 10-year period, and creative services accounted for US$89 billion, with an annual growth rate of 8.8 per cent during the 1996–2005 period. Trade in creative industries goods and services grew annually by 6.4 per cent over 1996–2005, with an annual rate of growth of 8.7 per cent over the 2000–2005 period (UNCTAD, 2008: 106–107). Table 5.1 below shows that developing countries accounted for 41 per cent of total exports of creative goods, suggesting that the developing world plays a significant role in the creative industries worldwide, but it must be noted that China alone accounted for 19 per cent. The largest export sector was design, but we must treat both this observation and the rise of China with some caution, as design includes low-value-added manufactured goods such

Table 5.1 Creative Goods: Exports by Economic Group and Region, 2000 and 2005

Economic Group and Region	Value ($ US million)		Change %
	2000	**2005**	**2000–2005**
Worldwide	**228,695**	**335,494**	**47**
Developed Economies	**136,643**	**194,445**	**42**
Europe	99,201	149,825	51
United States	20,703	25,544	23
Japan	4,803	5,547	15
Canada	`10,413	11,377	9
Developing Economies	**89,827**	**136,231**	**52**
Asia – South, Eastern, Southeastern (incl. China)	79,316	119,839	51
China	28,474	61,360	115
Western Asia	2,747	5,947	116
Latin America and Carribean	6.769	8,641	28
Africa	973	1,775	82
Least Developed Countries (LDCs)	648	211	–67
Small Island Developing States (SIDS)	133	153	15
Economies in Transition (post-communist Eastern Europe)	**2,226**	**4,818**	**116**

Source: UNCTAD, 2008: 109.

as toys, kitchenware and imitation jewellery, included alongside higher-value-added goods such as audiovisual media, music, new media and publishing.

If we control for this statistical bias, it is the case that 'the high-growth subgroups of creative industries with higher value added, such as audiovisuals and new media, are exported mainly by advanced countries' (UNCTAD, 2008: 108). It is also the case that most of the world's regions are net importers of creative goods and services, with the major exception being East and Southeast Asia, most notably China, primarily for reasons arising from data collection noted above. A worrying point to note is that while the level of creative goods exports grew by 73 per cent of developing economies overall between 1996 and 2005, the value of creative exports grew more slowly in Latin America and the Carribean and in the Small Island Developing States (SIDS), and actually declined in the Least Developed Countries (LDCs) between 2000 and 2005 (UNCTAD, 2008: 109). The rates of growth of imports of creative goods by type of good, and in terms of developed, developing or transitional economies (Eastern European and other post-communist nations that were formerly a part of the Soviet Union's trading bloc), are shown in Table 5.2.

It is anticipated that international trade in cultural goods and services will continue to grow over the coming years, both as a proportion of total world trade and relative to the growth in creative industries production and consumption overall. A number of reasons exist for this. Cultural goods are often seen as being subject to Engel's Law. This thesis, first developed by the nineteenth-century German economist and statistician Ernst Engel, proposes

Table 5.2 Creative Goods: Imports by Economic Group, 1996 and 2005 ($US million)

	Worldwide		Developed Economies		Developing Economies		Economies in Transition	
	1996	2005	1996	2005	1996	2005	1996	2005
All creative industries (incl. Creative Services)	190,492	350,884	163,257	282,558	27,074	60,759	161	7,568
Arts and crafts	15,679	25,091	12,680	20,174	2,984	4,390	15	527
Audiovisuals	333	650	255	526	78	116	0	7
Design	120,603	228,428	101,451	184,052	19,057	39,257	95	5,119
Music	4,851	16,419	4,442	13,737	406	2,413	3	269
New media	6,250	13,402	5,683	10,718	564	2,465	3	220
Publishing	31,242	45,783	28,225	34,740	2,973	9,735	44	1,308
Visual arts	11,534	21,111	10,521	18,610	1,011	2,382	2	118

Source: UNCTAD, 2008: 109.

that as people's overall income rises, their expenditure of food and other basics rises by a smaller proportion, meaning that they have more discretionary income to spend on luxury items. Put differently, it is proposed that many cultural goods have a positive income elasticity of demand, meaning that as global average incomes rise, and particularly as more people in developing nations acquire some form of middle-income status, it is anticipated that their demand for the products and services of the creative industries will increase. Globalisation may be seen as a factor promoting cultural trade, as greater exposure to the cultures of other nations through media, travel, education, etc. can act as a stimulus to consumption of their cultural products and services, overcoming an innate tendency towards parochialism in cultural consumption associated with language specialisation, a historic grounding in one's own culture, and a lack of awareness of the cultures of other nations (Schulze, 2003). New media technologies also act as a stimulus to cultural trade: as the Internet makes it easier to access books, music, video, etc. in an intangible format through digital downloads, the transaction costs associated with buying cultural products from other parts of the world are reduced dramatically. It should be noted, however, that one other consequence of this form of electronic commerce is that such transactions may be harder to track, as there is potentially less evidence of the transaction when it does not take the form of physical goods shipped from one place to another, but also because some of the downloads may be illegal or be circumventing copyright restrictions. There is also the question of what percentage of digital downloads are paid for by the end-user; Montgomery (2009) identified that 90–99 per cent of music consumed in China was either illegally downloaded or acquired from pirate sources.

Mainstream media economists begin from the theory of comparative advantage in explaining patterns in international cultural trade. First developed by political economist David Ricardo in the early nineteenth century, the theory of comparative advantage proposes that individual nations benefit from trade as it enables them to concentrate resources in those industries where they have the most efficient production processes, and import other goods and services, while being able to export the goods and services they produce most efficiently to other countries. Comparative advantage has been seen as deriving historically from different endowments of factors of production between nations, or the balance between land, labour, natural resources and other factors (e.g. climate) between nations. This cannot, however, explain comparative advantage derived from superior knowledge and/ or capital resources, and is of limited use in understanding trade differentials in the creative industries. Hoskins et al. (2004) argue that the reasons for US dominance of world audiovisual trade arises from the combination of a large population, high average per capita incomes, a common English language, and 'first mover' advantages deriving to Hollywood from being the first to industrialise film production processes and develop vertically integrated media businesses. Such advantages become mutually reinforcing as Hollywood has become a core knowledge cluster in film and television, attracting creative talent from all parts of the world and being a site where knowledge and resources are pooled to maximum advantage. It is also argued that openness to large-scale migration combined with a highly competitive industry generates popular content with broad-based audience appeal in both US domestic and international markets, and minimises the degree to which cultural discount occurs, whereby the appeal of imported film and television programming is diminished 'because viewers have difficulty relating to the way of life, values, institutions, and language' of the imported content (Hoskins et al., 2004: 318). From a more textually oriented perspective, Olson (2004) has proposed that Hollywood media content benefits in international markets from its narrative transparency, or 'the capability of certain texts to seem familiar regardless of their origin, to seem a part of one's own culture, even though they have been crafted elsewhere' (Olson, 2004: 120). As budgets for US media content have grown in recent decades, as outlined in Chapter Four, and the resultant need for sales in international markets has increased, pressures to generate texts with broad cross-cultural appeal have increased. By contrast, it is argued that films and other media content that arise primarily from forms of national cultural policy are less able to circulate in such a way internationally, as they are more reflective of policy makers' expectations for artistic merit and/or direct relevance to the national culture and polity (Cowen, 2002).

By contrast, political economists argue that these claims are at best naïve and at worst politically disingenuous. Miller et al. (2001) put this position most forcefully when they argue that while neoclassical media economists present 'the combination of high GDP, managerial sophistication, narrative clarity and the *lingua franca* status of English as factor endowments aiding Hollywood's hegemony', political economists such as themselves instead argue that 'Hollywood's hegemony is built upon and sustained by the internal suppression of worker rights, exploitation of a global division of labour, and the impact of colonialism on language' (Miller et al., 2001: 51). Grant and Wood argue that the 'winner takes all' characteristics of cultural products, combined with the need to secure local cultural production in order to establish whether consumer preferences for it over imported culture exists, mean that 'markets for cultural products do not behave like those for widgets and … the imposition of trade liberalization rules designed for ordinary commodities would simply institutionalize the stark imbalances that characterize the world of popular culture' (Grant and Wood, 2004: 4).

Joost Smiers (2004) has argued that the global spread of the Western copyright system presents the risk of freezing cultural development as it makes cultural products the property of a small number of well-established copyright owners, who are for the most part not the artists involved in their creation, while at the same time neglecting the value of cultural diversity in its own right, both within and between nations. At a more general level, international trade theory as applied to media is seen by its critics as both reinforcing the hegemony of the dominant players, most notably the United States, and failing to adequately acknowledge the dual nature of cultural goods as tradable commodities and as distinctive forms of cultural expression that are part of national societies and global cultural diversity.

The WTO, the GATS and the UNESCO Convention on Cultural Diversity

The historic antimony between culture as shared patrimony and artistic endeavour, and culture as commodity and commercial product, has sharpened in recent years with the finalising of the General Agreement on Trade in Services (GATS) in 1994 and establishment of the World Trade Organization (WTO) in 1995. The GATS built upon the General Agreement on Tariffs and Trade (GATT), signed by 23 countries in 1948 and by 123 countries by 1986, which had been credited with contributing to global economic growth by promoting sustained reductions in tariffs on manufactured goods, but by the 1980s momentum was building to extend its principles to service industries. The GATS framework had a particular potential to impact upon film, television and new media industries, constructing the audio-visual sector as part of the services industries, and hence subject to legal disciplines that can restrict the capacity of national governments to undertake policies that favour local media companies and service providers (Grant and Wood, 2004).

   The conclusion of the Uruguay Round of the General Agreement on Tariffs and Trade (GATT) negotiations in 1993, which led to the GATS in 1994, saw an unresolved rift between the European Union on the one hand and the United States on the other around the question of a cultural exemption for audiovisual services, and 40 WTO member countries (including the European Union as a single entity) took exemption to various clauses of the GATS as in relation to their audiovisual industries. Footer and Graber (2000) observed that while the European Union, Canada, Australia, India, Brazil and a number of other countries 'wished to preserve "cultural identity" and to recognize fundamental cultural differences, based on separate language, values and beliefs', the US position was one of 'labelling national cultural expression as an excuse for the continued protectionism of national film, television and media industries in those countries' (Footer and Graber, 2000: 119). One can see how different models of international trade in media and cultural goods can find concrete policy expression in international trade negotiations.

(Continued)

(Continued)

The provisions of the GATS that were seen as having the most impact upon domestic media and cultural policies were:

- Article II *Most-favoured-nation treatment*, whereby Members are required to 'accord immediately and unconditionally to services and service suppliers of any other Member treatment no less favourable than that it accords to like services and service suppliers of any other country';
- Article XVI *Market Access*, which requires that 'each Member shall accord services and service suppliers of any other Member treatment no less favourable than that provided for under the terms, limitations and conditions agreed and specified in its Schedule'. This Article also requires that, if the cross-border movement of capital is an essential part of the service, the Member is required to permit such capital movements;
- Article XVII *National Treatment*, which requires that 'each Member shall accord to services and service suppliers of any other Member, in respect of all measures affecting the supply of services, treatment no less favourable than it accords to its own like services and service suppliers'.

The reaction to the GATS and the WTO and its potential impact was particularly strong in the European Union, where an alternative tradition of media policy as a form of cultural policy has been fostered, based around a central role for public service broadcasting, state cultural policy initiatives to cater for cultural and linguistic diversity within nation-states, and a formative role for the development of citizens, as well as the promotion of European audiovisual industries as a counterweight to the dominance of the US media industries and cultural products (European Commission, 2005). The idea that the United States was using international trade forums to promote free trade in audiovisual services was seen as 'the latest manifestation of American cultural imperialism' (Palmer, 1996: 36). The French President, François Mitterand, said, 'Who could be blind today to the threat of a world gradually invaded by an identical culture, Anglo-Saxon culture, under the cover of economic liberalism?' (quoted in Miller, 1996: 72). Winseck (2002) has argued that the real significance of the WTO for global media and cultural policy lay less in its capacity to override national legislation than in the discursive shift it promoted. He argued that it was part of a wider trend towards thinking about media and communications as service industries, subject to generic forms of law such as competition policy, with a primary remit of delivering low-cost, innovative media and communications services to consumers worldwide, as distinct from adhering to traditional communication policy values such as freedom of expression, diversity, pluralism and the promotion of national culture and cultural identity.

Graber (2006) has observed that the 'cultural exception' position risked the accusation of being a cloak for protectionism as it did not invoke a positive conception of culture and the role of national cultural policy. By contrast, the concept of cultural diversity gained traction from the late 1990s, first through the European Union and then through UNESCO. Graber observed that 'in contrast to the negativism and latent "anti-Americanism" of the "cultural exception" rhetoric, the new concept has the advantage of being conceptually neutral. Diversity in audiovisual trade is something that can be analysed statistically – free from ideology and protectionist ulterior motives' (Graber, 2006: 555). Promotion of the principle of cultural diversity as a signpost for national cultural policies in an era of economic globalisation and trade liberalisation was central to the establishment of a Convention on the Protection and Promotion of the Diversity of Cultural Expressions (CCD) that was ratified at the 33rd UNESCO General Conference, adopted by a majority of 148 votes to two in 2005.

It was argued in the UNESCO Convention that cultures could be understood as akin to ecosystems 'made up of a rich and complex mosaic of cultures, more or less powerful [that] need diversity to preserve and pass on their valuable heritage to others'. Drawing a parallel with the Convention on Biodiversity, it was argued that 'Only adequate cultural policies can ensure the preservation of the creative diversity against the risks of a single homogenizing culture. Cultural diversity is the positive expression of the overarching imperative to prevent the development of a uniform world by promoting and supporting all world cultures' (UNESCO, 2003). Among the key propositions of the Declaration were:

- Article 8, which stated that as 'commodities of a unique kind', there was a need to pay particular attention to 'the diversity of the supply of creative work', and to recognise 'the specificity of cultural goods and services which, as vectors of identity, values, and meaning must not be treated as mere commodities or consumer goods';
- Article 9, which proposed that since cultural policies are 'catalysts of creativity', it is therefore the role of 'each State, with due regard to its international obligations, to define its cultural policy and to implement it through the means it considers fit, whether by operational support or appropriate regulations';
- Article 11, which argued that 'Market forces alone cannot guarantee the preservation and promotion of cultural diversity. Therefore, in promoting sustainable human development, the key role of public policy, in partnership with the private sector and civil society, must be reaffirmed'.

While the Convention provides a counterweight to the WTO in relation to matters of artistic and cultural expression, Graber (2006) concludes that at present the Convention does not adequately interface with the WTO framework, and there is a need to explicitly amend WTO law so that the dual nature of cultural goods as both tradable products and forms of cultural expression that are vital to the distinctive fabric of societies can be better recognised.

International trade agreements such as the GATS, organisations such as the WTO, and conventions such as the UNESCO Convention on Cultural Diversity have some influence upon what cultural goods and services are available to us. At the end of the day, however, such institutional infrastructures cannot themselves shape cultural consumption. In an era of economic and cultural globalisation, there is much work to be done on better understanding which products and services developed by the creative industries best 'travel' between nations and cultures, and which do not. We also need a better understanding of how consumer expectations are being shaped by the new technological infrastructures of distribution and consumption, particularly in the developing world and the emergent economies. One of the intentions of this chapter was to point to the complexities arising from such questions, which are not addressed simply by seeing consumption as the inevitable by-product of production, by denying the agency of consumers, or by seeing people as essentially subject to regimes of mass manipulation. Such models were characteristic of earlier theories of the cultural industries; understanding the creative industries requires that more attention is given to those at the consumption end of what UNESCO refers to as the culture cycle, as well as the production end.

Endnotes

1   The status of consumption *vis-à-vis* production has been a major source of disagreement between neoclassical economists and their Marxist critics. In the neoclassical approach, it is the desires and demands of individual consumers that drive production, as profit-seeking entrepreneurs identify opportunities arising from meeting these consumer wants, meaning that market economies are driven by *consumer sovereignty* (e.g. Friedman and Friedman, 1980). Importantly, the source of these consumer wants is taken to be outside the scope of economics; it is concerned only with their concrete manifestation as a willingness to pay certain prices to satisfy these wants. For Marxist critics (e.g. Mohun, 2003) this theory is ideological, as it ignores the extent to which a capitalist market economy, as distinct from an economy based upon simple commodity production, is driven by the demand for profit and the accumulation of capital, with the buying and selling of goods and services understood primarily as the means to that end.

2   Lee identifies Bret Easton Ellis's *American Psycho* (Ellis, 1991) as a case study of how such consumerism works in contemporary culture. A highly controversial novel when it came out in 1990 due to the graphic depictions of violence engaged in by the main character, Patrick Bateman, one reason why *American Psycho* retains interest that goes beyond shock value is the manner in which Bateman engages with the commodities he consumes in a completely blank, non-ironic manner. For Bateman, the worth of an individual can be gauged by the quality of their business cards; the lyrics of Phil Collins and Whitney Houston provide major insights into the human condition; toiletries need to be endorsed by major celebrities in order to be worth using; and no New York restaurant is worth having dinner at unless Donald Trump has eaten there.

3   In early 21st century globalised media culture, an obvious set of candidates for social emulation are celebrities, due to their visibility, ubiquity and their apparent possession of highly valued personal attributes. On the relationship between consumerism and celebrity culture, see Marshall (2006).

6 Globalisation, Cities and Creative Spaces

Globalisation became one of the key concepts of the 1990s and 2000s. From being a term that was rarely used prior to the 1990s, its influence had become such that it was argued that by the early 2000s 'globalisation, in one form or another, is impacting on the levels of everyone on the planet … globalisation might justifiably claim to be the defining feature of human society at the start of the 21st century' (Benyon and Dunkerley, 2000: 3); or, as Anthony Giddens put it, 'globalisation is not incidental to our lives today. It is a shift in our very life circumstances. It is the way we now live' (Giddens, 2003: 19). Although the term has many definitions, three of the most commonly used have been by sociologists Roland Robertson, Anthony Giddens, and David Held and Anthony McGrew:

> Globalization as a concept refers both to the compression of the world and the intensification of consciousness of the world as a whole … both concrete global interdependence and consciousness of the global whole. (Robertson, 1992: 8)

> Globalisation can … be defined as the intensification of worldwide social relations which link distant localities in such a way that local happenings are shaped by events occurring many miles away and vice versa … Local transformation is as much a part of globalisation as the lateral extension of social connections across time and space. (Giddens, 1990: 64)

> Globalization … denotes the expanding scale, growing magnitude, speeding up and deepening impact of transcontinental flows and patterns of social interaction. It refers to a shift or transformation in the scale of human organization that links distant communities and expands the reach of power relations across the world's regions and continents. (Held and McGrew, 2002: 1)

The globalisation literature is voluminous and difficult to summarise. For some, the key driving factor has been the globalisation of economic activity, which is seen as reducing the capacity of nation-states to regulate their national economies towards ends that are in the best interests of their citizens (e.g. Scholte, 2005a). In particular, those who focus on economic globalisation point to the rise of the multinational corporation (MNC) since World War II, which has large parts of its operations outside its home nation, and which increasingly outsources production through global production networks (Henderson et al., 2002); it is now estimated that internal transactions between different international branches of MNCs and related firms account for the majority of world exports (Held et al., 1999: 242). They also draw attention to the rapid globalisation of financial markets, where annual turnover is now over 30 times that of world GDP.

Other authors have drawn attention to the significance of cultural globalisation, particularly where it intersects with networked information and communications technologies (e.g. Giddens, 2003; Tomlinson, 2007). At the end of 2009, 1.733 billion people were on the Internet, or about 25.6 per cent of the world's population. There was a 360 per cent growth in the number of Internet users worldwide between 2000 and 2009, with the fastest rates of growth in developing countries in Africa, the Middle East, Asia and Latin America (Internet World Stats, 2010). The number of television viewers worldwide was about 4 billion in 2008; Hollywood film and television products provide internationally recognised signifiers of 'global culture'; and global media events and global media spectacles, such as the Olympics and World Cup football, continue to attract huge audiences (Kellner and Pierce, 2007; Hartley, 2008).

Some have also stressed the political dimensions of globalisation, such as the extent to which actions undertaken in one nation-state affect those in other states (e.g. environmental degradation, resource depletion, climate change, migration regulation, public health pandemics), leading to 'overlapping communities of fate' among political communities as the reach and impact of events with adverse consequences, as well as the proposed solutions, extend beyond nation-states (Held et al., 1999: 81). The rise of international civil society movements (also known as international non-governmental organisations (INGOs)) is one of the factors that means that the sovereignty of nation-states and effective political power are increasingly 'shared and bartered by diverse forces and agencies at national, regional and international levels' (Held et al., 1999: 80). Other forces promoting political globalisation include the rise of regional political and trade blocs such as the European Union, the growth of international treaties and the rise of international law, and the role played by the United Nations and others in brokering binding international agreements. In his influential formulation, Anthony Giddens (2003) proposed that globalisation was a three-fold set of processes acting from above, shifting economic and political power from nation-states to the supranational level; from below, in the promotion of new demands for local autonomy and recognition of local cultural identity (e.g. the rise of Scottish nationalism in the UK, or demands for Catalan or Basque autonomy in Spain); and 'sideways', by creating 'new economic and cultural zones within and across nations' (Giddens, 2003: 13). The rise of cities and regions as autonomous political actors is particularly driven by their growing integration into the global economy, as seen with city-regions such as the Hong Kong–Guangzhou-Shenzhen region of southern China (Pearl River Delta), Malaysia's Multimedia Super Corridor, and Hyderabad and Bangalore in India.

Greater global interconnectedness is a recurring theme of the globalisation literature, as is the claim that globalisation is weakening the power and sovereignty of the nation-state. Enthusiasts for free trade and open markets, such as Frances Cairncross (1998) and Thomas

Friedman (2005), have equated globalisation with 'the death of distance' and the 'inexorable integration of markets, nation-states and technologies' (Friedman, 2005: 9), while sociologists such as Malcolm Waters identified globalisation as 'a social process in which the constraints of geography on economic, political, social and cultural arrangements recede' (Waters, 2001: 5). From a Marxist perspective, Michael Hardt and Antonio Negri's influential formulation developed in their book *Empire* proposed that the current phase of global capitalism was one where 'large transnational corporations have effectively surpassed the jurisdiction and authority of nation-states', to the point where 'government and politics come to be completely integrated into the system of transnational command' (Hardt and Negri, 2000: 306, 307). In contrast, however, to those who are pessimistic about this loss of national sovereignty to transnational capital (e.g. Barber, 2000; Lloyd, 2000), Hardt and Negri's dialectical framework leads them to identify the global multitude, engaged with globally networked ICTs, as presenting the possibility for a true global democracy, uncompromised by the exigencies of sovereignty and the artificiality of nation-states and national cultures (Hardt and Negri, 2005). A similar conclusion was reached in earlier work by Nigel Harris (1984), who argued that the internationalisation of capital accumulation meant 'the end of capitalism in one country', pointing to an unresolved contradiction between capital and the nation-state (Harris, 1984: 229–237).

I have elsewhere (Flew, 2007; Flew and McElhinney, 2005) referred to such arguments as examples of the *strong globalisation* thesis. 'Strong globalisation' arguments go from the (relatively uncontentious) proposition that there have been important quantitative shifts in the world of the early 2000s associated with globalisation, which distinguish it from the world of the mid–late 1900s, to the more contentious claim that globalisation marks a qualitative shift in the pattern of economic, social, political and cultural relations within and between states and societies that is without historical precedent. Part of the problem is conceptual. Picking up on the observation that 'if globalisation means anything, it is the incorporation of societies globally into a capitalist modernity, with all the implications of the latter – economic, social, political, and cultural' (Dirlik, 2003: 275), a number of authors have argued that the trends identified could be seen as aspects of global capitalism as it has been theorised and conceptualised for some time, rather than requiring the entirely new conceptual apparatus of globalisation theories (Curran and Park, 2000; Sparks, 2007; Hirst et al., 2009). This proposition is supported empirically by the observation that capitalism as a world system has been marked by successive waves of global expansion and contraction, and that the growth of foreign trade, foreign investment and cross-border migration, identified as a driver of post-World War II globalisation, has clear historical parallels, most notably in the period from the 1850s to 1914 (Hirst et al., 2009). As there is a long history of conceiving of capitalism as a world system, with colonialism and imperialism as recognisable aspects of this system, there has been a recurrent problem with attempts to historicise claims about the newness of globalisation (Sklair, 2002; Robertson, 2007).

Moving from the conceptual to the empirical, I want to focus on two elements of the strong globalisation thesis that do not stand up to close scrutiny. These concern: (1) the claim that corporations are becoming increasingly transnational and 'placeless'; and (2) the argument that the powers of the nation-state are being weakened and sovereignty shifted to international governmental institutions. I have developed these arguments in more detail elsewhere (Flew, 2007: 58–65, 81–88), and my purpose here is not to add to the massive literature debating the pros and cons of globalisation as an analytical concept, but to draw attention to aspects of the economic geography of globalisation that are relevant to considering the rise of creative cities development strategies in the 2000s.

The assumption that multinational corporations (MNCs) increasingly operate as global giants unconstrained by geography, culture or local institutions is not borne out in the detailed studies undertaken of MNC conduct. Drawing upon data from the UNCTAD Transnationality Index (TNI), Dicken (2003a) found that the degree of transnationality of the world's top 100 non-financial corporations (the share of foreign sales, assets and employment as a percentage of the total) changed only marginally over the course of the 1990s (from 51.6% in 1993 to 52.6% in 1999), and that it varied substantially between corporations according to country of origin (MNCs from smaller countries have higher TNIs than those from large countries such as the US), and according to industry (mining and extractive industries, as well as established manufacturing industries such as motor vehicles, have considerably higher average TNIs than service and information-based industries).[1]

Dicken's contention that the bulk of the world's largest MNCs are 'national corporations with international operations', rather than global corporations defined as firms that 'have the power to co-ordinate and control operations in a large number of countries ... [and] whose geographically dispersed operations are functionally integrated' (Dicken, 2003b: 225), is supported by the literature on the organisational cultures of MNCs. The pioneering work of Doremus et al. (1998) on the influence of the cultural and institutional environment of their 'home base' continues to receive support from empirical case studies, leading Dicken (2003a) to observe that 'place and geography still matter fundamentally in the ways in which forms are produced and how they behave', and that 'country of origin continues to matter a lot for the behaviour of MNCs' (Dicken, 2003a: 41, 44). This is not to say that MNCs have identical organisational strategies for geographical expansion. Indeed, the 'global' strategy of maintaining tight central control over decisions, resources and information appears to be in decline relative to 'network enterprise' strategies that seek to tap into geographically dispersed knowledge-based assets and develop strategic alliances based on better local understanding of markets and regulatory arrangements (Dunning, 2000). This is reflective of the rise of what John Dunning refers to as *internalisation* advantages sought from foreign investment – as distinct from cost advantages or access to foreign markets – whereby MNCs can 'use their foreign affiliates and partners as vehicles for seeking out and monitoring new knowledge ... and as a means of tapping into national innovative or investment systems more conducive to their dynamic competitive advantages' (Dunning, 2000: 20). All of this reinforces Dicken's general observation that MNCs are 'products of the local "ecosystem" in which they were originally planted ... [and] "global" corporations are, indeed, a myth' (Dicken, 2003a: 44).

The proposition that the rise of MNCs weakens the power of nation-states has been long critiqued, as has the argument that national governments have ceded sovereignty to transnational institutions and systems of international law.[2] While the basis of power for MNCs lies in their capacity to take advantage of geographical differences in the availability and cost of resources and different state policies and regulatory regimes, it is the case that, once an investment is made in a location, there are significant sunk costs that present a barrier to relocating at a later date. Moreover, as Dicken observes, 'all the elements in transnational production networks are regulated within some kind of political structure whose basic unit is the national state' (Dicken, 2007: 304). As a result, there is a complex bargaining process always taking place between MNCs and governments, and 'the outcome of a bargaining process is highly contingent' (Dicken, 2007: 305).

This is consistent with Crotty et al.'s (1998) finding that the outcomes for host nations of foreign direct investment were contingent upon the 'rules of the game' in that nation and the relative bargaining strength of the two parties. Where economic demand is strong, governance arrangements are both well understood and readily enforced, and domestic and international competition in relevant markets is robust, then more positive outcomes are more likely to occur. Moreover, the case of 'developmental states' in East Asia demonstrates that governments can derive significant knowledge and technology transfers from MNCs as a part of the rules of the game associated with their investment decisions (Ernst and Kim, 2002; Henderson et al., 2002). If, however, foreign investment is sought as a desperate measure to revitalise a weak domestic economy, governance arrangements are weak, or shot through with corruption, or foreign competition is particularly likely to weaken local competitors, then the 'race to the bottom' scenario is more likely to prevail, where 'capital will increasingly be able to play workers, communities, and nations off against one another as they demand tax, regulation and wage concessions while threatening to move' (Crotty et al., 1998: 118).

Some of the issues facing MNCs in their dealings with national governments are being addressed through multinational institutions such as the World Trade Organization and binding multilateral agreements, and the role played by such global institutions and treaties has been criticised as weakening the sovereignty of the nation-state. Hirst et al. (2009) have argued that the problem with the metaphor of a spatial shift of state power from the national to the transnational level is that it simply misunderstands how international agreements are actually brokered and regulated by nation-states:

> The nation-state is central to this process of 'suturing': the policies and practices of states in distributing power upwards to the international level and downwards to sub-national agencies are the ties that will hold the system of governance together. Without such explicit policies to close gaps in governance and elaborate a division of control in regulation, then vital capacities will be lost. Authority may now be plural within and between states rather than nationally centralized, but to be effective it must be structured by an element of design into a relatively coherent architecture of institutions. (Hirst et al., 2009: 235)

The point here is not to say that nothing has changed, that globalisation is simply a myth, or that international capital or international institutions present no constraints for the freedom of action of national governments. It is rather to point out that an overly abstract or simplistic understanding of the multinational corporation, a failure to understand the institutional contexts and constraints that present themselves to MNCs, or an assumption that the power of the nation-state is in decline – all of which can be found in variants of the 'strong globalisation' thesis – do not assist us in advancing understanding of how globalisation is in fact shaping the development of industries and economies.

Globalisation and Cities

One aspect of globalisation that was not anticipated was its association with a greater role being played by cities. Cities have always been central to capitalist modernity. The rise of manufacturing industry and the factory system have been associated with the large-scale migration of people from the countryside to urban centres, where businesses have clustered to take advantage of economies of scale and diversity of resources such as land, labour, capital, infrastructure, institutions and knowledge. Cities have also been seen as exemplary spaces of cultural modernity, in so far as they have been sites for the incubation of new ideas, bringing together people from diverse cultures and backgrounds, generating new opportunities for entrepreneurial activity, and separating individuals – for better or worse – from the ties and boundaries associated with cultural tradition. As cities drew attention to 'the incredible diversity of experiences and stimuli to which modern urban life exposed us' (Harvey, 1989: 26), they have also been vital centres for the arts, literature, culture and entertainment more generally (Hall, 1998).

Cities have also been sites where many of the contradictory dimensions of capitalist modernity have been experienced at their sharpest and most concentrated. These include the co-existence of wealth and poverty, divisions based upon class, gender, race and ethnicity, and environmental degradation. This has meant that cities have frequently been centres of political revolt, violent repression, social movements, and campaigns for democratic reform. It has also meant that distinctive forms of urban policy and planning have evolved to address social problems that were seen to have a distinctively urban dimension. Bridge and Watson described the origins of modern urban planning in these terms:

> By the end of the nineteenth century the effects of industrialization on cities – the perceived disorder, pollution, ill health, chaos, and immorality – were increasingly erupting as a cause for public and moral concern. Discourses of cities as sites of moral degradation, unrest, and potential revolution were rife. In this context, the notions of progress, rationality and order which were embedded in the project of modernity were translated into planning ideas and the desire to find a way of organizing social and economic activities in cities in a rational, predictable, and aesthetically pleasing way. The aim was to improve the living conditions of urban populations without impeding economic progress and growth. (Bridge and Watson, 2003: 505)

A core concept in understanding the economic significance of cities is that of *clustering*. We need to distinguish between two economic drivers of clustering: those associated with localisation and industrial districts, and those associated with urbanisation and large-scale cities. Localisation refers to the clustering of firms in the same or related industries in a particular city or region, and the positive externalities that can arise from such co-location. The concept is generally attributed to the British economist Alfred Marshall, and his observations about how certain parts of Britain had become associated with particular industries, such as the Sheffield cutlery industries or the wool textiles industry in West Yorkshire (Marshall, 1990 [1890]). The resulting positive externalities include: labour market specialisation; the deepening of knowledge and craft skills; and reduced transaction costs between suppliers and producers. The risk arising for such 'Marshallian industrial districts' was that their economic destiny may become overly tied to the fate of particular firms and industries, as seen with the decline of Detroit, Michigan, after the heyday of the US car industry in the 1960s.

If specialisation provided the basis for the economic benefits of localisation, it is diversity that generated the positive externalities of urbanisation. Among the benefits commonly cited are: the possibility of innovation and new forms of collaboration arising from co-location with unrelated industries; the diversity of labour, skills, knowledge and ideas that can act as stimuli to entrepreneurship; the concentration of large-scale infrastructure in cities (particularly related to transport, communication and education); the incentives for professional services industries to cluster around urban centres; and the attractiveness of cities as sites for migration (Amin, 2003; Lorenzen and Frederiksen, 2008). It must be noted, however, that these benefits can turn into problems, with some of the more notable being rising land rents, environmental degradation, congestion, housing shortages, crime and overpopulation – the benefits from economies of scale can tip over into diseconomies of scale, providing different incentives to live or locate businesses outside major urban centres.

For many years in the twentieth century, the prognosis for cities was a pessimistic one. Technological and economic developments, such as electrification and motor vehicles, enabled greater geographical separation between home and work, and promoted suburbanisation. This was further enhanced in the post-World War II years as television viewing became the major use of leisure time and source of personal entertainment, and suburban shopping malls replaced city centres as the major sites of consumer spending (Clapson, 2003). Many businesses also identified the benefits of lower land rents outside the central business districts, and there was growing attention being paid to the crisis of inner cities, which were increasingly seen as areas associated with unemployment, poverty, crime and dereliction. This period also saw major cities, most notably New York, fall into major financial crises. Perhaps most importantly, the disaggregation of economic production processes, the rise of new export-based production centres in the developing world, the shift of manufacturing from high-wage industrialised economies to lower-wage economies such as China and other East Asian nations, and the rise of services and information-based industries all pointed towards a de-materialisation of the economy. With these developments went a decline in the salience attached to the aggregation economies associated with cities, that were in many cases tied to manufacturing industries now shifting production offshore or going bankrupt. Some referred to a de-territorialisation of the world economy (Harris, 1984), while others, such as Malcolm Waters (2001), argued that we were witnessing 'a social process in which the constraints of geography on economic, political, social and cultural processes recede', and that such a global shift was accelerated by the turn from a manufacturing to a cultural or more symbolically based economy, since 'symbols can be proliferated rapidly and in any location' (Waters, 2001: 5, 19).

The paradox has been that, from the late 1970s onwards, both globalisation and the rise of service, information-based and creative industries have been factors in the resurgence of cities. By the late 2000s, the majority of the world's population resided in cities, for the first time in the history of humankind (Worldwatch Institute, 2007). In his review of the literature on cities and globalisation, Ash Amin concluded that:

> There appears little evidence to support the claim that cities are becoming less impor-
> tant in an economy marked by increasing geographical dispersal ... [They] assert, in one
> way or another, the powers of agglomeration, proximity, and density, now perhaps less
> significant for the production of mass manufactures than for the production of knowl-
> edge, information and innovation, as well as specialized inputs. (Amin, 2003: 120)

According to Amin (2003: 117–120), the distinctive sources of competitive advantage that location in cities can bring to businesses in an increasingly globalised economic environment include:

- The advantages for professional services industries, such as business, financial and legal services, of being in locations that provide easy access to their principal clients and markets;
- Lifestyle attractors to professional and managerial workforces from location in urban centres, including access to a diverse range of cultural and entertainment options;
- Proximity to government decision-makers and public sector institutions such as universities and research centres;
- Opportunities for knowledge sharing, innovation and new entrepreneurial ventures that can arise from proximity to a diverse range of people, skills and industries.

One of the reasons why globalisation has been linked to the rise of cities rather than their decline arises from the dualistic nature of contemporary capitalist industry (Storper, 1997; Scott et al., 2001; Scott, 2008a, 2008b). One form of production rests upon highly routinised activities and codified knowledge, and is typically engaged in the production of standardised commodities. Globally networked production in this instance does entail developing an international division of labour, with the most routinised production activities being located in low-wage, low-cost locations, as labour requirements tend to be highly generic, and demand for these commodities highly price-sensitive. Advances in transport and communication enable these networks to be extended over large distances and for highly sophisticated global logistical planning to occur, leading to what can be termed de-territorialised economic development.

On the other hand, there are large areas of the contemporary global economy that 'involve activities where enormous uncertainty prevails, and where there are strong limits on pro-ducers' abilities to routinise or simplify their operations, especially in regard to their mutual interactions' (Scott et al., 2001: 15). These sectors produce de-standardised products and services, and require skilled and specialist labour in their creation and development.[3] In terms of their economic geography, these sectors frequently require territorialised economic development, defined as 'economic activity that is dependent on territorially specific resources' (Storper, 1997: 170), which include specific practices, routines and relationships that have evolved over time in particular locations. These form an element of what Storper terms *untraded interdependencies*, or 'the conventions, informal rules, and habits that coordinate economic actors under conditions of uncertainty … [and] constitute region-specific assets … in contemporary capitalism' (Storper, 1997: 4–5). As Storper's quote indicates, these are as likely to be found in particular regions as they are in cities, particularly those regions with a history as specialist industrial districts, or areas rich in particular agricultural or natural resources. What is distinctive about cities, however, is the higher propensity for new forms of untraded interdependencies to emerge. This can arise out of new patterns of corporate investment, public policy initiatives, or serendipitous interactions; as cities promote face-to-face contact and therefore trust, they are more likely to be both sites of 'buzz' (Storper and Venables, 2004). They are also sites for the large-scale migration of people, and they tend to have more diverse populations, both in terms of race and ethnicity and in terms of identity, culture and lifestyle factors.

Scott (2000, 2008a, 2008b; cf. Scott et al., 2001) has argued that such locationally specific assets based in cities are particularly important in the creative industries, or what he terms the cognitive-creative economy. Core elements of these locational resources that are central to creative industries include:

1 The contractual and transactional nature of production in knowledge-intensive and creative industries, which involves ongoing relationships between shifting networks of specialised but complementary firms. Geographical proximity reduces the transaction costs of joining and maintaining such networks across projects and over time.

2 Specialist workers engaged in these industries are drawn to such urban agglomerations as the centre of activity, thereby reducing job search costs; cities therefore act and as 'talent magnets' for those aspiring to work in such industries.

3 The resulting local system of production, employment and social life in turn generates learning and innovation, and 'a "creative field" or a structured set of interrelationships that stimulate and channel various kinds of creative energies' (Scott, 2008a: 313).

4 This dynamic is further promoted by the existence of complementary forms of 'social overhead capital' that includes the role played by universities, research centres, design centres, and other sites that generate specialist knowledge capital that can be applied in these sectors.

5 Provision of key institutional and infrastructural resources by public sector agencies, and an evolving relationship with local and regional governments that goes beyond either cultural development or industry development models, to ongoing relationships that focus upon the economic benefits of creative industries but also recognise their specificities both in cultural terms and in terms of their unique resourcing requirements.[4]

Global Cities and Creative Cities

There has been an extensive literature on what have been termed global cities or world cities. Saskia Sassen (2000, 2002, 2006) has argued that economic globalisation and new information and communication technologies have promoted global integration and the concentration of resources even as they have contributed to the global dispersal of activities, further consolidating and extending the role of global cities that are: (1) command points in the organisation of the world economy; (2) key locations and marketplaces for leading industries, most notably in the finance and professional services sectors; and (3) major production and innovation sites for these high-value-adding services sectors (Sassen, 2000: 4). In this respect, Sassen follows Hall's earlier definition of world cities as 'certain great cities in which a disproportionate part of the world's most important business is conducted' (Hall, 1966: 1). This has led to exercises in ranking world cities, including those developed by Friedmann (1995), Taylor (2004), and Beaverstock et al. (2006), that have developed various rankings of world cities based upon the extent to which particular cities are:

- Headquarters for multinational corporations;
- Headquarters for major international financial institutions;
- Headquarters for international institutions (e.g. United Nations agencies and major international governmental and non-governmental organisations);
- The size and rate of growth of business and professional services sectors;
- Their significance as a major transportation node (e.g. amount of airport activity and commercial shipping);
- The importance of the city as a manufacturing centre;
- Whether the city is a political capital;
- Population size.

Such a ranking exercise usually draws attention to particular core world cities (London, New York, Tokyo, Paris, Los Angeles, and increasingly Beijing and Shanghai), with a list of cities of varying size and significance below that: Beaverstock et al. (2006) identified 125 cities worldwide that had some 'world city' characteristics. More recent and additional indicators, such as levels of Internet traffic within and between cities, provide other ways of identifying global city status (García, 2002).

World Cities

There have been a number of significant research activities undertaken into world cities. John Friedmann proposed that the rise of world cities would be a key feature of a world economy where the largest corporations were organising their activities on a global scale and breaking from the territorial boundaries of national economies and nation-states (Friedmann, 2006;

Friedmann and Wolff, 2006). For Friedmann, world cities would not only be the headquarters for these multinational corporations, but would also become the centres for the investment of 'surplus' capital in areas such as real estate. For Friedmann, 'world cities are the control centres of the global economy ... they become the major points for the accumulation of capital and "all that money can buy". They are luxurious, splendid cities whose very splendour obscures the poverty on which their wealth is based' (Friedmann, 2006: 61). He proposed that one could test the world-city status of particular cities by the extent to which they had generated clusters of employment based around: (1) business, professional and financial services; (2) real estate, entertainment services, the media and luxury shopping; (3) international tourism; (4) specialist manufacturing; (5) government services; and (6) an 'informal' or 'street' economy based around the floating migrant populations that are drawn to world cities as much as skilled professionals are, and who fill low-wage jobs (e.g. domestic services, retail and hospitality) that are complementary to the growth of high-wage jobs.

Subsequent to Friedmann's work, the Globalisation and World Cities (GaWC) research network was established at the University of Loughborough in Great Britain (http://www.lboro.ac.uk/gawc/). A defining feature of the Globalisation and World Cities project has been that while considerable attention has been given to the internal features and dynamics of world cities, less attention had been given to external relations, or the relations between world cities. The GaWC project starts from the proposition that 'connections are the very raison d'être of cities [and] there is no such thing as a city operating on its own' (Taylor, 2004: 1–2). This has meant that their project has sought to identify world city networks, or the ways in which world cities are interconnected, and not simply the world cities themselves. Their project has given a primary role to professional business services as being at the centre of these networks, which include accountancy, banking and finance, advertising, management consultancy, law and insurance. Other relevant indicators include global media organisations, the network connectivity of international government and non-government organisations, aircraft traffic and, most recently, Internet traffic (Taylor et al., 2002; Taylor, 2004; Beaverstock et al., 2006). Through such data measures, they have developed sets of what they have termed *alpha* (most connected), *beta*, *gamma* and *delta* world cities. The most connected (*alpha*) world cities in the late 1999s according to this work were: London, Paris, New York, Tokyo, Chicago, Frankfurt, Hong Kong, Los Angeles, Milan and Singapore. *Beta* world cities included: San Francisco, Sydney, Toronto, Zurich, Brussels, Madrid, Mexico City, Sao Paolo, Moscow and Seoul (Taylor et al., 2002: 100).

Other influential approaches to world cities/global cities research have come from Saskia Sassen (2000, 2002, 2006) and Manuel Castells (1996). Sassen notes that while global cities such as New York, London and Tokyo tend to be major economic, political and cultural centres, it may also be the case that cities acquire ascendancy in some of these but not others. For example, Geneva is a major city for international politics but not so central to global economic flows, while Los Angeles is a global cultural centre but less central to world politics. Sassen also observes strong pressures towards

(Continued)

increasing inequalities within global cities as they simultaneously generate high-wage and low-wage jobs, so that 'the expansion of the high-income workforce in conjunction with the emergence of new cultural forms has led to a process of high-income gentrification that ultimately rests upon the availability of a vast supply of low-wage workers (Sassen, 2006: 86). Castells' concept of the global space of flows (Castells, 1996) noted the possibility for disjunctures between the economic, political and cultural domains in the context of globalisation – particularly between increasingly globalised and de-territorialised economic flows and the continuing attachment of political power to nation-states and defined territorial spaces – but also observes that all of these domains are being impacted upon by digitisation and networked ICTs, which are themselves seen as globalising and de-territorialising forces, meaning that the relationship between the global and the local is always in flux. Both Castells and Sassen identify the emergence of transnational elites, ideas and policy agendas that are thinking about how to shift key areas of decision-making, especially in the economic realm, from national governments to transnational institutions, and who also make divisions between 'cosmopolitans' and 'nationalists' an increasingly significant political fault-line in the twenty-first century (Castells, 1998).

One observation of the work on global cities is that it has tended to frame discussions about globalisation and cities primarily through 'networks of urban places that are arranged hierarchically in terms of their relative importance as sites of corporate control' (Timberlake and Ma, 2007: 265). The focus has been upon their place in terms of economic globalisation. But this leaves open a question of whether cities that are centres of commerce and corporate power are also centres of culture and creativity. In some cases the two can be seen to intersect: Landry (2005) and Currid (2007) argue persuasively that the global centrality of London and New York arises as much from their histories of punk rock and disco, their vibrant live theatre districts, the visual arts and fashion scenes, and their multicultural diversity, as they do from the corporate headquarters located in the City of London or Manhattan. But the further down the world cities list one goes, the more complicated the picture becomes. Frankfurt and Paris are both major international financial centres and transportation hubs, but few would see the two cities as having equivalent international standing as cultural centres. Los Angeles and San Francisco are the two dominant urban centres of the US West Coast, but the two have evolved very differently in a cultural sense, with the hippie movement, counter-culture and gay culture being key drivers of San Francisco's cultural development, as compared to Hollywood, media industries and celebrity culture in the case of Los Angeles. Equivalent questions can be identified in other places: how do we compare Manchester and Glasgow as creative cities? Barcelona and Madrid? Beijing and Shanghai? Sydney and Melbourne?

Some urban centres rise as creative cities, while others face crisis and decline. The 'Korean Wave' (*hallyu*) of films, TV programmes and digital media cultural products exported from

Korea to the rest of East Asia over the 2000s saw Seoul being identified as a major global cultural centre for the first time (Choi, 2008). However, it has been argued that Hong Kong has struggled to gain the cultural ascendancy it once had since the handover of sovereignty to China in 1997 (Donald and Gammack, 2007). There is also the argument that smaller cities can concentrate cultural resources more effectively than larger ones. In large cities, there is the perpetual danger of gentrification and the shortage of affordable housing driving out artists, musicians and other cultural workers, thereby destroying the loosely formed social and cultural networks that had constituted what Charles Landry termed the 'soft infrastructure' of urban creativity (Landry, 2000; cf. Hamnett, 2003, on gentrification). By contrast, the United States in particular has a thriving network of 'college towns', smaller urban centres typically dominated by a major university where vibrant cultural scenes exist and where the university can be a major factor in incubating creative talent: such cities include Austin (Texas), Bloomington (Indiana), and Boulder (Colorado), which all contrast in significant ways to the major cities that they are near – Dallas-Fort Worth, Indianapolis and Denver.

At a general level, what this potential lack of correspondence between economic indicators of global cities and the characteristics of cultural or creative cities points to is a wider set of problems arising from the reading of culture as being largely determined by economic forces. John Tomlinson points to the common assumption in globalisation literature that 'it is the *economic* sphere, the institution of the global capitalist market, that is ... the *sine qua non* of global connectivity'. As a result, we find 'common expressions like "the *impact* of globalisation on culture" or "the cultural *consequences* of globalisation" contain a tacit assumption that globalisation is a process which somehow has its sources and its terrain of operation *outside* of culture' (Tomlinson, 2007: 353 – emphasis in original). The role that is played by cities as incubators of culture and creativity has long been acknowledged; Peter Hall (1998) argued that because the city 'continues to attract the talented and ambitious ... it remains a unique crucible of creativity' (Hall, 1998: 7). But the question has gained a renewed intensity over the last two decades, as culture is increasingly conceived of as both constituting a set of wealth creating industries in their own right (as with the creative industries), or as a resource that urban policy makers can tap into to promote their cities as global leaders. Hall has observed that the decline of manufacturing industries throughout Europe has seen those engaged with the planning and development of cities 'become more and more preoccupied by the notion that cultural industries ... may provide the basis for economic regeneration, filling the gap left by vanishing factories and warehouses, and creating an urban image that would make them more attractive to mobile capital and mobile professional workers' (Hall, 1998: 8).

We therefore find an interesting collection of reasons that have emerged for policies designed to support and develop creative cities. Amin and Thrift (2007) identify four sets of arguments that connect cities to development of the cultural economy. First, there is the mutually reinforcing relationship found in global cities between being centres of business, finance, professional services and government on the one hand, and being centres of arts, cultural and entertainment activities on the other, as well as being the places where major media organisations tend to have their head offices. Second, culture is seen as being central to the relational assets that are found in cities, and is seen as the touchstone for resources which are key to a post-industrial, knowledge-intensive economy, such as reflexivity, trust and sociality. This is the much talked about (but notoriously hard to quantify) 'buzz' factor that arises out of extended opportunities for face-to-face interaction with a diverse network of people, which cities can enable and which cultural activities may facilitate (Storper and Venables, 2004). Third, there is the idea of the city itself providing a range of amenities and a series of cultural and entertainment activities that can be consumed; this extends the vision of the city as a site for cultural tourism that can include the everyday experience of its own population as well as actual visitors to the city (Miles and Miles, 2004). Finally, there is the significance of cities as the primary sites of cultural production, and the spatial relations associated with cultural production chains (Pratt, 2004b, 2008; Power and Scott, 2004). The last issue points to the significance not only of mapping current cultural activities and levels of employment, income and trade in the creative industries – which local authorities have typically done poorly, but which has been improved considerably over the last two decades – but also of identifying potential attractors for new investment in the creative industries. (Landry and Wood, 2003)

Creative Clusters

The concept of clusters has a long, if uneven, history in economic geography. As noted earlier, Alfred Marshall's identification of positive externalities arising from the co-location of firms and workers in related businesses drew attention to the geographical dimensions of industrial specialisation, although his insight was not for the most part taken up by economists, as it had the potential to challenge neoclassical equilibrium modelling by pointing towards 'winner takes all' economic outcomes (Warsh, 2006: 77–84). The concept was picked up elsewhere in work such as: French economist François Perroux's concept of growth poles, designed to assist policy makers in understanding how particular regions developed economic dynamism based on industrial specialisation; Swedish economist Gunnar Myrdal's concept of cumulative causation used to explain why particular regions could experience ongoing growth based on the agglomeration of industries and skilled labour at the expense of other regions; and Albert Hirschman's 'unbalanced growth' model of development economics, focused on developing forward and backward linkages in key industries as a driver of early industrialisation.

The cluster concept experienced a resurgence in the 1990s through the work of business management theorist Michael Porter from the Harvard Business School. Porter defined a cluster as 'a geographically proximate group of interconnected companies and associated institutions in a particular field, linked by commonalities and complementarities', observing that 'the geographical scope of a cluster can range from a single city or state to a country or even a group of neighbouring countries' (Porter, 2000: 254). In extending his competitive advantage model from firms to cities, regions and nations (Porter, 1998, 2000), Porter argued that dynamic and sustainable sources of competitive advantage derived less from lower costs and production efficiencies than from elements that promote productivity growth and innovation over time. In particular, following Marshall, Porter was interested in the spillover benefits that can emerge from being in particular locations, including the presence of related and supporting industries, and the positive externalities arising from location within a cluster. In particular, Porter argued that location within particular clusters is able to provide three sources of competitive advantage to the firms that are a part of them:

1 Productivity gains, deriving from access to specialist inputs and skilled labour, access to specialised information and industry knowledge, the development of complementary relationships among firms and industries, and the role played by universities and training institutions in enabling knowledge transfer;

2 Innovation opportunities, derived from proximity to buyers and suppliers, sustained interaction with others in the industry, and pressures to innovate in circumstances where cost factors facing competitors are broadly similar;

3 New business formation, arising from access to information about opportunities, better access to resources required by business start-ups (e.g. venture capitalists, skilled workforce), and reduced barriers to exit from existing businesses.

The notion of creative clusters lent itself well to strategies of culture-led urban regeneration that were becoming a particularly prominent feature of post-industrial cities in Europe in particular, stimulated by European Union initiatives such as the European City of Culture programme, as well as the high-profile redevelopment of cities such as Barcelona, Dublin and Glasgow during the 1980s and 1990s (Mommaas, 2009). Cluster development had a strong appeal to urban policy makers, as it could be undertaken at sub-national levels of government, in a context where city and regional governments have sought to become greater managers of cultural policy in an era of economic globalisation (Schuster, 2002; Stevenson, 2004). Creative cluster formation developed a strong momentum in countries where a collectivist ethos had long been cultivated by governments, such as Singapore and China, as it pointed to a homology between the cluster literature where 'social networks, tacit knowledge and trust relationships are valorized' (Kong, 2009: 70), and state ideologies that promote working together around shared problems and common goals, in contrast to Western liberal individualism (Keane, 2009).

Most importantly, in a field where, as Graham Evans has observed, the literature is 'heavily reliant on proxies but light on theory or hard evidence' (Evans, 2009: 1005), cluster theory generated no shortage of potentially relevant international exemplars. These typically include the fashion districts of Paris and Milan, the design and advertising clusters of London, the high-technology clusters of 'Silicon Valley' and Bangalore, and the film industry clusters of Mumbai and – most famously – Hollywood. Hollywood is seen here as more than simply the most successful film and television production location in the world (Wasko, 2003; Scott, 2005). It is seen as having developed the template for project-based work in the cultural economy, drawing upon 'geographical proximity ... face-to-face collaborations ...the co-location of specialised activities ... low transaction costs, thick networks of social business activities, high levels of competence and specialisation, innovation, and a pool of skilled labour' (De Propris and Hypponen, 2008: 268). Its reputation as the centre of the global film industry has meant that it also acts as a talent magnet for actors and filmmakers from across the United States and around the world. It has also generated considerable capacity for reflexivity and the generation of new knowledge about film and TV production and distribution. Given that key elements of film production include high up-front costs and profound uncertainty about consumer demand, Hollywood possesses a deep repository of tacit knowledge about what works with audiences as well as the economic and institutional capacity to produce a large repertoire of films, even if – as critics argue – this can lead to 'recycled creativity' and formulaic, risk-averse cinema (De Propris and Hypponen, 2008: 275–281).

The motivations behind creative cluster development have been many and varied, and the mix of policy rationales has generated some recurring tensions. One is that clusters are often easier to describe and observe than to draw from in order to provide a policy formula for their development. Frith et al. observe that 'cluster theory ... is an entirely convincing *post facto* analysis – a successful cultural industry must, of course, have a locale – but rather more problematic as a prescriptive or diagnostic tool, a guide to what needs to be done to produce a successful cultural sector' (Frith et al., 2009: 79).[5] A further issue is that it is unlikely that a whole city would constitute the basis for an industry cluster. Indeed, in the earlier discussion of the difference between localisation and urbanisation economics, it was observed that the latter are differentiated from the former by virtue of having a diversity of industries, hence avoiding the 'all eggs in one basket' problem of specialist industrial districts. One response has been to develop specialist cultural quarters in cities. In his review of cultural quarters in Europe, Simon Roodhouse defines a cultural quarter as:

> a geographical area of a large town or city which acts as a focus for cultural and artistic activities through the presence of a group of buildings devoted to housing a range of such activities, and purpose designed or adapted spaces to create a sense of identity, providing an environment to facilitate and encourage the provision of cultural and artistic services and activities. (Roodhouse, 2006: 22)

In his review of creative clusters in the Netherlands, Mommaas (2004) identified five distinctive sets of motivations lying behind creative cluster development:

1 Promoting the brand identity, attraction power and market position of places, particularly for investors and affluent professionals;
2 Stimulating a more entrepreneurial approach to arts and culture, particularly in terms of reaching younger audiences through a more market-oriented and less subsidy-dependent approach to maintaining the sustainability of cultural organisations;

3 Stimulating creativity and innovation through strategies to assist the formation of micro-businesses in the creative industries;

4 Finding new uses for old buildings and derelict industrial-era sites (warehouses, power stations, etc.) as arts centres, apartment buildings and creative work spaces;

5 Stimulating cultural democracy and cultural diversity by providing alternative spaces for those marginalised from the arts establishment.

Given such an eclectic range of motivations and the extent to which creative clusters has become a 'fuzzy concept' (Mommaas, 2009: 52), it is not surprising that the scorecard for such initiatives is mixed, and much depends upon what city or region you are referring to and what its governance structure was (Pratt, 2005). One attempt to evaluate these policies has been made by Bassett et al. (2005), who point to some of the benefits of these initiatives as being:

1 A more central role being given to the cultural dimensions of urban development strategies;

2 A broader and more inclusive understanding of culture than simply the performing and visual arts, or 'high culture';

3 Greater recognition of lifestyle factors and consumption activities in urban planning;

4 The development of new cultural infrastructures that have renovated the image of cities and acted as attractors of tourism and – possibly – investment.

Problems with creative cluster policies identified by Bassett et al. include:

1 Blurring of distinctions between arts and cultural sectors and those of the entertainment, leisure and service industries;

2 Possibly contradictory policy agendas between economic development and social inclusion;

3 Instances of 'capture' of the urban renewal agenda by private developers and real estate interests;

4 The possibility that the drive to create distinctive creative clusters in inner-urban post-industrial sites has the paradoxical effect of promoting greater urban homogeneity.

Problems exist with the cluster concept itself, which has developed in such a loose and all-inclusive manner that, as Ron Martin and Peter Sunley have observed, 'it is impossible to support or reject clusters definitively with empirical evidence, as there are so many ambiguities, identification problems, exceptions and extraneous factors' (Martin and Sunley, 2003: 31). One basic problem is a conflation between geographical and industrial definitions of a cluster, so that there is a failure to distinguish between clusters where a number of firms in the same industry have co-located (horizontal clusters), such as the successful wine industries of Northern California in the United States and the Barossa Valley in Australia, and those where a value chain of buyers and suppliers has emerged (vertical clusters), such as the ICT/electronics hub of Silicon Valley. While both types of cluster enable knowledge transfer to occur, they do so in quite different ways, and this is blurred by the concept of creative clusters being associated with a highly diverse and in many ways disconnected set of 'creative industries'. While one can see how the film industry and digital effects (DFX) industry would be part of a Hollywood film cluster, this would not make a loose aggregation of jewellers, fashion designers and visual artists in a newly developed cultural quarter evidence in itself of an industry cluster.

Agglomeration is not *prima facie* evidence of clustering in the manner that Porter referred to. Gordon and McCann (2001) distinguished between what they referred to as simple agglomeration, where co-location in particular areas reduces overall costs (e.g. transport and catering businesses clustering around an airport), and those where it is social networks and embedded ties that are critical to locational decisions: it would only be in the latter case where clustering would be strongly connected to innovation through knowledge flows. The experience of policy-driven creative clusters in the 2000s has not confirmed or ruled out the possibility of developing them outside of global cities such as London, New York and Paris, but such cities do possess the advantages associated with large-scale urban agglomeration, 'first mover' advantages in developing cultural infrastructure, and large numbers of well-paid professionals. Mommaas's study observed that more consumption-oriented clusters developed *ex nihilo*, tend to have more top-down governance structures, as compared to 'more production-oriented clusters tending towards a higher input from the historically formed cultural infrastructure itself' (Mommaas, 2004: 516). Scott (2008a: 318) has observed that it is precisely the top-down approaches based upon directive planning that are most likely to fail, particularly in cities and regions that lack a strong, pre-existing base of cultural production.

A major failing of the whole discussion of creative clusters has been its failure to focus sufficiently on questions of market demand. While there is no doubt that agglomerations of cultural producers will generate cultural product pretty much by definition this provides no foundation for assuming that this will better meet the demands of cultural consumers than what would occur in the absence of such initiatives. Some of the problems arising from wholesale uptake of the creative clusters concept can be seen in China, where cities such as Shanghai have declared themselves to have up to 75 creative industries clusters. These proto-culsters have been formed by 'urban growth coalitions' of developers, Communist Party officials, city planners and – with widely varying degrees of enthusiasm – artists and cultural producers, but much of the revenue derived from changing patterns of land use rather than growth in the sales of cultural products *per se* (Zheng, 2010).

London as a Creative City

London is the archetypal global city, sitting at the centre of international business and finance, politics and culture. It has more foreign banks than any city in the world, and over half of the world's secondary bond market. It has been the top European city for business location, with the most available qualified staff, the most languages spoken, and also the best transport and communications links. Its largest sector is business services, which added £32 billion in 2007, and its second largest sector was the creative industries (CI), estimated to be worth £21 billion annually in 2007. The creative industries sectors employ about 554,000 people, accounting for 12.2 per cent of all London's jobs. London dominates the British creative industries, with London and the South-East region accounting for 57 per cent of all British creative workforce jobs (all figures from Knell and Oakley, 2007).

The creative industries concept took off quickly in London, because it both played to the city's strengths and broadened London's base of appeal. Many in the UK dislike the influence of bankers and financiers associated with 'The City' over the national economy and policy makers, as seen in the wake of the role played by banks and the finance indus-try in the 2008 global financial crisis. Creative industries were associated with well-paying post-industrial jobs that London required, as it has long ceased to be a manufacturing centre; it had obvious connections, for example, to the tourism industry. As the first Mayor of London from 2000 to 2008, Ken Livingstone was particularly enthusiastic about devel-oping London's creative industries, having pioneered a focus on cultural industries devel-opment when he headed the Greater London Council from 1981 to 1986. A broadened appeal for London based on its arts and culture would also prove to be advantageous in its successful bid for the 2012 Olympics, where it prevailed over cities such as Paris and Madrid.

Landry (2005) developed a series of arguments for developing the creative industries in London that went beyond the purely economic focus on jobs, output, trade, etc., to consider the interrelationships offered between culture, creativity, the city's 'brand' and identity, as well as economic and social development. These arguments were:

1   Cultural activities, both traditional and contemporary, create meaning and are there-fore vitally important to how a community understands a place and their relationship to it, both historically and in the current conjuncture;
2   Cultural activities are inextricably bound up with innovation and creativity, and crea-tive skills associated with the arts – including creative problem solving as well as craft skills (e.g. in multimedia) – are increasingly sought by business. Cities have histori-cally been major incubators of innovation and creativity as well as culture;
3   Culture is vital to the image of a place, and in a world where the global circulation of images is now central, the culture of a city that is projected internationally, as well as the presence of prominent individuals and institutions in the arts, media and cultural sectors, are attractors to international businesses and an internationally mobile pro-fessional workforce;
4   Culture and tourism are fundamentally connected, and tourism that offers a focus upon cultural activities can constitute the basis for more ongoing relationships between individuals and a place, such as relocation or new investment;

(Continued)

5 There are important links between publicly supported arts activities (e.g. theatre and the performing arts), the more commercially driven film and television industries, and the higher education institutions that are primary sources of education and training in the arts, media and cultural sectors (cf. Holden, 2009). There is also greater attention being given to intersections between ICTs and arts and cultural practices (cf. Mitchell et al., 2003);

6 Cultural activities can contribute to a higher degree of social cohesion and greater social inclusion, by assisting in personal and community development and enhancing awareness of different cultures. This is particularly important in a multicultural city such as London, where people from over 200 countries now live, and where there has been a history of racial and ethnic conflicts.

In their assessment of London's creative industries agenda over the 2000s, Knell and Oakley argued that their development was 'more a symptom of London's inherited economic success, [rather] than a sustainable cause of future growth' (Knell and Oakley, 2007). In particular, they pointed to the following as significant weaknesses in creative industries (CIs) policy over the 2000s:

- A failure to give sufficient attention to small CI firms, meaning that there was high 'churn' among small firms with significant costs to those involved, as well as a loss of the small-scale base through which skills and innovation emerge. As more and bigger players seek to develop their own creative clusters (China being a major example here), relying primarily upon big companies and foreign investment creates new risks for London, and competing at this level is considerably more costly than developing local talent.
- The London CIs lack connections to the rest of Great Britain, meaning that they can 'suck' creative talent from other regions, while at the same time failing to fully develop national capacity and national markets. This can also give them a very partial understanding of 'British culture', as seen in criticisms made of London-centric media.
- The predominance of 'precarious employment' in the CIs is a particular problem for those living in London, which has by far the highest housing and other living costs in Britain.
- Ethnic minorities are significantly underrepresented in the creative industries as compared with the London workforce as a whole, and this has shown few signs of changing.
- Cultural policy remains bifurcated between arts funding that has a strong focus upon established cultural organisations and the non-profit sector, and industry development programmes that continue to struggle to understand the nature of commercial cultural businesses.

- More attention needs to be given to how the infrastructure of the city, which ranges from its universities to its transport system, feeds into the 'creative ecology' of London, and how it connects its citizens to its cultural institutions and activities.

There is also the problem, which exists across the British economy but is particularly apparent in the creative industries, of London increasingly functioning as a 'city-state', cut off from the rest of Britain, except as an absorber of talent and resources and a projector back of ideas and culture. As Knell and Oakley observe, 'the more London drifts away form rest of the UK, the less its cultural production will reflect the reality of life in the UK and the more its metropolitan media and political conversation will fail to resonate outside the M25' (Knell and Oakley, 2007: 13). It is worth noting that the change in political leadership did not diminish the focus on developing London as a creative industries centre, and that it was not seen solely as a Labour priority. The Conservative Mayor of London, Boris Johnson, who became Mayor in 2008, has been a supporter of London's creative industries, and expressed concern about the impact on the London economy of cuts to arts and cultural funding after the Conservative–Liberal Democrats coalition came to power in the UK in 2010.

Creative Cities and the 'Creative Class'

Lou Reed's famous account in his 1972 song 'Walk on the Wild Side' of Andy Warhol's 'Factory' in 1960s New York, and the 'superstars' who came from across the USA to be a part of the Warhol 'scene', captured the extent to which New York City acted as a 'talent magnet' for a very diverse range of people seeking to leave small-town America in pursuit of new opportunities and experiences. In one respect, Warhol's Factory can be referred to as a creative cluster in the sense that we now use the term: it was a centre of art, photography, music, film, fashion and much more. Similarly, one could interpret Warhol's Factory as a component of New York's arts and cultural economy, which is now estimated to account for about 4 per cent of all jobs in New York City (Currid, 2007: 49). But such an industrial focus would miss a larger point. The attractiveness of New York City to its denizens, such as those who gravitated to Warhol's Factory, came from the sense of creativity, dissidence and celebration of identities marginalised from 'mainstream' society – homosexuals, transsexuals, musicians, artists, drug users and others – who could only thrive in a large cosmopolitan city such as New York. Moreover, this was marginality not only from 'straight' society, but from much of the art world of the time. Bockris (1989) documents the extent of the hostility that Warhol's work attracted among artists, curators and others during the 1960s. However mainstream it may appear now, Warhol and The Factory were associated with a set of developments that were very much 'bottom-up' and at the fringes of the society and culture of its time, and whose originality and coherence is more apparent in retrospect than it was at the time. Indeed, Lou Reed's 1972 hit single 'Walk on the Wild Side', capturing people (transsexuals) and activities (drug use, oral sex in back rooms) that rarely appeared in the pop charts of the time, came after Reed's association with the Velvet Underground, who came out of Warhol's Factory and have been hugely influential in the history of rock music, although they sold relatively few records at the time they were together. Such a contingent set of developments do not arise out of standard models of urban policy or cultural policy, whether they take the form of creative clusters or some other 'top-down' urban cultural planning strategy.

In her account of the cultural economy of New York City, Elizabeth Currid identified the similarities and differences between how cities work as a catalyst to arts, culture and entertainment, as compared to their role as centres for traditional businesses and service industries. Whereas for other industries informal social environments (hanging out, living in the same neighbourhoods, etc.) are the by-product of agglomeration processes whose primary drivers were economic (density of supplier networks, a geographically proximate labour market), such environments are 'the central force, the *raison d'être*' of the arts, culture and entertainment industries. For Currid:

> The cultural economy is most efficient in the informal social realm, and its social dynamics underlie the economic system of cultural production. Creativity would not exist as successfully or efficiently without its social world – the social is not the by-product – it is the decisive mechanism by which cultural products and cultural producers are generated, evaluated and sent to the market. (Currid, 2007: 4)

Currid draws upon the account of cities in history, and the critique of modernist urban planning developed by Jane Jacobs. For Jacobs, the factors that make for a culturally dynamic and economically prosperous city are difficult to define and quantify, but emerge out of a complex mix of proximity, sociality and diversity that are inherent features of large cities. It is difficult for urban planners to capture these elements – though urban planning can certainly do harm to them – but an openness to new ideas and a city structure that is based on mixed uses and is 'amenable to serendipity' are some elements that can be promoted (Currid, 2007: 74).

This focus upon the role of sociality, cultural intangibles, and the unpredictable relationship of the arts to creativity lay behind Richard Florida's analysis of the influential role of cities in the rise of what he refers to as the *creative class*. Florida proposed that, just as the nineteenth and early twentieth century was the heyday of industrial capitalism, and the mid-to-late twentieth century was dominated by bureaucratic organisations, the twenty-first century has seen creativity become 'the decisive source of competitive advantage' in the global economy. This conclusion is derived from new growth economics developed by Paul Romer of Stanford University, which presented new ideas and knowledge as the primary drivers of economic growth (Romer, 1990; Warsh, 2006: 195–226). Florida argued that creativity is a paradoxical source of human capital since 'it is not a "commodity". Creativity comes from people. And while people can be hired or fired, their creative capacity cannot be bought or sold, or turned on and off at will' (Florida, 2002: 5). Defining creative work as that which 'produces new forms and designs that are readily transferable and widely useful' (Florida, 2002: 7), Florida argued that the creative class, has grown in size from 10 per cent of the US workforce in 1900 to 30 per cent by 1990, thus making it a numerically larger group than the traditional working class (Florida, 2002: 73, 330). He argued that the creative sectors accounted for 47 per cent of wealth generated in the US economy, so this creative class is making a disproportionately large contribution to contemporary economic growth (Florida, 2007: 29).

Florida's theory of the rise of the creative class intersected with cities and urban planning around the concept of the power of place. In contrast to the orthodoxy of urban economic geography that people moved to where jobs are, and the associated policy implication that city policy makers needed to attract businesses that were large employers, Florida argued that creative people sought out places that were rich in urban amenity, had a vibrant and varied nightlife and cultural 'scene', and offered a range of experiences and opportunities to meet with a diverse range of people. Inverting the standard job-creation script, Florida's thesis was that creative people can create their own economic opportunities, and that the most economically successful US cities were also those that were also the most culturally vibrant and demographically diverse. He developed what was termed the 'Three T's Index' – technology, talent and tolerance – to argue that places with the highest concentrations of creative class workforce where characterised by: (1) the presence of high-technology firms and industries; (2) a highly educated population and significant levels of migration, both from other countries and from other parts of the United States; and (3) a high proportion of gays and lesbians among their population, as well as artists and 'bohemians' (Florida, 2002: 249–251). The last of these, measured by what Florida termed the 'Gay Index' and the 'Bohemian Index', has been the most contentious, and debate about it has perhaps overshadowed the wider claim that 'regional economic growth is powered by creative people who prefer places that are diverse, tolerant and open to new ideas. Diversity increases the odds that a place will attract different types of people with different skill sets and ideas' (Florida, 2002: 249). In Florida's creative class thesis, the most dynamic cities in the United States are those such as San Francisco, Boston, Seattle, Portland and Austin. Extending this framework internationally, Florida argued that we lived in an increasingly 'spiky' world, where large city-regions are becoming disconnected from the nations of which they are a part:

> While in the aggregate statistical sense, it often seems to be nations that compete for creative talent, when it comes down to it, creative people choose regions. They don't simply think of the United States versus England, Sweden versus Canada, or Australia versus Denmark. They think of Silicon Valley versus Cambridge, Stockholm versus Vancouver, or Sydney versus Copenhagen. (Florida, 2007: 10)

In light of their widespread influence, Florida's arguments have been ferociously debated. There is considerable dispute about the size and significance that he attaches to the creative class, and on closer examination, the category of creative professionals largely consists of those in business and professional services, or in management and sales-related occupations.[6] As a result, the findings of Florida's research look similar to those developed by Edward Glaesar (2000), about positive correlations existing between the level of human capital in a city (the proportion of its population with higher levels of education and skills) and its economic growth, which in turn relates to the role played by factors identified in the global cities literature about where professional and business services are located. As a result, it is not clear beyond the largely anecdotal level what difference the renovation of downtown areas and the 'hipsterisation' strategies – the mix of bike paths, pedestrian-friendly main streets, outdoor cafés, live music venues, funky galleries and art spaces that have been at the core of the script on how to attract the creative class – advocated by Florida and his associates are a significant independent variable in shaping migration patterns for skilled professionals, as distinct from whether they are of benefit to the urban environment in its own right. It may also be the case, common in creative industries literature, that a strategy to benefit the arts is being conflated with one that will benefit the wider economy, without the link ever being tangibly established.[7] Jamie Peck (2005) has observed, in relation to the influence of Florida's ideas among US urban policy makers:

> Investment in the 'soft infrastructure' of the arts and culture are easy to make, and need not be especially costly, so the creativity script easily translates into certain forms of municipal action. Whether or not this will stimulate creative economic growth, however, is quite another matter. (Peck, 2005: 749)

Critics of Florida, such as Joel Kotkin (Kotkin, 2006, 2007), argue that a far more significant trend in cities worldwide has been the new suburbanisation, and the outward expansion of cities to accommodate young families seeking stand-alone residential blocks. For this group, development of the inner-city is largely irrelevant, as their culture is very much car-based and home-centred, as they work, shop and consume leisure outside the inner-city. Kotkin also disputes Florida's claims about the most economically successful American cities, pointing to places such as Phoenix (Arizona), Las Vegas (Nevada), and Riverside (California), as places whose growth has exceeded that of creative class favourites such as San Francisco.[8] At the same time, critics of Florida such as Peck (2005) and Slater (2006) identify a pervasive lack of concern in creative cities arguments for those who may be displaced by the 'hipsterisation' of urban areas and 'reinvestment designed for the middle-class colonization of urban neighbourhoods' (Slater, 2006: 756).

One of the difficulties with these debates is that a representational geography that dichotomises hip, inner-urban areas and boring, homogeneous suburbs has been overlaid upon a set of assumptions about who works in the creative industries, in ways that ignore both the large and growing number of creative workers who live and work in the suburbs of major cities (Collis et al., 2010), and the different ways in which such workers and industries operate outside the major metropolitan centres (Waitt and Gibson, 2009; Brennan-Horley et al., 2010). Just as observation about the connection between globalisation and cities does not bear out the case for investing in creative clusters, even though we can observe the importance of both clustering and cultural activity to the contemporary dynamism of cities, chasing the allegedly flighty desires and consumption habits of a hard-to-define creative class would not appear to be the most effective policy route to developing the creative industries (Flew, 2012). The case for less speculative theorising, more grounded empirical work on actual creative industries production trends, consumption patterns and labour markets, and for more evidence-based policy making, would all appear to be a strong one.

Endnotes

1   The Transnationality Index was developed by UNCTAD to determine the extent to which non-financial corporations operate outside their nation. It measures the percentage of sales, assets and employment that companies have outside their home base, and divides the total by three. The aim is to minimise biases that can arise from the use of a single indicator, such as assets.

2   This is by no means a new debate. As early as 1971, Robin Murray wrote in *New Left Review* about the challenge presented by the internationalisation of capital for the capacity of nation-states to perform their economic functions (Murray, 1971). Bill Warren responded by challenging the claim that internationalisation weakened nation-states, instead proposing that the power of nation-states was increasing, and they were themselves promoting the international expansion of 'their' national capitals (Warren, 1971).

3   It is important to understand that this is not a dualistic model. Highly skilled and specialised activities can co-exist with deskilled activities in global production value chains, as seen in sectors as diverse as animation and fashion. These are not necessarily stable in terms of where they happen: China has been notable in recent years in seeking to 'move up the value chain' from low-cost manufacturing to the higher-value-adding activities associated with design, marketing and brand development.

4   Such forms of assistance can range from the relatively mundane, such as assistance with procuring and managing sites for location shoots, to more sophisticated forms of assistance with film marketing and the provision of specialist business services. Coe and Johns (2004) discuss how such activities can be dispersed across regional value chains.

5   Frith *et. al.* observe that the success of Glasgow-based bands Snow Patrol, Franz Ferdinand and Belle and Sebastian led to proclamations far and wide in 2004 that Glasgow was the centre of an internationally significant music scene (Frith et al., 2009: 80). Something similar occurred with Manchester in the late 1980s after the success of New Order, the Stone Roses, Happy Mondays and others (Brown et al., 2000).

6   The *super-creative core* are classified as those working in: computing and mathematical occupations; architecture and engineering occupations; life, physical and social science occupations; education, training and library occupations; and arts, design, entertainment, sports and media occupations. *Creative professionals* are those working in: management occupations; business and financial operations occupations; legal occupations; healthcare practitioners and technical occupations; and high-end sales and sales management (Florida, 2002: 328).

7   Independently of Florida's work, there has been a movement developing in the United States that focuses on the role that artists can play in the creative economy of cities,

which differs from traditional arts and cultural policy approaches in its focus on artists rather than arts organisations, and can be part of an integrated local response to cultural globalisation (Wyszomirski, 2008). It needs to be noted that this work is not making wider claims about the capacity of such strategies to attract those from other areas of the professions.

8 In the United States context, such debates are invariably overlaid with the culture wars. An obvious feature of Florida's list of preferred creative-class cities is that they are solidly Democrat in their voting patterns and very much liberal in their social and cultural values. As a result, Florida is frequently accused by conservative critics of promoting a 'pro-gay' and 'anti-family' agenda. The other relevant issue is that much of this research preceded the 2008 US financial crisis, which hit all West Coast cities particularly hard as these had large numbers of over-indebted mortgagees, as well as the fiscal crisis of the Californian government. The implications of the financial crisis for urban cultural policies in the USA was not clear at the time of writing.

7 Creative Industries and Public Policy

An argument can be made that the historical origins of cultural policy lie with the French Revolution. One of the key acts of the French Revolution of 1789 was the transfer of the Royal art collections from the Palace of Versailles to the Louvre, alongside a program of collecting historically significant art works from the palaces of the nobility and moving them to the new public museums and galleries (Hobsbawm, 1990). The idea that art treasures and monuments were to become the property of the nation and the responsibility of the state – *patrimoine culturel*, or common cultural heritage – was consistent with both an opening up of the institutions of cultural display to the whole population, and what Tony Bennett described as the transformation of institutions such as galleries and museums into 'an instrument which, through the education of its citizens, was to serve the collective good of the state' (Bennett, 1995: 89). This enlisting of culture 'as a resource that might be used to regulate the field of social behaviour' (Bennett, 1995: 20) was a recurring theme of governmental practice in Europe throughout the nineteenth century, as the provision of public museums, free libraries, events and festivals, etc. was seen simultaneously as enabling large-scale public education, a low-cost exercise improving the habits and morals of the population (particularly the lower classes), and strengthening the authority of the nation-state and the loyalty of citizens to it through the inculcation of a common culture.

This deployment of culture as a source of national integration has been a theme of cultural policy from times before the term was even in circulation. Michael Schudson has observed that 'nation-states cannot be understood, or even defined, apart from their achievement of some degree of cultural identity. If we ask not what force integrates a society but what defines or identifies the boundaries of the society to which individuals are integrated, cultural features are essential' (Schudson, 1994: 65). Modern nation-states have self-consciously used language policy, formal education, and collective rituals such as national events and public holidays to enable populations to recognise themselves as national citizens. Such vernacular and mass-popular forms of cultural policy can be seen as part of what Ernest Gellner referred to as 'the striving to make culture and polity congruent, to endow a culture with its own political roof, and not more than one roof at that' (Gellner, 1983: 43).

Cultural policy as we understand it today, however, primarily took shape in the middle decades of the twentieth century. In Britain, the Council for the Encouragement of Music and the Arts (CEMA) was established during World War II, and it would become the Arts

Council of Great Britain in 1946. Its first Chairman, the famous economist John Maynard (Lord) Keynes, was a great believer in the inherent qualities of the arts, and saw the purpose of arts policy as being to promote creative excellence, with government providing a limited financial and infrastructural scaffolding to ensure that this would always occur. At the same time, he recognised that while the purpose of public patronage was to enable non-profit-making activities to take place, he saw good arts management as being central to ensuring the widest possible public access to and appreciation of music, drama and the visual and per-forming arts (Skidelsky, 2000: 286–299). Although Keynes died before British arts policy was fully established, he had already flagged many of the themes that would be central to cultural policy: the relationship between private patronage and state subsidy; tensions between promoting excellence and broadening access; the role of cities in the nurturing of creative talent; and the significance of regional diversity in arts funding policies (Skidelsky, 2000: 288–299). More generally, Keynes saw the arts as a higher-order social good, and believed that as economists and social reformers such as himself could address the scourges of poverty and unemployment, there would be more scope for a wider cross-section of society to enjoy the arts as part of a better life for all.

In France, the establishment of the Fifth Republic from 1958 opened up a particularly fertile period for cultural policy development. Under the leadership of Charles de Gaulle, there was the creation of the *Ministère d'Etat chargé des Affaires culturelles* (Ministry of State in charge of Cultural Affairs), with the famous author Andre Malraux as head of this new Ministry. Malraux's broad trajectory for cultural policy identified three clear tasks for a national cultural policy: heritage, creation and democratisation. The concept of *heritage* foresaw a role for the state in distributing the 'eternal products of the imagination' through-out the national population: the construction, and renovation, of museums, galleries and other exhibitionary spaces both within and outside the major cities was one of the major tasks of a national cultural policy. Further, the state had an ongoing role in promoting the *creation* of new artistic and cultural works, and needed to use public funding to provide a catalytic role to the creation of new works, and the associated need for financial support for artists and cultural workers. Finally, and perhaps most controversially, the objective of *democratisation* constituted an activist role for cultural policy in redressing socio-economic inequalities by cultural means. Such a critique raised the issue of whether cultural policy largely entailed *action culturelle*, or cultural policy makers identifying and supporting cultural activities and institutions in ways that bring these closer to people, communities and societies, critics saw this as being essentially about the national distribution of 'great works', or *l'action socioculturelle*, whereby culture is understood as being principally constituted by the autonomous and self-motivated activities of people and communities, with cultural policy makers needing to realign their understandings of the role and purpose of cultural policy accordingly (Looseley, 1995). Such visions were highly influential in the formation of UNESCO, which developed various policy manuals and protocols for the development of a national cultural policy, particularly for the newly independent states of the developing world (Mattelart, 1994). UNESCO defined the purpose of cultural policy as being to 'establish conditions conducive to improving the means for the expression and participation of the population in cultural life' (UNESCO, 1982: 9).

While perhaps shaped by less dramatic historical forces, media policy has certainly played a central role in the development of media in all of its forms, as governments have sought to regulate the ownership, production, distribution and content of media in order to achieve particular policy goals. While the rhetoric of media has been that of the 'Fourth Estate', as an independent and impartial watchdog of governments and other powerful interests, the freedom to communicate has in practice been constrained both by general civil and criminal laws, and by media-specific laws and regulations, including those governing defamation, copyright, *sub judice*, racial and other forms of vilification, obscenity, blasphemy and – the ultimate mark of state capacity to influence the media – sedition. Media organisations are also subject to a series of technical regulations as well as industry-specific regulations governing ownership, content and standards, by virtue of both their unique role as a means of public communication, and the perceived adverse consequences that may be associated with: potential impacts on children and other 'vulnerable' individuals (Hutchinson, 2004); tendencies towards monopoly and oligopoly and a lack of diversity of content and voices arising from the ability to exploit economies of scale and scope (Picard, 1989; Doyle, 2002); and the question of whether commercial media will under-provide content to minority audiences, more specialist media content, and higher-cost programming (Herman, 1997). Historically, print media have generally been less subject to industry-specific forms of regulation and government control than broadcast media, due in part to the implied rights of public communication arising from use of the broadcast spectrum as a common resource (Streeter, 1995). More extensive regulation of broadcast media has also been reflective of public good elements of the media commodity, such as non-rivalrous and non-excludable consumption and the lack of a clear relationship between costs of production of individual programmes and services and the overall costs of access to broadcast media for consumers (Collins et al., 1988). Some characteristic elements of media regulation are outlined in Table 7.1.

A useful distinction can be made between *input-based* forms of policy intervention, which typically involve public subsidy of cultural activity, and *output-based* forms, involving regulations designed to manage media ownership and media content (Flew and Cunningham, 1997). As a general rule, input-based approaches have tended to prevail in the arts, where the often one-off or artisanal nature of creative production processes is met by special purpose grant assistance. By contrast, the more industrialised sectors of broadcast media have tended to have output-based regulations applied, such as local content, minority programming or children's programming requirements, where less attention is given to overseeing the actual content produced. At the same time, the mix of public support mechanisms provided to the audiovisual media sectors often has a mix of input-based and output-based approaches, as governments have identified film and television to be part of a national audiovisual space that requires at least some forms of what Philip Schlesinger (1991) termed *communicative boundary maintenance*. The most notable manifestation of this has been the support for public service broadcasting worldwide, which has been driven not only by the provision of public information and the promotion of public communication on a universal basis, promoting citizenship, community and 'common knowledge' within the nation, but also by producers and distributors of quality or innovative local content, or local content targeted at under-served audiences and communities (Graham and Davies, 1997).

Table 7.1 Government Media Regulations

Area of government regulation	Policy goals	Policy instruments
Control of entry	Planned development of media services	Licensing of media (e.g. broadcasters)
	Viability and stability	Controls over new entrants and new services
Ownership and control	Limiting concentration of media power	Limits on concentration of ownership
	Local control of media services	Limits on cross-media ownership (e.g. newspapers and TV stations)
	Responsiveness to local communities	Limits on foreign ownership
Media content	Promoting national culture	Local content quotas
	Catering to minorities (e.g. linguistic minorities) and specialist audiences (e.g. children)	Quota requirements for programme types
		Specialist media channels (e.g. children's TV service)
	Providing opportunities for local media producers	Grants and subsidies for local content production
Community standards	Ensuring fair, accurate and responsible coverage of matters of public interest	Programme classification standards
	Respecting community standards	Advertising standards (e.g. limits on 'junk food' advertising)
	Protecting children from harmful material	Time restrictions on programme content
		Requirements for news and current affairs programmes

Following Freedman (2008: 13–14), we can distinguish three levels of media policy: media policy proper, media regulation and media governance:

- Media policy refers to both the goals and norms that inform and underpin relevant media legislation, and the intentions and instruments associated with shaping the structure and behaviour of actors in a media system.
- Media regulation focuses on the operations and activities of specific agencies that have responsibility for overseeing the media policy instruments that have been developed to manage the media system.
- Media governance refers to the totality of institutions and instruments that shape and organise media systems – formal and informal, national and supranational, public and private, large-scale and smaller-scale.

It is important to make these distinctions for a number of reasons. 'Media policy' can cover everything from the approach taken to audiovisual trade in bilateral and multilateral trade agreements, to how a regulator such as the Federal Communications Commission in the United States or Ofcom in Great Britain deals with a complaint that a televised item was obscene or offensive to some viewers, or that a particular news item or documentary programme lacked 'balance'. It is also important because a feature of the period since the 1980s in particular has been that media policy questions have increasingly overlapped with those of previously distinct policy domains, such as telecommunication policy and information policy. This policy covergence has been the result of technological convergence, the rise of the Internet, and what Sandra Braman (2004) has referred to as the 'blending of communicative styles', so that 'the directly communicative functions of the media are now a relatively small proportion of the overall role of information technologies in society … [and] conceptually, the field of media policy can be considered co-extant with that of information policy, broadly defined as all policy pertaining to information creation, processing, flows and use' (Braman, 2004: 153). Moreover, as Raboy (2002) has argued, media policy is no longer being solely developed by government agencies or within nation-states: there is instead what he refers to as an emerging global policy 'map', where 'communications policy is no longer "made" at any clearly definable location [and] is increasingly the result of a vast array of formal and informal mechanisms working across a multiplicity of sites' (Raboy, 2002: 7).

There is also the question, to be considered in this chapter, of whether there has been a wider discursive and cognitive shift in media and cultural policy. From the 1940s to the 1970s, it has been argued that media policy was broadly shaped by what Robert Horwitz has referred to, with particular reference to the US context, by the 'progressive' belief that 'democratic governmental power reconciled the tension between the needs of powerless consumers and the productive might of the corporation', and that 'the administrative process [operated] not only to protect powerless consumers, but also to effect rationality and fairness in the economy generally' (Horwitz, 1989: 25, 26). Authors such as Des Freedman have argued that this 'public interest' conception of the pluralistic and regulatory state was usurped by a neo-liberal model which, as Freedman describes it, seeks to 'bring all human action into the domain of the market … [and] shapes both the objectives of government action and the structures and policies that emerge (in part) from this action' (Freedman, 2008: 37). Assessing arguments for and against this proposition, that media and cultural policy in the 2000s was dominated by discourses of neo-liberalism, particularly as it relates to the rise of creative industries policy discourse, will be addressed in detail in this chapter.

Drivers of Change in Media and Cultural Policy

The landscape of media and cultural policy in the 21st century possesses both similarities to and profound differences from that which prevailed for much of the twentieth century. Many of the objectives remain broadly similar: enabling public participation and communication; ensuring accountability and setting limits to market power; promoting local creative activity and national identity; encouraging excellence and innovation in the arts and related fields;

and broadening the reach and remit of culture to the population as a whole. But some are profoundly different – media and cultural policy as it was in the 1970s did not have to address such factors as economic globalisation, the rise of the Internet, creative industries policies or international trade agreements. Copyright was not as central to discussions then as it is now, and we still lived in a world of relative information scarcity, where newspapers were delivered to the home before breakfast, the news was watched in the early evening or not at all, and there was a limited range of TV and radio channels available. While there was some debate about assumptions concerning 'quality' and 'excellence' in the media, the tsunami of questioning of literary canons and cultural hierarchies associated with the rise of cultural studies was yet to have anything other than marginal significance, and most nations assumed that 'national culture' was understood in the singular – multiculturalism was only beginning to emerge.

In this section, I will outline ten drivers of change in media and cultural policy, arising in a period that is broadly from the 1980s to the late 2000s. The ten factors that I wish to consider – briefly in each case, as much more could be said about each – are:

1 Technological change;
2 The impact of budget constraints;
3 Broadening definitions of culture;
4 The impact of political shifts;
5 Revaluing the arts;
6 Globalisation and international trade agreements;
7 Growing interest in content industries as growth industries;
8 Rethinking innovation policy;
9 The implications of information abundance;
10 The new politics of copyright.

1. Technological Change

The development of new technologies can act as a constant driver of change. As we noted in Chapter Six, the most significant technological changes – the rise of clusters of innovation associated with meta-technologies that form part of a new techno-economic paradigm – tend to emerge at certain periods of time. There seems little doubt that the changes associated with information and computing technologies, information processing, digitisation, communications networks and microelectronics, which begin to have a substantive impact on how businesses operate and what people are consuming from the 1980s onwards, mark one of these watershed periods.

The first major set of disruptive technological changes for media policy arose from new delivery technologies for television, such as satellite and broadband cable, which enabled multichannel services to be provided across distances without additional use of spectrum. The impact of satellite TV was very marked in Europe, where the number of terrestrial TV channels went from 62 in 1980 (44 of which were public service broadcasters (PSBs)) to 244 by 1995 (64 of which were PSBs), while many European homes had additional access to up to 262 satellite TV channels and 463 cable TV channels (Cairncross, 1998: 69). Satellite TV had a major impact throughout Asia, with the number of homes accessing the satellite TV provider StarTV growing from 3 million in 1992 to 93 million in 2001 (Thomas, 2006: 58). In countries such as India and regions such as Europe, this marked the end of a public broadcaster monopoly, as PSBs now faced major commerical competition for both programming and audiences, which would in turn challenge their historic remit (Siune and Hulten, 1998).

The major technological changes of recent times relate to the Internet. While all major media companies responded relatively quickly in the second half of the 1990s to the challenge of making content available online, the 2000s have seen both the rise of new user-driven media content distribution channels such as *YouTube* (Burgess and Green, 2009) and a plethora of new publishing and distribution practices associated with social media. While these do not in themselves mean the end of mass media, let alone the decline of the big media corporations, they do challenge many of the underlying assumptions that have informed mass communication as it developed in the twentieth century, as shown in Table 7.2 below.

2. The Impact of Budget Constraints

The period from the early 1970s onwards witnessed a global economic downturn, triggered by rising oil prices and the onset of 'stagflation' (low rates of economic growth and rising unemployment combined with high inflation levels) throughout the advanced capitalist

Table 7.2 Mass Communications Media and Social Media

	Mass communications media (20th century)	Convergent media/Web 2.0 (21st century) 2.0
Media distribution	Large-scale distribution; high barriers to entry for new entrants	Internet dramatically reduces barriers to entry based on distribution
Media production	Complex division of labour; critical role of media content gatekeepers and professionals	Easy-to-use Web 2.0 technologies give scope for individuals and small teams to be producers, editors and distributors of media content
Media power	Assymetrical power relationship – one-way communication flow	Greater empowerment of users/ audiences enabled through interactivity and greater choice of media outlets
Media content	Tendency towards standardised mass appeal content to maximise audience share – limited scope for market segmentation based on product differentiation	'Long tail' economics make much wider range of media content potentially profitable; demassification and segmentation of media content markets
Producer/ consumer relationship	Mostly impersonal, anonymous and commoditised (audiences as target mass markets)	Potential to be more personalised and driven by user communities and user-created content (UCC)

Source: Flew, 2009b: 95.

economies (Marglin and Schor, 1990; Glyn et al., 1991). This meant that many of the assumptions that had held during the 'Golden Age' of capitalism during the 1950s and 1960s could no longer be taken for granted, with a key one being the assumption that rising levels of government social expenditure could be readily accommodated by increasing taxation revenues arising from economic growth. Many nations experienced rising budget deficits during this period, which worsened problems of inflation and high interest rates, and in the case of two major industrial economies – Britain and Italy – the International Monetary Fund was called in to advise on how to reorganise state finances to ensure that debts could be repaid. Such constraints would become harder with the rise of doctrines of 'smaller government', such as the monetarist economic policies associated with Milton Friedman from the University of Chicago, during the 1970s (Friedman and Friedman, 1980). The changed economic climate meant that it could no longer be taken as a given that more public funding would be made available to the arts and culture, including public broadcasting. It meant that the combination of merit-good arguments that had justified public support for the arts – that the arts should be publicly supported because their outputs are intrinsically valuable to a society – and an associated disdain towards financial and performance-based measures of cultural worth, were not longer as self-evident as they once appeared, and questions concerning the uses of public funds to support the arts and culture became more prominent. As questions of how much subsidy, who should receive it, and what purposes it should be used for became more central, it became apparent that there were many conflicting goals and competing claimants in arts policy, and decision-makers were faced with increasingly complex criteria on which to base cultural policy rationales and cultural funding decisions (Rowse, 1985). Moreover, Ruth Towse (2010: 277–278) identifies the pervasiveness of principal-agent problems in cultural policy, where subsidised organisations can exercise undue power in funding arrangements due to their capacity to control information, and mobilise others to defend their own interests against the demands of funding agencies, creating structural biases towards preservation of the *status quo* in arts funding, even if this conflicts with other cultural policy goals, such as decentralising funding or promoting new creative works.

3. Broadening Definitions of Culture

The rise of cultural studies was associated with the insistence that understandings of culture could no longer be isolated to the arts or to aesthetics, but needed to incorporate the full dimensions of everyday life that had been associated with its anthropological definition (Williams, 1976). Grossberg et al. defined cultural studies as 'an interdisciplinary, transdisciplinary, and sometimes counter-disciplinary field that operates in the tension between its tendencies to embrace both a broad, anthropological and a more narrowly humanistic conception of culture' (Grossberg et al., 1992: 4). This meant that:

> In cultural studies traditions, then, culture is understood both as a way of life – encompassing ideas, attitudes, languages, practices, institutions, and structures of power – and a whole range of cultural practices: artistic forms, texts, canons, architecture, mass-produced commodities, and so forth. (Grossberg et al., 1992: 5)

The rise of cultural studies as an intellectual movement was associated with the growth in demands for greater cultural democracy (Trend, 1997). Cultural democracy can be understood in three senses. First, there was the rise of the community arts movement, which sought to challenge the 'equation between subsidy and Art, with a very large capital "A" [and] the connotations which surround arts funding ... that what gets money, and therefore legitimation, are superior, high or fine cultural activities' (Hawkins, 1993: 6). The community arts movement and its supporters instead sought decentralisiation of both funding and engagement, to make access and participation mean something because it could reduce the social distance between those who decide on the provision of a cultural item and those who are said to benefit from it (Rowse, 1985; Williams, 1989; Kelly, 2003). Second, the challenge of increasing cultural diversity within nation-states, arising from both large-scale migration and the demands of minority cultures for 'the right to recognition as distinct cultural collectivities within the nation-state' (Castles and Davidson, 2000: 124), has given rise to multiculturalism as a component of contemporary cultural policies. Tony Bennett (1998: 104) has argued that where multiculturalism has been adopted in state cultural policies, this entails 'a range of programs that are concerned explicitly with managing cultural resources in ways calculated to achieve ... outcomes' of cultural maintenance, the promotion of respect for cultural diversity, and the enabling of better intercultural dialogue and communications. Finally, broadening definitions of culture as applied through media and cultural policy inevitably raised the issue of whether popular media and cultural forms require greater recognition in such policies, challenging the 'discursive differentiation' (Dominguez, 2000: 22) between those forms of cultural activity that fall within the ambit of cultural policy and those which do not. In so far as the question of recognition is connected to funding, this returns us to many of the debates that have informed creative industries policies, as such interventions typically work with the market rather than in contra-distinction to it.

4. The Impact of Political Shifts

The 1970s and early 1980s are often identified as the period in which parties broadly of the left (social democratic and Labour parties, as well as the US Democrats) experienced a downturn in their political fortunes, as the nature of the economic downturn, with its combination of rising unemployment and high inflation, undercut confidence that government spending could in itself reverse economic fortunes. This was accompanied by a series of intellectual shifts whereby the hegemony of both Keynesian economic theories and traditional public interest rationales for regulation were challenged by a resurgent set of market-oriented theories, from monetarism to public choice theory, that have been termed neo-liberalism (Horwitz, 1989; Streeter, 1995; Harvey, 2005).

In the United States and Britain, where this shift was probably strongest, this led to some interesting inversions of traditional attitudes towards both the arts and broadcast media. Miller and Yúdice (2002) traced how the position of the U.S. Republican Party shifted between the 1970s and the 1990s from one broadly supportive of public subsidy of high culture to become a party that sought to de-fund the National Endowment for the Arts, based upon both a political impulse to wind back public support for artists and cultural groups seen as hostile to their interests, and a libertarian set of arguments that arts funding entailed transfers from working-class 'taxpayers' to middle-class 'elites'. Streeter (1995) observed parallels between neo-conservative and left-libertarian arguments to open up broadcasting to new cable services, while the *Peacock Review of Public Broadcasting* in Britain was underpinned by a perception among a vocal group of economic liberals that British broadcasting in general, and the BBC in particular, operated along paternalist lines and were unresponsive to popular tastes.

5. Revaluing the Arts

The sense that arts advocacy increasingly operated in a more difficult political and economic climate acted as a catalyst for new arguments about the value of the arts and cultural sectors, increasingly framed around 'managerial efficiency and economic benefits in terms of employment, tourism and image enhancement' (O'Connor, 2007: 26). Myerscough's (1988) advocacy of the economic impact of the arts in the UK led to a proliferation of economic impact studies, largely used to buttress existing institutions and funding arrangements. These arguements have been critiqued by cultural economists (e.g. Seaman, 2000; Towse, 2010: 282–286), and had most likely reached their use-by date in terms of usefulness and credibility by the mid-1990s.

While economic impact studies fell out of fashion, creative industries discourses provided a new impetus to what Kieran Healy has referred to as 'bullish defence[s] of the arts in economic terms' (Healy, 2002: 101), particularly where they intersected with new economy discourses (Miller, 2004). But economic arguments were among a plethora of new claims being made about the value of the arts and culture to education (Robinson, 2001), social cohesion and social inclusion. Jermyn (2001) identified 20 claims that had been made about the social, community or educational value of the arts in a range of studies undertaken in Great Britain between 1996 and 2001.

The idea that the arts have a 'therapeutic' role to address social exclusion and other problems always had its critics (e.g. Mizra, 2006), and it could be argued that a list such as the one in Table 7.3 represented the overblown thinking about arts policy under New Labour in the UK, where nebulous performance indicators generated a rent-seeking mindset among arts and cultural organisations (pitching to whatever are the perceived policy priorities of the day) as well as 'diverting them from their mission and speciality in order to fulfil the list of performance indicators' (Towse, 2010: 280). It could also be argued that the Conservative–Liberal Democrats coalition is unlikely to be as indulgent in the face of Britain's public debt crisis. But the UK Conservatives under David Cameron sought to distance themselves from the earlier claims by Margaret Thatcher that 'there is no such a thing as society' (McSmith, 2010), by proposing a 'Big Society', where power would be devolved from the state to local authorities and community organisations. Although it is too early to be sure, it would be no surprise to see arts and cultural organisations placing themselves at the forefront of UK 'Big Society' initiatives, most likely with a retooled version of the list of benefits of the arts provided in Table 7.3.

Table 7.3 Claimed Impacts of the Arts for Individuals, Communities and Society

- Develops self-confidence and self-esteem
- Increases creativity and thinking skills
- Improves skills in planning and organising activities
- Improves communication of ideas and information
- Raises or enhances educational attainment
- Increases appreciation of arts
- Creates social capital
- Strengthens communities
- Develops community identity
- Decreases social isolation
- Improves understanding of different cultures
- Enhances social cohesion
- Promotes interest in the local environment
- Activates social change
- Raises public awareness of an issue
- Enhances mental and physical health and well-being
- Contributes to urban regeneration
- Reduces offending behaviour
- Alleviates the impact of poverty
- Increases the employability of individuals

Source: Jermyn, 2001: 13.

6. Globalisation and International Trade Agreements

It was observed in the previous chapter how the finalising of the GATS agreement and the establishment of the WTO in 1995 had created a new element in developing policies for domestic creative industries, particularly those in highly tradable goods and services such as the audiovisual media sector. This marks a major development in the 'sharing and bartering' (Held et al., 1999) of policy making sovereignty in relation to developing national media industries, including forms of cultural policy such as subsidies and local content policies for the film and television industries. Both the reach and the significance of such agreements remain sources of ongoing tension because of their threat to democratic decision-making within nation-states and the perceived lack of accountability of multilateral institutions. Woods (2002) observes that:

> Large sections of the public do not buy the idea that they are represented in institutions such as the IMF, the World Bank, the UN Security Council, or the WTO ... representation and accountability have always been weak in these multilateral institutions. Now, however, the weaknesses are glaring because the institutions are being called on by their powerful members to intrude much more deeply into areas which were previously the preserve of national government. (Woods, 2002: 30)

The catch for national governments is that forces associated with economic globalisation, such as the rise of global media corporations, the role of the Internet and digital media in facilitating faster global communication, the availability of a much wider range of cultural products, and the growth in cosmopolitan consumer preferences, mean that national media invariably face greater competition in home markets from imported media and cultural products. One response has been regional trade agreements that harmonise rules and reduce or eliminate trade barriers between member nation-states within a particular geographical region. Examples include the North American Free Trade Agreement (NAFTA); the Central American Free Trade Agreement (CAFTA); the MERCOSUR agreement involving Brazil, Argentina, Uruguay and Paraguay; the Closer Economic Relation between Australia and New Zealand; and – most famously – the European Union (EU).

Of these, it has been the EU (previously the European Commission) that has been most active in the media and cultural policy domains. It introduced the 'Television Without Frontiers' agreement as early as 1989, which set a 'European Works' programme content quota of 50 per cent, binding upon all EU members, with the aim of creating a 'pan-European audiovisual space' (Schlesinger, 1997) that could enable European producers to realise the scale economies made possible by access to larger markets by liberalising audiovisual trade within Europe, while strengthening barriers to content from outside the EU, most notably that of the United States. The 'Television Without Frontiers' agreement is unusual in that it approaches Europe as a coherent cultural entity on the basis of its capacity to act as a collective political and diplomatic entity. Schlesinger (1997) has questioned this strategy, as it relies upon a dichotomy existing between European 'culture' and American 'entertainment', and because commitments to European culture and identity among its national populations are thin when compared to their national allegiances. Galperin (1999) has observed that the degree of cultural distance among member states in such agreements is a critical variable. Taking NAFTA as an example, Galperin argued that NAFTA disadvantaged Canadian cultural producers, as they competed directly with US cultural products on the basis of a shared language and common cultural reference points, but offered advantages to Mexican cultural producers, who have significant linguistic and cultural barriers to US material, while the agreement gave them better access to the large Spanish-speaking population within the United States.

7. Content as a New Growth Industry

Technological convergence and the digitisation of news, information and entertainment led the OECD and others to identify content as a new growth industry in the 1990s (OECD, 1998). While some of this enthusiasm waned with the bursting of the 'dot.com bubble', with the precipitous fall of the high-technology NASDAQ in 2001 confounding the 'Content is King' mantra of the 1990s (Odlyzko, 2001; Flew, 2008), the renewed focus on developing digital content industries had a number of lasting legacies on media and cultural policy.

One has been the push towards creative industries policies, and in countries such as Australia, South Korea and Taiwan, policy makers saw digital content as being at the forefront of these sectors (Department of Communications, Information Technology and the Arts (DCITA), 2004). Second, it opened up questions of whether media constitutes a distinctive policy realm, as media industries and media content increasingly blur with and bleed into other sectors, such as information, telecommunications and computing. The issue of whether media should be thought of as 'not just another business' (Schultz, 1994) was challenged by those who increasingly understood media as being in the realm of convergent service industries, generating a new set of pressures for deregulation of media industries and a turn from sector-specific to more generic forms of industry regulation (Productivity Commission, 2000; Cunningham and Flew, 2002).

Finally, one of the challenges presented by digital content industries to established media is that the major players rise and fall more quickly, with considerably fewer degrees of state subvention than incumbents have in the print, broadcast and telecommunications industries (OECD, 2006). The rise of new industry players such as Google, Facebook, Skype and the digital games industry is far more characteristic of Schumpeterian waves of creative destruction and disruptive innovation than the oligopolistic world of the traditional large media players, who have frequently been able to rely upon various forms of industry regulation and protection of economic rents as a *quid pro quo* for their contribution to national culture and other pro-social goals (Flew, 2006). The likelihood of clashes between traditional media industry and cultural policy goals and other goals, such as the promotion of competition, innovation and new digital products and services, will be an ongoing source of policy tensions as strategies to develop digital content industries are further developed.

8. The Changing Nature of Innovation Policy

There have been important shifts in thinking about how innovation occurs, and their policy implications in recent years that have come to have an indirect influence upon the arts, media and culture. Dodgson et al. (2005: 32–38) refer to five generations of innovation process as a way of mapping these shifts, which can be represented as shown in Table 7.4.

Charles Leadbeater (2008) contrasts open innovation to what he terms the pipeline model, where 'innovation was seen as a linear and sequential process from invention through development to application [and] consumers waiting at the end of the pipeline played little role other than deciding whether or not to use the product' (Leadbeater, 2008: 92). By contrast, open innovation emphasises the 'the use of purposive inflows and outflows of knowledge to accelerate internal innovation, and expand the markets for external use of innovation, respectively. [This paradigm] assumes that firms can and should use external ideas as well as internal ideas, and internal and external paths to market, as they look to advance their technology' (Chesbrough, 2006: 14). Leadbeater identifies open innovation as part of a larger paradigm shift in 21st century market economies, driven by collaborative impulses that are enabled by the Internet and digital media technologies, and exemplified by social media innovations such as *Wikipedia* and *YouTube*, where 'the irresistible force of collaborative mass innovation will increasingly be meeting the immovable object of entrenched corporate organisation' (Leadbeater, 2008: 90). One of the challenges of innovation policies

Table 7.4 Five Stages of Innovation Policy

Historical phase	Innovation model	Core feature	Government policy implications
First Generation (1950s–1960s)	Science Push	Supply-driven focus on new inventions	Government investment in 'big' R&D (e.g. nuclear engineering, space exploration)
Second Generation (1970s–1980s)	Market Pull	Consumer demand-driven	Make science more responsive to industry
Third Generation (1980s–1990s)	Coupling	Interaction between science push and market pull	Promote partnering between industry, government and research institutions (e.g. universities)
Fourth Generation (1990s–2000s)	Integrated	Integration between science, markets, suppliers and customers	Promoting clustering as a source of competitive advantage ('Silicon Valley model')
Fifth Generation (2000s–2010s)	Network Model	New sources of knowledge, creativity and learning are highly distributed	Promoting open innovation models and engaging in 'global competition for talent'

Source: Dodgson et al., 2005.

in such an environment is to resist the impulse to defend the well-organised incumbents against the smaller and more dispersed challengers, which is to side with open systems over closed models where possible, and to move from the problem of twentieth-century corporate, governmental and other institutions that 'often in the name of doing things for people ... end up doing things to people' (Leadbeater, 2008: 240).

A particularly important element of this is the politics of copyright, to be considered below. Another that is particularly relevant to the arts and culture is that creative practices are being identified as central elements of this innovation ecology. Mitchell et al. (2003) emphasised the degree to which transformations in ICT enabled more sustained interaction between creative practices associated with the arts and design with business practices and scientific practices.

In order to fully realise such possibilities for arts and culture in the innovation ecology, there is a need, as Bakhshi et al. (2010) observe, to overcome two entrenched prejudices. One is the exclusion of the arts and culture from thinking about research and development, as R&D tends to be equated exclusively with the science, engineering and technology sectors. The second is the tendency for those within the arts and cultural sectors to rely upon a conception of creativity that mystifies its sources and processes in ways that render it virtually unknowable. From an innovation perspective, the problem with this conception of creativity is that innovation policy necessarily points not only to the importance of knowledge creation, but also to knowledge application and knowledge diffusion (Mytelka

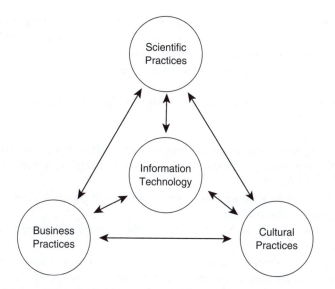

Figure 7.1 ICTs and Creativity in the Arts, Business and Science

Source: Mitchell et al., 2003: 25.

and Smith, 2002). Creative practices themselves need to be open to adaptation and social learning, and not operate as closed systems only able to be understood by a small elite with requisite forms of cultural capital.

9. Information Abundance

One of the most obvious implications of the rise of the Internet and digital media technologies has been the exponential proliferation in the sources of information that are now widely available through the population. This is not to say that information is synonymous with knowledge. Brown and Duguid (2000) pointed out that knowledge has a personal dimension, whether it resides in those who possess it or in the learning process through which others acquire it, and that it is not replicable in information systems: organisations have needed to recognise that 'knowledge lies less in their databases than in their people' (Brown and Duguid, 2000: 121).

At the same time, there are questions to be asked about the implications of moving from a world of information scarcity to one of information abundance. Brian McNair (2006) has argued, in the context of news and journalism, that we have been moving from a *control* paradigm that was dominant for much of the twentieth century, where it made sense to emphasise the structural role played by media in maintaining existing relations of power and hierarchy, to a *chaos* paradigm, where there is exponentially more news and journalistic information available which moves more quickly and circulates more widely, and to a much wider proportion of the world's population, than ever before. For McNair, the chaos paradigm:

acknowledges the desire for control on the part of elites, while suggesting that the performance, or exercise of control, is increasingly interrupted and disrupted by unpredictable eruptions and bifurcations arising from the impact of economic, political, ideological and technological factors on communication processes. (McNair, 2006: 3)

He identifies eight constituent elements of this shift from a control to a chaos paradigm (McNair, 2006: 199–204):

1 From information scarcity to information surplus, enabling a potential 'power-shift from the traditionally information-rich to the no-longer so information-poor mass' (McNair, 2006: 199);
2 From closed to open information systems, with much greater 'leakage' of information from powerful institutions;
3 Greater transparency in how the sources and mechanisms of power are seen to be operating;
4 Greater accessibility of information to a much wider range of the population;
5 Greater diversity and heterogeneity of information sources, or a move from mass media to more personalised information flows and greater access for more people to minority and/or dissident sources of information;
6 The growth of networked information flows and knowledge sharing through social media, as compared to hierarchical, top-down mass communications models;
7 Greater interactivity and a relative flattening of hierarchies between information producers and consumers. Bruns (2008) has referred to this as the rise of the *produser* and collaborative, open, self-governing information systems such as that generated by Wikipedia;
8 Greater competition between information sources and across platforms, between traditional media outlets and new providers, between media professionals and what Leadbeater and Miller (2004) termed 'pro-ams', and between locally or nationally based media and global media and information sources.

10. The New Politics of Copyright

Copyright and intellectual property law has become a crucible for a range of legal, policy and political issues in recent times, as the rise of creative industries generates new momentum for intellectual property as a primary source of revenue,[1] while technological changes associated with digital media and the Internet have dramatically reduced the cost of reproducing, distributing and accessing digital content in all of its forms across electronic networks. The tension between the moral and economic rights of creators to derive returns from their original forms of creative expression, and the value of information to the community as the lifeblood of both democracy and commerce (and as the basis of new knowledge and creativity), has always existed in copyright law. Historically, copyright law has divided up the possible rights in and uses of a work, giving control over some of these rights to the creators and distributors, and control over others to the general public as conditions of 'fair use' (Litman, 2001). Authors such as Bettig (1996), Vaidhyanathan (2001) and Perelman (2002) have argued that whereas copyright law was originally framed around a conception of content creators, distributors and users as relatively equal parties, the twentieth century saw the distributors of creative content gain power dramatically as the major media industries asserted ownership and control over copyrighted works. As a result, they argue, the interests of the 'copyright industries' now sit over and above – and frequently in opposition to – the much larger but far more dispersed collectivity of end-users of copyrighted or copyrightable material (Flew, 2008: 227–228).

As well as technological changes and the rise of intellectual property as a source of wealth, other factors that are rendering copyright law ever more significant yet complex include the extent to which copyrighted products are at the core of an increasingly image-based global popular culture (Coombe, 1998), and the globalisation of copyright and intellectual property law through international agreement. The Trade-Related Aspects of Intellectual Property Rights (TRIPS) agreement was signed by over 100 nations in 1994, and saw the establishment of the World Intellectual Property Organization (WIPO) as a supranational body responsible for promoting regulatory harmonisation and settling disputes arising between nations. The period since the 1990s has seen regulatory provisions protecting copyright increased significantly around the world, at a time when new media has dramatically enhanced the capacity of content users – both creators and consumers – to circumvent copyright through the use of various ICTs. What this generates is a massive social fault-line as a range of everyday behaviours (music downloading, posting videos on *YouTube*) became illegal, while at the same time artists and creative workers are increasingly drawing upon remix culture and derivative works as the basis for new creative products (Lessig, 2004; Jenkins, 2006). As copyright law is increasingly internationalised, such tensions increasingly play themselves out on a world scale, most notably in ongoing trade wars between the United States, as the economy that derives the greatest trade surplus from intellectual property, and China, as the world's largest manufacturer of copyrighted products and for its critics a haven for breaches of intellectual property (Montgomery, 2009).

What has been emerging quite rapidly since the late 1990s has been the new politics of copyright. With origins in the cyber-libertarian critique of all forms of proprietary control over digital content (Barlow, 1996), it has evolved into critical legal movements such as Creative Commons, which aims to make copyright material more accessible, and its terms of access more open and less costly, by enabling content creators to generically give permission in advance to certain forms of reuse of their content (Fitzgerald, 2006). The general argument is that recent developments in copyright and intellectual property law have given too much control over digital content to existing rights holders – who are typically the large corporations that profit from media distribution, rather than the direct content creators – and that this has a series of adverse consequences. Some of the most important are economic, as it is argued that extending copyright protection not only makes transactions more costly and enables existing rights holders to extract monopoly rents, but also that it can inhibit the capacity of 'follow-on' and 'second' innovators to build upon existing copyrighted innovations ('Standing on the shoulders of giants'), thus dampening the overall scope for innovation by artificially restricting the public domain. This is because information is not only a public good, thus warranting government oversight over how it is produced and distributed, but is in fact a *metapublic good* that generates positive benefits to a community when freely available in ways that are impossible to calculate in advance, since the uses of existing information to produce new information, and the value of that new information, are endemically hard to 'guesstimate'. Michael Perelman observed that:

> Information is not scarce, except to the degree that society allows agents to create artificial scarcity through secrecy and property rights … as the economy becomes increasingly dependent on information, the traditional system of property rights applied to information becomes a costly fetter on our development. (Perelman, 2002: 178)

The new politics of copyright has been connected to new public interest theory (Benkler, 2001, 2006; Rennie, 2003; Lessig, 2004). The key here is to recognise that the Internet and digital media have come to be associated with new forms of peer production and collaboration, which Benkler (2006) terms *social production*. The extent to which these are forms of production not driven by traditional market signals (e.g. receipt of income as the condition for contributing one's labour and ideas), or whether they are more elaborate forms of market signalling behaviour, has been the subject of considerable debate, particularly among economists (Quiggan and Potts, 2008). What they do favour, as a general principle, is greater openness of culture, more opportunities for the free exchange of information, and the removal of artificial barriers to co-operation and collaboration, in ways that cut across traditional left/right divides shaped by attitudes to the capitalist market economy. They do, however, share a common concern with the capacity of the *ancien régime* of existing rights holders and other stakeholders from the mass communications economy to use copyright law and other devices to stifle the public information domain and opportunities for new players, arguing that 'as economic policy, letting yesterday's winners dictate the terms of tomorrow's economic competition is disastrous. As social policy, missing an opportunity to enrich our freedom and enhance our justice while maintaining or even enhancing our productivity is unforgivable' (Benkler, 2001: 90).

Creative Industries and the Neo-Liberalism Debate

It has been observed at various points in this book that identifying the emergence of creative industries policy discourse as a response to wider trends in media and cultural policy is only one possible reading of its rise. There is another argument, arising from the critical humanities in particular, that sees creative industries less as a descriptive category or a distinctive way of framing media and cultural policy questions, but instead as an ideological category. In particular, the turn to creative industries is seen as a concrete manifestation of neo-liberalism, understood as a global ideological project with its roots in the United States and Britain, that has aimed to shift power and resources to corporations and wealthy elites through the privatisation of public assets, removal of 'public interest' regulations over large corporations, and tax cuts targeted towards the highest income earners. The rise of media and cultural industries to greater prominence coincides with the 'Great Downturn' of the world economy in the 1970s and 1980s, generating a policy response focused upon marketisation, or 'the process by which market exchange increasingly came to permeate the cultural industries and related sectors' (Hesmondhalgh, 2007a: 110). This is consistent with neo-liberalism as defined by the Marxist geographer David Harvey as:

A theory of political economic practices that proposes that human well-being can best be advanced by liberating individual entrepreneurial freedoms and skills within an institutional framework characterized by strong private property rights, free market, and free trade. The role of the state is to create and preserve an institutional framework appropriate to such practices. (Harvey, 2005: 2)

Through a series of waves of such policies being advanced through the global system, neo-liberal globalisation is seen as emerging, defined by Scholte (2005b) as 'an economically driven process that should proceed on first principles of private property and uninhibited market forces', and where 'other economic rules and institutions are reduced to a minimum' (Scholte, 2005b: 1). Fuchs has argued that 'the capitalist nation-state has been transformed ... into a neo-liberal competitive state', whose consequences have included 'on the one hand the extension and intensification of economic colonization – the commodification of everything – and ... the extension and intensification of alienation – the almost entire loss of control over economic property, political decision making, and value definition ... in all realms of life' (Fuchs, 2008: 108–109).

A number of critical theorists have argued that media and cultural policy in the 1990s and 2000s has largely involved the implementation of neo-liberalism, often under the rubric of creative industries. Through the association of creative industries with neo-liberal globalisation, David Hesmondhalgh argued that 'neo-liberalism and the neo-classical conception of the market have made huge advances in the cultural sphere', so that 'strong traditions of public ownership and regulation ... were abandoned or severely limited during the neo-liberal turn' (Hesmondhalgh, 2007a: 135). In his analysis of US and UK media policy in the 1990s and 2000s, Des Freedman identified a decisive shift from pluralism to neo-liberalism in media policy, associated primarily with 'a much narrower and more consumer-oriented role for the media', and 'conceptualizing media policy ... towards a focus on the largely economic benefits that may accrue from the exploitation of the media industries' (Freedman, 2008: 219). Freedman linked the rise of creative industries policy discourse in the UK to the 'the neo-liberalization of media policy' which 'is designed to transform the existing balance of power ... to assist the expansion of private accumulation and to undermine the legitimacy and existence of non-profit and public service media provision' (Freedman, 2008: 224). In a similar vein, Andrew Ross referred to creative industries policy discourse in the UK as '"old wine in new bottles" – a glib production of spin-happy New Labourites, hot for naked marketisation but mindful of the need for socially acceptable dress' (Ross, 2008: 18). Justin O'Connor (2009) has critiqued recent theorisations of creative industries, such as social network markets (Potts et al., 2008), as involving 'the annexation ... of the cultural value of cultural goods to the evolution of the knowledge economy' (O'Connor, 2009: 389). Toby Miller argued that 'neo-liberalism is at the core of the creative industries' (Miller, 2009a: 270), that 'neo-liberal creative industries discourse' has been promoted by 'carpet-bagging consultants' (Miller, 2009b: 188), and that 'neo-liberalism [has] understood people exclusively through the precepts of selfishness [and] it exercised power on people by governing them through market imperatives' (Miller, 2009a: 271).

One of the difficulties in addressing arguments that refer to neo-liberalism is that, in a manner akin to that of postmodernism in the 1990s, the range of possible meanings and interpretations has been ballooning outwards. Nonini has made the observation that 'the term "neo-liberal" has recently appeared so frequently, and been applied with such abandon, that it risks being used to refer to almost any political, economic, social or cultural process associated with contemporary capitalism' (Nonini, 2008: 149). To take a small smattering of examples from a voluminous literature, neo-liberalism has been associated with: the growing popularity of Bollywood-style weddings (Kapur, 2009); the prevalence of violence in recent Australian cinema (Stratton, 2009); the financial difficulties of the University of California (Butler, 2009); the death of politics (Giroux, 2005); standardised national educational curricula and national testing (Apple, 2004); the performative sexuality of the character of Mr Garrison in the animated comedy series *South Park* (Gournelos, 2009); and the privileging of access to databases over space for books in Australian public libraries (McQueen, 2009). In spite of the concern raised by early analysis of neo-liberalism to avoid 'a tendency to reify neo-liberalism and to treat it as a phenomenon which manifests itself everywhere and in everything' (Gamble, 2001: 134), this does indeed seem to have happened in the academic literature on the concept. This tendency has been reinforced in recent years by a propensity to conflate neo-liberalism with neo-conservatism (Brown, 2006). This means that a very broad gamut of ideas and movements, from religious conservatism and the 'Tea Party' movement in the United States to the 'Third Way' sociology of Anthony Giddens (Giddens, 1998), are all seen as emanating from broadly similar intellectual sources. The other point to be made is that the term is now almost invariably used in a negative sense. Neo-liberalism refers to the bad ideas that others hold; it is never the intellectual position of the author writing about it. For instance, of the 45 articles published in Australia with the words 'neo-liberalism' in the title – accessed from the Informit database in May 2009 – only one, published in 1995, could be said to have been written by someone supporting a neo-liberal policy position (Kirchner, 1995). It has quite explicitly been defined in pejorative terms in most literature on the subject, as seen in Brown's equation of neo-liberalism with 'a radically free market: maximized competition and free trade achieved through economic de-regulation … and a range of monetary and social policies favorable to business and indifferent toward poverty, social deracination, cultural decimation, long term resource depletion and environmental destruction' (Brown, 2003).

There are two branches within this broad church of critics of neo-liberalism. For Harvey, Hesmondhalgh, Freedman, Scholte and Fuchs, neo-liberalism can be understood in straightforwardly Marxist terms, as an ideology imposed on behalf of dominant class and big business interests through their control over the state and public policy, whether directly, through explicitly pro-market governments such as the Conservatives in Britain or the Republican Party in the USA, or by 'Third Way' administrations, such as those of the

Clinton Democrats and the British 'New Labour' governments of Tony Blair and Gordon Brown. For others, such as Jodi Dean (2008), Wendy Brown (2003, 2006) and Toby Miller (2009a, 2009b, 2010), neo-liberalism is understood through a synthesis of neo-Marxist critiques of political economy with the later work of Michel Foucault on governmentality and liberal political rationality (Foucault, 1991a, 2008). Dean draws upon Foucault to argue that neo-liberalism 'inverts the early [liberal] model of the state as a limiting, external principle supervising the market to make the market form itself into the regulative principle underlying the state', thereby 'reformatting social and political life in terms of its ideal of competition within markets' (Dean, 2008: 48, 49). Brown has argued that 'neo-liberalism casts the political and social spheres both as appropriately dominated by market concerns and as themselves organised by market rationality ... the state itself must construct and construe itself in market terms, as well as develop policies and promulgate a political culture that figures citizens exhaustively as rational economic actors in every sphere of life' (Brown, 2006: 694). Miller proposed that the 'grand contradiction of neo-liberalism was its passion for intervention in the name of non-intervention ... calling for the generation of more and more markets by the state while insisting on fewer and fewer democratic controls, and hailing freedom as a natural basis for life that could only function with the heavy hand of policing by government to administer property relations' (Miller, 2010: 56).

This latter group of authors rightly identify the analysis developed by Michel Foucault in his 1978–1979 lectures at the *Collège de France*, published as *The Birth of Biopolitics* (Foucault, 2008), as being ahead of its time in its interest in neo-liberalism. Foucault's interest in the German *Ordoliberal* theorists and the economists of the Chicago School in the USA identifies a development in the history of ideas that was only beginning to be noted in the 1970s, but which would generate a voluminous literature by the 2000s, under the general critical thematic of neo-liberalism. At the same time, there is something anachronistic about the readings of Foucault developed by authors such as Dean, Brown and Miller, as they appear to be crediting Foucault for anticipating their own critiques of the Bush administration in the United States in the 2000s. To make this point is not to make the trite observation that we no longer live in the time of Foucault; we no longer live in the time of Marx, Freud, Weber or Aristotle, but this would not be the basis on which we would judge the value of their ideas. It is instead to observe that the engineering of a synthesis of Marx and Foucault, as seen in formulations of neo-liberalism such as 'the commodification of identity within a liberal framework, in which freedom, success, rights, and politics become fully integrated into a system of commodity and governmentality' (Gournelos, 2009: 290), may well be at odds with Foucault's own intentions in his writings at this time. For while neo-liberalism was a minority discourse in this period, Marxism most definitely was not; in France in the 1970s, Marxism was the dominant intellectual strand in the humanities, and it received some degree of concrete political form – in ways that have long been inconceivable in the United States – in the programmes of the Socialist Party (PS), the French Communist Party (PCF), and a range of smaller Trotskyist, Maoist and other Marxist political groupings. Foucault's intellectual work was consistently at odds with dominant Marxist formulations, particularly in relation to ideology, power and the state, and this opposition to Marxism became particularly marked in the 1970s (Barrett, 1991; Foucault, 1991c).[2]

In *The Birth of Biopolitics*, Foucault's interest is in the 'art of government', and in particular how economic liberalism from Adam Smith onwards has existed as an immanent challenge to what he refers to as 'reason of state' (*raison d'État*), by presenting the perpetual question of liberal government as that of 'frugal government', where 'a government is never sufficiently aware that it always risks governing too much, or a government never knows too well how to govern just enough' (Foucault, 2008: 17). It is an approach that starts, not from questions of sovereignty, the nature of the state, and the rights of citizens, but from governmental practice itself, and what Foucault refers to as the paradoxical management of freedom in liberal forms of government. As Foucault puts it, 'The problems of what I shall call the economy of power peculiar to liberalism are internally sustained ... by this interplay of freedom and security' (Foucault, 2008: 65). He rejects a theory of the state as he would 'forego an indigestible meal' (Foucault, 2008: 77), and chides socialists for failing to develop suitable models of governmental practice that can best further their ends, arguing that:

> What socialism lacks is not so much a theory of the state as a governmental reason ... that is to say, a reasonable and calculable measure of the extent, modes and objectives of governmental action. In actual fact, and history has shown this, socialism can only be implemented when connected up to diverse modes of governmentality. (Foucault, 2008: 91–92)

As Behrent (2009) has observed, this presents the interesting possibility that, rather than engaging with neo-liberalism in order to present a radical critique of it, Foucault's interest stemmed from a qualified endorsement of the indirect measures for exercising governmental power preferred by the neo-liberals, particularly when contrasted to the top-down 'social statism' of the PS and PCF. He appears in these essays to endorse the compromise with liberalism and the 'game of governmentality' that the German Social Democratic Party had engaged in since the 1960s, contrasting it favourably to the rhetorical anti-capitalism of the French left.

At any rate, as Guala (2006) has observed, Foucault rejects the easy critique of neo-liberalism as ideology in these lectures, choosing not to present it as 'a convenient cover for an underlying reality of oppression and domination' or as 'pseudo-science, to be exposed and condemned as the servant of whatever power is in place' (Guala, 2006: 433). Rather, he takes seriously the transformation of liberal arts of government associated with the rise of neo-liberalism, which shift the focus of governmental action away from identifying domains that are demarcated between the market and the state, or the question of state intervention versus laissez faire, towards the generalisation of competition and the enterprise form as guides to governmental practice, and the perpetual practice of critique of whether there is 'too much' or 'too little' government involvement in a vastly expanded range of policy domains.

In relation to creative industries, an important implication of Foucault's approach to governmentality and the 'art of government' is the need to differentiate the question of whether creative industries policy discourse introduced new tools and techniques to the governance of arts, media and cultural activity, from the question of whether it was a Trojan Horse for malign neo-liberalism. Pratt (2005) saw the rise of creative industries in Britain as being associated with new modes of cultural governance, observing that he 'prefer[s] the term "governance" rather than "policy" as it encompasses policy, the definition of artefacts and their production, as well as the legitimization and implementation of policy' (Pratt, 2005: 39). While Pratt does not describe such an approach as Foucauldian, the intention to move from standard cultural policy models, which have typically focused upon cultural economics and the cost–benefit analysis of state support for the arts and culture – an economically liberal approach in its classic sense – to consideration of wider questions surrounding 'the different institutional orders' that cultural governance has to address. This in turn raises the need to 'extend the notion of governance beyond that which the state and the market seek to control' (Pratt, 2005: 39, 41) and points in the direction of more nuanced approaches to the evaluation of creative industries policies. One example would be the paradoxes arising for these sectors from new ways of calculating their economic value: on the one hand, this gives greater visibility to these sectors, and enables policy discussions to enter on to a new plane, but on the other it has led to the setting of inappropriate 'performance targets' and the enmeshing of cultural organisations into a wider 'audit culture' that was commonly identified as a key problem of 'New Labour' policies in the late 1990s and 2000s. Another example would be the implications of creative industries being associated with an innovation agenda rather than simply public subsidy (Potts et al., 2008), which is likely to be of more direct benefit to some types of creative industries, such as those dealing with digital media content, than others, such as the visual arts and crafts.

Observing paradoxes of cultural governance, and questions of what may involve 'too much' or 'too little' government support, or poorly designed or managed government support, is different from 'the neo-liberalisation of media policy' or 'the commodification of everything'. In these critical accounts one can observe some recurring problems with the application of Marxist state theory to public policy, where public policy is seen largely in terms of the application of ideologies such as neo-liberalism to promote dominant class interests. Following Dunleavy and O'Leary (1987), three problems with such analyses can be identified. The first is that of functionalism, or the propensity to attribute a diverse range of phenomena to a single causal factor, such as the preproduction of capitalist class rule. In critiquing the claim by Harvey (2005) that China has become neo-liberal since 1978, Nonini observes the circularity of claims that 'flexible capitalism dictates its own conditions of existence to the political systems of the nation-states it is organized within' (Nonini, 2008: 150), and that this is no less true of China, Russia or India than it is of the United States, Britain, Scandinavia or Western Europe. The second and related problem is that of instrumentalism, or the assumption that whatever the differences in institutional form or the values and ideologies of dominant political parties in different countries, they nonetheless converge in practice around the control over state agencies and functions by a relatively unified ruling class that is both conscious of its own interests and able to exercise them through public policy. In such accounts, those responsible for the design, enacting and implementation of various forms of public policy appear simply as 'administrative elites [that are] simply functionaries who make policy according to the rational interests of the capitalist class' (Dunleavy and O'Leary, 1987: 239). In such accounts, questions such as how this occurs, or why it changes from one period to the next, or from one government to another, tend either to be glossed over, or to be presented largely as involving the capture of state agencies by particular ideological interests. The final set of problems arise from what Dunleavy and O'Leary refer to as a cipher model of the state and policy agencies, where the actual conduct of such agencies is largely shaped by forces external to them – such as the power of dominant business interests – and 'the state is a passive mechanism controlled from outside of the formal political sphere, and that ultimate power lies with groups in civil society' (Dunleavy and O'Leary, 1987: 327–328). Where Foucault's account of governmentality provides a useful corrective to such tendencies is in its ability to identify the capacity of state agencies and policy makers to be innovators in their own right, to generate new forms of policy discourse and governmental practice that reshape the institutional spaces and discursive practices within particular policy domains. It would seem that the emergence of creative industries as a distinctive way of articulating relations between institutions, policy and discourses, in what had hitherto been the discrete domains of arts, media and cultural policy, marks precisely this kind of innovation and activism within the policy process, rather than simply being the reflex adaptation of cultural policy to better serve dominant corporate-cultural interests.

Endnotes

1   As was noted in Chapter Three, the creative industries are sometimes referred to as the *copyright industries*, which are 'engaged primarily in the generation, production, and dissemination of new copyrighted material' (Siwek, 2006: 9).

2   As a student in the aftermath of World War II, Foucault was greatly influenced by Marxism, as were most French intellectuals of that generation. He was a member of the PCF in the first part of the 1950s, but left for reasons connected in part to the Party's uncritical support for Stalin's rule in the Soviet Union. Eribon (1991) tracks the complex development of Foucault's political positions during the 1970s, from a position that was well to the left of the PCF in the early 1970s, to a growing frustration with the parties of the French left in the late 1970s and early 1980s. He was consistently critical of the Soviet Union and supported Eastern European dissident movements, and frequently defined his own political thought in opposition to Marxism. Gordon (1991) argues that Foucault's growing interest in the concept of governmentality arose from his frustration with the absence of a distinctive socialist art of governing and the electoral failings of the PS and PCF in the 1970s.

Conclusion

This study concludes at an interesting historical juncture in both theory and practice with the creative industries. The creative industries concept is unique, at least in terms of cultural theory, in having its origins in policy discourses, particularly those of the 'New Labour' governments of Tony Blair and Gordon Brown in Britain in the 1990s and 2000s. Given these origins, it may appear reasonable to surmise that the concept departs the scene with these administrations. Yet the set of developments which the concept of creative industries has sought to capture, particularly the growing economic importance of activities relating to creativity and innovation, and the reflexive and mutually determining relationships this points to between economy and culture, have not gone away at all. In fact, every indication is that this has become more important in terms of public policy, particularly if we understand creative industries broadly to also incorporate entertainment industries more generally. The proliferation of statistical and mapping exercises that have taken place around the world over the 2000s, and the greater global integration of cultural statistics being led by agencies such as UNESCO internationally, as well as by regional entities such as the European Union, point to a set of developments that are moving to the front and centre of policy makers' thinking. Ideas associated with the rise of creative industries have also permeated cultural policy, urban planning and innovation policy worldwide to a degree that will not be reversed simply as a result of political changes in Britain.

This book has sought to navigate a path through the complex policy, empirical and analytical debates that have surrounded the rise of creative industries. While such an exercise can be tedious, it is nonetheless necessary, as a variety of different terms have been developed to describe these phenomena. In the course of providing an overview of the field for economic geographers, Jeff Boggs makes this point:

> Collectively, these industries take many names: cultural industries, creative industries, cultural-products industries, the creative economy, and the cultural economy. While individual authors are often consistent in the terms they use (at least within a single manuscript), when viewed collectively, these terms appear as an imprecise muddle ... However, these competing definitions make it difficult to evaluate the claims of individual scholars and to provide well-founded policy recommendations. Do scholar A and scholar B mean the same thing when they both say creative industry? Does scholar B mean creative economy when scholar C means cultural industries? In a perfect world, one term would emerge that corresponds to these kinds of industries, and what they are called collectively. But given scholars' penchant for inventing new names for concepts ... this hope will probably remain unfulfilled. One must muddle through the existing concepts, which are useful ones despite their imprecision. (Boggs, 2009: 1484)

So we muddle through with vague but useful concepts! It is of course hoped that this book has made these concepts less vague, as well as indicating how they may be useful. What certainly can be noted is that we have greater clarity as to the industries that we are referring to, as well as better data from which to make comparisons between countries and over time, which will certainly assist with ongoing policy formation. In this respect, the advances made in such reports as UNESCO's revised *Framework for Cultural Statistics* (UNESCO, 2009) will continue to have an impact, particularly in the developing world, thereby also confirming that creative industries is not simply a 'First World' or rich nation concept.

Thinking about this diverse range of sectors and activities – arts to architecture, performance to publishing, music, games, publishing, broadcasting, film, design, writing, journalism, and so on – as creative industries presents a series of distinctive empirical challenges. Some relate to the 'missing middle': sectors where there are large global corporate conglomerates and myriad individual entrepreneurs and small businesses, but an apparent shortage of medium-sized businesses; or to the 'hourglass' structure of many of these sectors, with large numbers of producers and consumers and a concentration at the level of distribution, wherein economic and other forms of power reside in the sectors. Some relate to the unpredictable nature of creativity in terms of realisation of financial gain, and the ways in which contracts and industrial organisation emerge as ways of seeking to manage, but never fully resolving, questions of endemic risk and uncertainty. Other issues concern the centrality of intrinsic motivators to many creative people and creative activities, and to people who resist being disciplined by bureaucracy, policy or industrial organisation, and how the combination of 'Fame Academy' artistic and creative ideals bump up against the risks that flexible labour markets bring, particularly in industries with strong propensities towards 'winner takes all' outcomes. Finally, there are issues surrounding a possible mismatch between the traditional instruments and priorities of arts and cultural policy, focused upon protecting the best elements of human endeavour and creativity from the predations of the market (at least in some areas), and the new focus upon innovation cultures, creative cities and wealth derived from intellectual property, or the capitalisation of new ideas for economic gain. As Tom O'Regan has observed in his commentary on the rise of creative industries policy discourse, 'even "creativity" seemed too important to be left up to cultural policy institutions and frameworks' (O'Regan, 2002: 23).

If creativity raises one set of questions, the idea of industries raises others. Empirically, the Standard Industrial Classifications (SIC) were developed in the heyday of manufacturing employment, and what we refer to today as the creative industries, along with other service industries more generally, tend to be spread across a diverse range of categories, including the arts, media, services, information, culture and leisure (Flew, 2004c; Hartley, 2005). Moreover, and reflective of these origins, the term industry itself tends to imply mass production, standardisation, the separation of the mind and the hand, assembly lines, etc. Adorno and Horkheimer's critique of the culture industry turned around precisely the concern that cultural production was being industrialised in the age of monopoly capitalism, alongside counter claims – most notably by Lash and Urry (1994) – that other industries are now being increasingly 'culturalised', do little to dispel the perception that being involved in an industry entails losing control over one's creativity and individual autonomy. But this concern is neither new nor is it unique to cultural sectors, and it is not universally held by those engaged in cultural activities. To take sub-sections of the creative industries as case studies, people who are involved in making films or television programmes have tended to be more comfortable with the idea that they work in the film industry or the television industry than, say, painters, sculptors, writers or photographers may be about being said to be working in the arts industry, the writing industry or the photographic industry. They would more likely be referred to as artists, writers or photographers. A parallel could be drawn here with universities. People who teach, research or study in universities do not typically refer to themselves as working in the education industry. They refer to themselves as academics, teachers, researchers, scholars, or a term that captures their individual occupational identity. But there are clearly instances when it makes sense to refer to the education industry, while acknowledging that it does not cover the totality of practices taking place within universities. To take an example, in Australia in 2009–2010 there were a series of bashings of Indian students in Melbourne, including one death; these incidents were widely reported in India, and led to a significant reduction in the number of those travelling from India to study in Australian universities. This has a negative impact on the Australian higher education industry, but does not – at least not in any direct sense – impact on how teaching is taking place, what research projects are being supported, or a myriad of other activities that take place in Australian universities. Reference in this instance to the education industry, like that of the creative industries, provides us with a handle with which we can grasp some aspects of a broadly defined field, without claiming to be the only prism through which such activities can be observed or comprehended.

At the same time, I would argue that there is a wider animating force to debates surrounding creative industries that goes beyond the empirical and the definitional. It goes to the heart of questions about the underlying purposes of intellectual work, and it has its strongest force in the critical humanities, particularly cultural studies. There would appear to be a degree to which creative industries – at least from some understandings of the role of cultural studies and the critical persona of the cultural studies intellectual – constitutes by its very nature a discursive field that is simply incommensurable with it. This is different from the question of whether it is best to refer to cultural industries or creative industries, or whether those who analyse the creative industries should apply greater critical scrutiny to the practices of the firms that constitute these industries, such questions of labour exploitation in the digital games industry or self-exploitation in industries such as fashion design (McRobbie, 2005; Neff et al., 2005; Miller, 2008). It relates to what Jean-François Lyotard referred to as the différend, or the impossibility of reconciling one set of claims with another:

> A différend would be a case of conflict between (at least) two parties, that cannot be equitably resolved for lack of a rule of judgement applicable to both arguments. One side's legitimacy does not imply the other's lack of legitimacy. However, applying a single rule of judgement to both in order to settle their différend as though it was merely a litigation would wrong (at least) one of them … A wrong results from the fact that the rules of the genre of discourse which one judges are not those of the judged genre or genres of discourse. (Lyotard, 1988: xi)

An example of such a différend can be found with Jim McGuigan's view of creative industries as selling out to the business school, developed in his book *Cultural Analysis* (McGuigan, 2009a) and elsewhere. McGuigan associates talk about the creative industries – he largely avoids questions of whether they have influence in the broader economy – with a trajectory associated with what he identifies as the 'cultural populist' strand of cultural studies – approaches that champion engagement with popular cultural texts and media rather than identifying them as sites for his preferred methodology of 'critical intervention'. Indeed, McGuigan's bugbear with creative industries arises not only from its being insufficiently critical of popular culture; it also arises from its wish to engage with policy makers, whose horizons are, for McGuigan, inevitably limited by their indebtedness of what he refers to as 'recipe knowledge', and their inability or unpreparedness to transcend their administrative horizons in order to acquire critical knowledge (McGuigan, 1996; for a critique, see Bennett, 2007). A similar set of arguments can be found in Simon During's *Exit Capitalism* (During, 2010). For During, creative industries talk is indicative of a turn to reformism in cultural studies, which can only seek to 'manage capitalism's crises and growth spurts in the interests of social justice and the alleviation of suffering' (During, 2010: 158), turning away from a 'Great Refusal' of capitalism, the administrative state and reformism that During establishes as the *sine qua non* of a critical cultural studies practice, from which (for During) it has been unfortunately deviated from a putative Marxist heyday in the mid-1970s.

This vision of cultural studies as engaged in an existential anti-capitalist struggle is best described in terms of what Michael Lowy refers to as *revolutionary romanticism*, which he identifies as the most powerful legacy of the post-1968 New Left. Noting its long history, Lowy identifies romanticism as 'a structure of feeling and a world view ... defined as a rebellion against modern capitalist society ... [and] as a protest against the modern disenchantment of the world, the individualist/competitive dissolution of human communities, and the triumph of mechanization, mercantilization, reification, quantification' (Löwy, 2002: 95). Noting that romanticism can be both nostalgic and reactionary, and utopian and forward-looking, Löwy observes that it is not driven by crises in the capitalist economy: he points out that the high point of the New Left in the late 1960s and early 1970s was also the high water-mark of post-World War II Western capitalist economies. Rather, it exists as a form of what Daniel Singer termed 'total rebellion', and Herbert Marcuse described as the 'Great Refusal', of capitalist modernisation, consumer society and hierarchical authority (Löwy, 2002: 97).

Interventions to influence government policy, reshape markets, reorganise industries, or promote local cultural products or firms are, from this perspective, not part of a solution but a fundamental part of the problem, as they can only serve to make capitalism work more effectively, thereby further entrenching its hold over the social imaginary. During is explicit about this in his critique of social movement activism, arguing that 'even when successful, such activism is easily absorbed by democratic state capitalism thought of as an integrated and global system, and indeed tends to strengthen the system by the old logic of reformism' (During, 2010: 133). Moreover, as Boltanski and Chiapello (2005) observe in relation to creativity and the 'new spirit of capitalism', not only does social reformism become absorbed back into the system, but so too does the artistic critique of capitalism, whose demands for freedom and authenticity are repackaged as the 'no-collar' workplace, counter-cultural commodity branding, and the bohemian lifestyles of the 'creative class'. It is therefore not surprising that During would find creative industries to be doing the bidding of what he terms 'democratic state capitalism', for 'the grounds for making an anti-reformist refusal are finally … ethical and irrational' (During, 2010: 158). To seek to reform social and cultural relations from within the system is, according to this perspective, to be complicit in systems and structures of domination. Such a position stands in notable contrast to traditions of academic involvement in industry policy in other sectors, most notably manufacturing, where it has been seen as a necessary complement to strategies to protect existing jobs and promote new ones, to the benefit of people, regions, nations and communities.

The perspective of revolutionary romanticism is not the perspective undertaken in this book. The analysis developed here is concerned with capitalisms in the plural, rather than Capitalism in the singular. While one can identify a set of common features of capitalist economies – production for profit, the role played by markets, legally sanctioned private property relations, etc. – it is maintained that the differences between capitalist economies are as important as their similarities, and that tendencies towards convergence over time are counter-balanced by the continuing significance of national differences that are historically and institutionally grounded (Perraton and Clift, 2004). This is a key factor setting limits to the globalisation thesis: the differences between cities, regions and nations are not being negated by multinational capital. The rise of China as the world's fastest-growing economy from the late 1970s to the late 2000s, with its political culture of state orchestration of socio-economic relations in order to maintain power and sovereignty in the face of the foreign 'barbarians', should be a salutary reminder that the forces of global capital do not invariably trump nation-states, nor do they flatten the distinctive features of national polities and cultures. Rather, close analyses of how multinational corporations operate in practice reveals their propensity to work with the grain of historically defined differences between one place and another, rather than seek to flatten such differences in the name of global homogeneity. Moreover, when we seek to identify factors that continue to generate differences between places, culture and policy emerge as two of the key intervening variables. It is not surprising, therefore, that even where we are seeing policy transfer of ideas from one place to another, of which creative industries can be seen as a case study, the national, regional and local variations on the theme continue to be highly significant (Flew and McElhinney, 2005).

This distinction between capitalism as social totality that absorbs all forms of non-revolutionary critique, and institutionally variable capitalisms shaped by variances in culture, history and forms of public policy, plays itself out in differing conceptions of neo-liberalism. We noted in Chapter Seven that neo-liberalism has ballooned out as a concept over the 2000s, from its origins as a form of economic theorising associated with writers such as Friedrich von Hayek and Milton Friedman, to a Moloch-like entity responsible for everything from Bollywood weddings to cinematic violence to the digitisation of library collections. Moreover, it can only be conceived of negatively: neo-liberalism is a term with 'negative normative valence' (Boas and Gans-Morse, 2009), a term used to critique the bad ideas associated with others – particularly economists but also politicians and policy makers – even if they may not recognise such a categorisation themselves. It is, in short, an ideology, in the sense defined by John Thompson as 'a system of ideas which expresses the interests of the dominant class but which represents class [and other social – TF] relations in an illusory form' (Thompson, 1991: 37). For critics such as Hesmondhalgh (2008), Freedman (2008), Miller (2009a) and McGuigan (2009a), creative industries is read as an instantiation of neo-liberalism in the cultural sphere. As Toby Miller puts it, 'neo-liberalism is at the core of creative industries' (Miller, 2009a: 270).

In thinking through claims about the influence of neo-liberalism over the last 30 years, there is a need, as Andrew Gamble observed, to resist a tendency 'to reify neo-liberalism and to treat it as a phenomenon which manifests itself everywhere and in everything … [and] to deconstruct neo-liberalism into the different doctrines and ideas which compose it, and relate them to particular practices and political projects' (Gamble, 2001: 134). If we adopt this approach – of being specific about neo-liberalism rather than using it as a synonym for the market economy or a scare-word for something the author does not like – there are three interconnected layers from which neo-liberalism as a political-economic project can be understood:

1   The coalescing of a diverse range of economic schools, united in the first instance by an opposition to Keynesian economics and socialist economic planning, through forums such as the Mont Pelerin Society (Peck, 2008). These most famously include the Austrian economists such as Freidrich von Hayek and his mentor, Ludwig von Mises, and the 'Chicago School' of economists such as Milton Friedman, George Stigler and Gary Becker. An extension of this family of economists into a wider formation would also include the German *Ordoliberals* discussed by Foucault (2008), economists at the London School of Economics such as Lionel Robbins, and the 'Rational Expectations' and 'Public Choice' schools of political economy that emerge in the United States from the 1970s.
2   Transformations in the political sphere, associated in the first instance with the rise of Margaret Thatcher in Britain and Ronald Reagan in the USA, that saw conservative politics move decisively towards the 'New Right' position of reducing the size of government, deregulating markets and privatising public assets (Dunleavy and O'Leary, 1987: 72–135). This would give conservative thought a more overtly economistic and ideological character, and would in turn come to influence liberal/social democratic politics, as seen with Bill Clinton's 'New Democrats' in the USA, and Tony Blair's 'New Labour' and the 'Third Way' in Britain, which accepted large parts of the New Right agenda and consolidated the turn away from post-World War II 'liberal corporatism' (Curran and Leys, 2000; Gamble, 2004; Wilentz, 2008);
3   The globalisation of neo-liberalism, or what is also referred to as neo-liberal globalisation, with the influence of the 'Washington Consensus' in policy advice to developing countries tied to funding from the International Monetary Fund or the World Bank (Stiglitz, 2002) and, more generally, the influence of international free trade agreements and entities such as the World Trade Organization (Scholte, 2005b).

All of the factors outlined here have been of great significance over the last 30 years, particularly as the economic downturn on the 1970s was successfully attributed by the

New Right to the impact of Keynesian economics, big government and the power of trade unions (Marglin and Schor, 1990; Armstrong et al., 1991). Some have argued that the global financial crisis of 2008 similarly marks the harbinger of a turn away from such untrammelled faith in free markets and deregulation (Quiggan, 2009). But we need to be wary, as Abercrombie and Turner observed many years ago in relation to Marxist theories of a dominant ideology (Abercrombie and Turner, 1978), of attributing all prevailing belief systems and power relations to an overarching system of ideological control. For example, neo-liberalism tends to be associated with individualism, but individualism, defined as a social theory advocating the liberty, rights or independent action of the individual, can co-exist with a number of political ideologies. Historically, markets as mechanisms for the allocation of economic resources have operated across a very diverse range of social formations, and a strong argument exists that attempting to eliminate markets altogether was the greatest economic mistake of twentieth-century communist societies (Nove, 1983; McMillan, 2002). As social democrats such as Australia's Hugh Stretton have observed:

> Wherever they [markets – TF] work as they should, especially where they work without generating undue inequalities of wealth or power, Left thinkers should value them as highly as any privatiser does. Indeed, more highly: the Left has such necessary tasks for government, and so much to lose from inefficient or oppressive bureaucracy, that it should economise bureaucracy every way it can. (Stretton, 1987: 27)

The critique of neo-liberalism also seems to possess some conceptual confusion about liberalism. As a body of thought, liberalism runs all the way from the individualist utopians such as von Hayek to social democratic traditions such as those associated with John Maynard Keynes, so it is often hard to gauge where the critics of neo-liberalism stand on liberalism more generally. In the United States, for instance, to be termed a liberal is to be placed on the left, not the right, of the political spectrum. It is important to note that the tradition of the New Left discussed earlier has tended to be anti-Leninist, and therefore to often see socialism as a democratic extension of liberalism, rather than the overthrow of the liberal-democratic state in the name of a collectivist social order. Authors such as Ernesto Laclau and Chantal Mouffe were quite explicit in arguing that socialist struggles involved the democratic extension of liberalism: 'The task of the Left therefore cannot be to renounce liberal-democratic ideology, but on the contrary, to deepen and extend it in the direction of a radical and plural democracy'. (Laclau and Mouffe, 1985: 176)

The claim that neo-liberalism has spread as a hegemonic ideology across the globe is less persuasive than it may first appear. While one can acknowledge, with Stiglitz (2002), the profound influence of neo-liberal economic doctrines in places such as Russia in the 1990s, the clear international counter-weight to such claims is China. Contrary to Harvey's (2005) account of China since 1980 as 'neo-liberalism with Chinese characteristics', scholars such as Kipnis (2007) and Nonini (2008) have argued that the depth of both popular and official commitment to such principles as private property rights, free markets and free trade are limited, contingent and reversible, indicative of both the historical weakness of liberalism as a political philosophy in China and the extent to which the Communist party-state has sought to manage economic reform in ways that preserve its own leadership, so that 'the strong version of neo-liberalism does not exist in China as a hegemonic project' (Nonini, 2008: 168). While China may be an exceptional case, it is a pretty large exception, given its size, its rapid growth rates since 1978, and its significance in the global economy. Moreover, there are parallels between the Chinese case and the more general model of the developmental state that continues to play a critical role in East Asia (Weiss, 2003; Yeung, 2004). Turning from Asia to Europe, it is worth reminding ourselves that while Foucault identified the German *Ordoliberals* as playing a leading role in translating neo-liberalism from moral philosophy to governmental practice in Germany in the late 1940s and 1950s, the resulting German social market economy is today understood by many as an exemplar of the neo-corporatist alternative to neo-liberalism that is based on consensus culture. For critics of Anglo–American neo-liberalism such as Michael Pusey, neo-corporatist nations such as Germany 'have managed structural economic change with far fewer social costs and presently enjoy the best quality of life in the world' (Pusey, 2009: 141). My point here is not to champion German capitalism, or indeed French, Scandinavian, Chinese or Japanese capitalism, over the models that have evolved in the United States or Britain. It is rather to point again to the ongoing significance of national variations in institutional formations and political economic dynamics, and to question arguments asserting that these have been swept aside by a tide of global neo-liberalism.

Excessive use of the term neo-liberalism resembles a problem identified by the French writer Alain Lipietz in the 1980s with the concept of imperialism (Lipietz, 1984). Drawing upon Umberto Eco's *The Name of the Rose* (Eco, 1983), Lipietz observed that just as William of Baskerville comes to the Benedictine monastery to investigate a series of murders which the monks have become convinced are signs that the Beast of the Apocalypse is among them, the work on imperialism that he surveyed found that imperialism could function as a kind of master category capable of explaining anything and everything happening in the Third World, and that no crimes or atrocities were beyond its malevolent reach. It could, for instance, be held responsible for driving industrial development in Brazil or the 'tiger economies' of East Asia, just as it could be held responsible for the lack of industrial development in sub-Saharan Africa. Unfortunately, the concept of neo-liberalism has acquired a similar conceptual elasticity. For example, Fuchs (2008: 108) associates neo-liberalism with 'the withdrawal of the state from all areas of social life', while Nick Couldry (2010: 61) identifies growing state surveillance of citizens as a feature of the neo-liberal state. The point is not so much that these propositions are right or wrong, but whether anything is added to the claim, other than a rhetorical flourish and a burnishing of one's radical credentials, by putting all such propositions under the banner of neo-liberalism. Even if we take a basic tenet of neo-liberalism – Milton Friedman's maxim that the happiness of the citizenry is inversely related to the size of the public sector – the evidence of the United States and Britain in the 2000s is unequivocal. The size of the public sector in both countries grew significantly over the 2000s – and over the whole decade, not just after the 2008–2009 bank bailouts – and it grew by more in these apparently neo-liberal countries than in countries such as France and Germany (*The Economist*, 2010). So the evidence of whether we are in an era of neo-liberalism remains decidedly mixed, not least because there seems to be little agreement on what evidence of it would be, aside from comments made at the highest level of generality and abstraction.

In light of these problems with the concept of neo-liberalism, I think it is reasonable to say that, whatever other issues or problems arise with the concept of creative industries as either analytical concept or policy discourse, the criticism that it is emblematic of or furthers neo-liberalism is one that now needs to be discounted. This is not to say that the concept of neo-liberalism does not itself raise important debates about contemporary public policy – and the translation of Michel Foucault's 1978–1979 lectures adds depth and richness to these in the English-speaking world – but that it has come to be a much-abused term that too easily lends itself to a poorly theorised condemnatory stance towards whatever happens to be a particular author or presenter's bugbear at that point in time.

Having rejected the claim that creative industries is primarily a product of a malign neo-liberalism, or that it was a politically driven fad whose historical moment has passed, we conclude with consideration of what may be the most pressing developments in the creative industries field in the near future. Definitional questions remain important, with an important question being the porosity of the boundaries between what we refer to as the creative industries on the one hand, and the whole range of entertainment industries that include activities related to tourism and sport as well as live performance and public exhibitions, on the other. This becomes particularly significant as we see how major events such as the Olympics and football World Cups are structured in such a way as to be catalysts for the development of other arts and media-related activities, as well as being central to the branding of cities and nations (Kornberger, 2010).

Another issue will be the ongoing relationship between creative industries policy discourse and cultural policies. Cultural policy since the 1970s has been moving, albeit with many fits and starts, from a supply-side, artist-centred approach that was primarily focused upon the flagship cultural institutions, to one that gave stronger consideration both to the diversity of forms of creative practice, and to questions of consumer demand and cultural markets (Flew, 2005b). Nonetheless, it remains implicitly framed by what we have referred to in this book as the 'hourglass' structure of the creative industries, where a relatively small number of gatekeepers – be they major performing arts companies and centres, large media corporations, or cultural funding bodies – constitute a distributional 'bottleneck' between the large number of prospective creative content producers and their potential audiences. The Internet and social media are an important force breaking up this linear pattern of cultural production and consumption, and by no means the only ones, yet there remains a mismatch between the large and growing numbers of individuals, small groups and SMEs engaged in the cultural sector, many of whom are quite new to the field and are pursuing 'portfolio careers', and the political power and lobbying clout of the incumbents in the sector, be they large corporations, established trade unions and producer organisations, or traditional cultural funding bodies. The challenge will be how to tap into the loosely configured, emergent networks of cultural producers – that increasingly include the consumers as well – which are increasingly the mainspring of innovation in the arts, media and cultural sectors, in ways that differ from the traditional focus of cultural policies on large-scale and highly visible institutions and interests.

A final issue that will keep emerging relates to the boundaries of an industry itself, and the relationship between the creative industries and other sectors of the economy. As we have seen, the early list-based approach taken by UK policy makers, where you could identify 13 sectors and declare them to be 'the creative industries', based upon a loose alignment of assumptions about creativity and the application of intellectual property regimes, has proved inadequate. While measurement and classificatory technologies have become more rigorous and sophisticated, the question continues to remain of why we are saying that creativity is uniquely applied and valued in these particular domains, when the wider implication of the arguments being developed is that creativity needs to be applied across all industries and domains in an increasingly knowledge-based economy and society (Hartley, 2009). The switch in the late 2000s from talk about the creative industries to that of a creative economy reflected this to some extent, although the sectoral silos and interest group alignments associated with policy formation continue to keep pushing creative industries policies towards designated arts, media and cultural sectors, and other parts of the economy towards their own designated domains, such as information technology policies or manufacturing industry policies.

An even more radical conception of the challenge, developed by the Chinese scholar Li Wuwei, is to ask whether we should in fact be thinking about a creative society? (Wuwei, 2011) If it is the case that socially valued applications of creativity come, not from abstract entities such as industries or 'the economy', but from the original and independent initiatives of people, then should the development of the creative potential of people be our starting point? Such arguments take the debate out of the logical *cul-de-sacs* that arise when one attempts to quantify the value of the arts, or consider whether software development should be considered a part of the creative industries, and into wider questions around the future of education, knowledge, lifelong learning, and the evolving social compact between citizens and the state. Thinking in such terms also brings us back to the original remit of cultural studies, which sought to transform the study of culture from the close reading of a canon of privileged texts to an understanding of the social, historical and spatial dynamics of cultural behaviour and practices of whole communities and societies. In this respect, creative industries moves from being a niche field within the domain of cultural policy, to being central to debates about the ongoing development of 21st century culture and policy.

References

Abercrombie, N. and Turner, B. (1978) The Dominant Ideology Thesis. *British Journal of Sociology* 29(2): 149–170.

Adorno, T. and Horkheimer, M. (1979) The Culture Industry: Enlightenment as Mass Deception. In J. Curran, M. Gurevitch and J. Woollacott (eds.), *Mass Communication and Society*. London: Verso, pp. 349–383.

Albarran, A. (1996) *Media Economics: Understanding Markets, Industries and Concepts*. Ames, IA: Iowa State University Press.

Albarran, A. (2010) *The Media Economy*. Hoboken, NJ: Taylor & Francis.

Albarran, A. and Dimmick, J. (1996) Concentration and Economies of Multiformity in the Communication Industries. *Journal of Media Economics* 9(4): 41–50.

Aldridge, A. (2003) *Consumption*. Cambridge: Polity Press.

Americans for the Arts (2008) *Research Services: Creative Industries*. Retrieved April 10, 2008 from www.artsusa.org/information_services/research/services/creative_industries/default.asp.

Amin, A. (2003) Industrial Districts. In E. Sheppard and T. Barnes (eds.), *A Companion to Economic Geography*. Oxford: Blackwell, pp. 149–168.

Amin, A. and Thrift, N. (2004) Introduction. In A. Amin and N. Thrift (eds.), *The Blackwell Cultural Economy Reader*. Malden, MA: Blackwell, pp. x–xxx.

Amin, A. and Thrift, N. (2007) Cultural-Economy and Cities. *Progress in Human Geography* 31(2): 143–161.

Amsden, A. (1989) *Asia's New Giant: South Korea and Late Industrialisation*. Oxford: Oxford University Press.

Anderson, K. (2008) Cultural Geography: An Account. In T. Bennett and J. Frow (eds.), *The SAGE Handbook of Cultural Analysis*. London: Sage, pp. 46–65.

Apple, M. (2004) Schooling, Markets and an Audit Culture. *Educational Policy* 18(4): 614–621.

Appleby, J. (2003) Consumption in Early Modern Social Thought. In D. B. Clarke, M. A. Doel and K. M. L. Housiaux (eds.), *The Consumption Reader*. London: Routledge, pp. 31–39.

Armstrong, P., Glyn, A. and Harrison, J. (1991) *Capitalism since 1945*. Oxford: Basil Blackwell.

Arthur, W. B. (2009) *The Nature of Technology: What it is and How it Evolves*. New York: Free Press.

Bagdikian, B. (2004) *The (New) Media Monopoly* (6th edn). Boston, MA: Beacon.

Bakhshi, H., Desai, R. and Freeman, A. (2010) *Not Rocket Science: A Roadmap for Arts and Cultural R&D*. Brisbane: Australian Research Council Centre for Creative Industries and Innovation.

Banks, M. and Hesmondhalgh, D. (2009) Looking for Work in Creative Industries Policy. *International Journal of Cultural Policy* 15(4): 415–430.

Banks, M. and O'Connor, J. (2009) After the Creative Industries. *International Journal of Cultural Policy* 15(4): 365–373.

Barber, B. (2000) Jihad versus McWorld. In F. J. Lechner and J. Boli (eds.), *The Globalization Reader*. Malden, MA: Blackwell, pp. 21–26.

Barlow, J. P. (1996) Selling Wine without Bottles: The Economy of Mind on the Global Net. In P. Ludlow (ed.), *High Noon on the Electronic Frontier*. Cambridge, MA: MIT Press, pp. 9–34.

Barrett, M. (1991) *The Politics of Truth: From Marx to Foucault*. Cambridge: Polity Press.

Barrowclough, D. and Kozul-Wright, Z. (2008) Voice, Choice and Diversity through Creative Industries: Towards a New Development Agenda. In D. Barrowclough and Z. Kozul-Wright (eds.), *Creative Industries and Developing Countries: Voice, Choice and Economic Growth*. London: Routledge, pp. 3–38.

Bassett, K., Smith, I., Banks, M. and O'Connor, J. (2005) Urban Dilemmas of Competition and Cohesion in Cultural Policy. In N. Buck, I. Gordon, A. Harding and I. Turok (eds.), *Changing Cities: Rethinking Urban Competitiveness, Cohesion and Governance*. Basingstoke: Palgrave Macmillan, pp. 132–153.

Baudrillard, J. (1988) For a Critique of the Political Economy of the Sign. In M. Poster (ed.), *Jean Baudrillard: Selected Writings*. Cambridge: Polity Press, pp. 57–97.

Bauman, Z. (2000) *The Individualized Society*. Malden, MA: Polity Press.

Beaverstock, J., Smith, R. and Taylor, P. (2006) World–City Network: A New Metageography? In N. Brenner and R. Kell (eds.), *The Global Cities Reader*. London: Routledge, pp. 96–104.

Beck, U. (2000) *The Brave New World of Work*. Cambridge: Polity Press.

Becker, H. (1982) *Art Worlds*. Berkeley, CA: University of California Press.

Beckett, C. (2008) *Supermedia: Saving Journalism so it Can Save the World*. Malden, MA: Blackwell.

Behrent, M. (2009) Liberalism without Humanism: Michel Foucault and the Free Market Creed 1976–1979. *Modern Intellectual History* 6(3): 539–568.

Beilby, W. T. and Beilby, D. D. (1994) 'All Hits are Flukes': Institutionalised Decision Making and the Rhetoric of Network Prime-Time Program Development. *American Journal of Sociology* 99(5): 1287–1313.

Beng Huat, C. and Iwabuchi, K. (2008) East Asian TV Dramas: Identifications, Sentiments and Effects. In C. Beng Huat and K. Iwabuchi (eds.), *East Asian Pop Culture: Analysing the Korean Wave*. Hong Kong: Hong Kong University Press, pp. 1–12.

Benkler, Y. (2001) The Battle for the Institutional Ecosystem in the Digital Environment. *Communications of the ACM* 44(2): 84–90.

Benkler, Y. (2006) *The Wealth of Networks*. New Haven, CT: Yale University Press.

Bennett, T. (1982) Theories of Media, Theories of Society. In M. Gurevitch, T. Bennett, J. Curran and J. Woollacott (eds.), *Culture, Society and the Media*. London: Methuen, pp. 30–55.

Bennett, T. (1992) Putting Policy into Cultural Studies. In L. Grossberg, C. Nelson and P. Tresichler (eds.), *Cultural Studies*. New York: Routledge, pp. 23–37.

Bennett, T. (1995) *The Birth of the Museum: History, Theory, Policy*. London: Routledge.

Bennett, T. (1998) *Culture: A Reformer's Science*. Sydney: Allen & Unwin.

Bennett, T. (2007) Intellectuals, Culture, Policy: The Technical, the Practical, and the Critical. In T. Bennett, *Critical Trajectories: Culture, Society, Intellectuals*. Oxford: Blackwell, pp. 141–162.

Bennett, T., Emmison, M. and Frow, J. (1999) *Accounting for Tastes: Australian Everyday Cultures*. Cambridge: Cambridge University Press.

Benyon, J. and Dunkerley, D. (2000) General Introduction. In J. Benyon and D. Dunkerley (eds.), *Globalisation: The Reader*. New York: Routledge, pp. 1–33.

Bettig, R. (1996) *Copyrighting Culture: The Political Economy of Intellectual Property*. Boulder, CO: Westview Press.

Bianchini, F. (1987) GLC RIP, 1981–1986. *New Formations* 1: 103–107.

Bilton, C. (2007) *Management and Creativity: From Creative Industries to Creative Management*. Oxford: Blackwell.

Bilton, C. and Leary, R. (2002) What Managers can do for Creativity? Brokering Creativity in the Creative Industries. *International Journal of Cultural Policy* 8(2): 49–64.

Blair, T. (1999) Foreword. In National Advisory Committee on Creative and Cultural Education, *All Our Futures: Creativity, Culture and Education*. Report to the Secretary of State for Education and Employment, and the Secretary of State for Culture, Media and Sport. Retrieved June 10, 2010, from www.cypni.org.uk/downloads/alloutfutures.pdf.

Bloustein, G., Peters, M. and Luckman, S. (eds.) (2008) *Sonic Synergies: Music, Identity, Technology and Community*. Aldershot: Ashgate.

Boas, T. and Gans-Moore, J. (2009) Neo-Liberalism: From New Liberal Philosophy to Anti-Liberal Slogan. *Studies in Comparative International Development* 44(1): 137–161.

Bockris, V. (1989) *The Life and Death of Andy Warhol*. New York: Bantam Books.

Bocock, R. (1993) *Consumption*. London: Routledge.

Boggs, J. (2009) Cultural Industries and the Creative Economy – Vague but Useful Concepts. *Geography Compass* 3(4): 1483–1498.

Boltanski, L. and Chiapello, E. (2005) *The New Spirit of Capitalism*. Trans. G. Elliott. London: Verso.

Bonner, F. (2003) *Ordinary Television*. London: Sage.

Bourdieu, P. (1984) *Distinction: A Social Critique of the Judgement of Taste*. Trans. R. Nice. London: Routledge.

Boyd-Barrett, O. (1995) The Political Economy Approach. In O. Boyd-Barrett and C. Newbold (eds.), *Approaches to Media: A Reader*. London: Arnold, pp. 186–192.

Braman, S. (2003) Technology. In J. Downing, D. McQuail, P. Schlesinger and E. Wartella (eds.), *The SAGE Handbook of Media Studies*. Thousand Oaks, CA: Sage, pp. 123–144.

Braman, S. (2004) Where Has Media Policy Gone? Defining the Field in the Twenty-First Century. *Communications Law and Policy* 9: 153–176.

Brennan-Horley, C., Luckman, S., Gibson, C. and Willoughby-Smith, J. (2010) GIS, Ethnography and Cultural Research: Putting Maps Back into Ethnographic Mapping. *The Information Society* 26(2): 92–103.

Bridge, G. and Watson S. (2003) City Interventions. In G. Bridge and S. Watson (eds.), *A Companion to the City*. Malden, MA: Blackwell.

Brown, A., O'Connor, J. and Cohen, S. (2000) Local Music Policies within a Global Music Industry: Cultural Quarters in Manchester and Sheffield. *Geoforum* 31: 437–451.

Brown, J. S. and Duguid, P. (2000) *The Social Life of Information*. Boston, MA: Harvard Business School Press.

Brown, W. (2003) Neo-Liberalism and the End of Liberal Democracy. *Theory and Event* 7(1). Available online at: http://muse.jhu.edu.ezp01.library.qut.edu.au/journals/theory_and_event/v007/7.1brown.html. Retrieved April 4, 2009.

Brown, W. (2006) American Nightmare: Neoliberalism, Neoconservatism and De-Democratization. *Political Theory* 34(6): 690–714.

Browne, Lord (2010) *Securing a Sustainable Future for Higher Education: An Independent Review of Higher Education Funding and Student Finance*. London: UK Government. London: HMSO.

Bruns, A. (2008) *Blogs, Wikipedia, Second Life and Beyond: From Production to Produsage*. New York: Peter Lang.

Bryman, A. (2004) *The Disneyization of Society*. Thousand Oaks, CA: Sage.

Bulow, J. and Summers, L. (1986) A Theory of Dual Labour Markets with Application to Industrial Policy, Discrimination, and Keynesian Unemployment. *Journal of Labor Economics* 4(3): 376–414.

Bureau of Transport and Communications Economics (1991) *Economic Aspects of Broadcasting Regulation*. BTCE Report 71. Canberra: Australian Government Publishing Service.

Burgess, J. and Green, J. (2009) *YouTube*. Digital Media and Society Series. Cambridge: Polity Press.

Butler, J. (2009) Save California's Universities. *The Guardian*. 4 October. http://www.guardian.co.uk/commentisfree/cifamerica/2009/sep/30/california-university-berkeley-budget-protest.

Cairncross, F. (1998) *The Death of Distance: How the Communications Revolution will Change Our Lives*. London: Orion Business Books.

Callon, M., Méadel, C. and Rabeharisoa, V. (2004) The Economy of Qualities. In A. Amin and N. Thrift (eds.), *The Blackwell Cultural Economy Reader*. Oxford: Blackwell, pp. 58–79.

Campbell, C. (1983) Romanticism and the Consumer Ethic: Intimations of a Weber-Style Thesis. *Sociological Analysis* 44(4): 279–295.

Carter, M. (2003) *Fashion Classics from Carlyle to Barthes*. Oxford: Berg.

Castells, M. (1996) *The Rise of the Network Society*. Vol. I of *The Information Age: Economy, Society and Culture*. Oxford: Blackwell.

Castells, M. (1998) *The Power of Identity*. Vol. II of *The Information Age: Economy, Society and Culture*. Oxford: Blackwell.

Castles, F. and Davidson, A. (2000) *Citizenship and Migration: Globalization and the Politics of Belonging*. London: Macmillan.

Caust, J. (2003) Putting the 'Art' Back into Arts Policy Making: How Arts Policy has been 'Captured' by the Economists and the Marketers. *International Journal of Cultural Policy* 9(1): 51–63.

Caves, R. (2000) *Creative Industries: Contracts between Art and Commerce.* Cambridge, MA: Harvard University Press.

Centre for International Economics (CIE) (2009) *Creative Industries Economic Analysis: Final Report.* Prepared for Enterprise Connect and the Creative Industries Innovation Centre. Canberra and Sydney: Centre for International Economics, 30 June.

Chesbrough, H. (2006) Open Innovation: A New Paradigm for Understanding Industrial Innovation. In H. Chesbrough, W. Vanhaverbeke and J. West (eds.), *Open Innovation: Researching a New Paradigm.* Oxford: Oxford University Press, pp. 1–16.

Choi, J. (2008) The New Korean Wave of U. In H. Anheier and Y. Raj Isar (eds.), *The Cultural Economy.* Los Angeles, CA: Sage, pp. 148–154.

Christensen, C. (2003) *The Innovator's Dilemma.* New York: Harper Collins.

Clapson, M. (2003) *Suburban Century: Social Change and Urban Growth in England and the USA.* London: Berg.

Clegg, S., Kornberger, M. and Pitsis, T. (2005) *Managing and Organisations: An Introduction to Theory and Practice.* London: Sage.

Coe, N. and Johns, J. (2004) Beyond Production Clusters: Towards a Critical Political Economy of Networks in the Film and Television Industries. In D. Power and A. J. Scott (eds.), *Cultural Industries and the Production of Culture.* New York: Routledge, pp. 188–206.

Collins, R., Garnham, N. and Locksley, G. (1988) *The Economics of Television: The UK Case.* London: Sage.

Collis, C., Felton, E. and Graham, P. (2010) Beyond the Inner City: Real and Imagined Places in Creative Place Policy and Practice. *The Information Society* 26(2): 104–112.

Considine, M. (1994) *Public Policy: A Critical Approach.* Melbourne: Macmillan.

Cooke, P. and Lazzeretti, L. (2008) Creative Cities: An Introduction. In P. Cooke and L. Lazzeretti (eds.), *Creative Cities, Creative Clusters and Local Economic Development.* Cheltenham, UK: Edward Elgar, pp. 1–22.

Coombe, R. (1998) *The Cultural Life of Intellectual Property: Authorship, Appropriation, and the Law.* Durham, NC: Duke University Press.

Couldry, N. (2010) *Why Voice Matters: Culture and Politics after Neoliberalism.* London: Sage.

Court, D. (1994) Capture Theory and Cultural Policy. *Media Information Australia* 73, August: 23–25.

Cowen, T. (2002) *Creative Destruction: How Globalization is Changing the World's Cultures.* Princeton, NJ: Princeton University Press.

Coyle, D. (1998) *The Weightless World.* London: Capstone.

Craik, J. (1996) The Potential and Limits of Cultural Policy Strategies. *Culture and Policy* 7(1): 177–204.

Craik, J. (2007) *Re-Visioning Arts and Cultural Policy: Current Impasses and Future Directions.* Canberra: ANU E-Press.

Crotty, J., Epstein, G. and Kelly, P. (1998) Multinational Corporations in the Neo-liberal Regime. In D. Baker, G. Epstein and R. Pollin (eds.), *Globalization and Progressive Economic Policy*. Cambridge: Cambridge University Press, pp. 117–143.

Cunningham, S. (1992) *Framing Culture: Criticism and Policy in Australia*. Sydney: Allen & Unwin.

Cunningham, S. (2002) From Cultural to Creative Industries: Theory, Industry and Policy Implications. *Media International Australia* 102: 54–65.

Cunningham, S. (2005) Creative Enterprises. In J. Hartley (ed.), *Creative Industries*. Malden, MA: Blackwell, pp. 282–298.

Cunningham, S. (2007) Creative Industries as Policy and Discourse outside the United Kingdom. *Global Media and Communication* 3(3): 347–352.

Cunningham, S. (2009) Creative Industries as a Globally Contestable Policy Field. *Chinese Journal of Communication* 2(1): 13–24.

Cunningham, S. (2010) *In the Vernacular: A Generation of Australian Culture and Controversy*. Brisbane: University of Queensland Press.

Cunningham, S. and Flew, T. (2002) Policy. In T. Miller (ed.), *Television Studies*. London: British Film Institute (BFI).

Cunningham, S. and Potts, J. (2009) New Economics for the New Media. In G. Goggin and L. Hjorth (eds.), *Mobile Technologies: From Telecommunications to Media*. London: Routledge, pp. 131–142.

Cunningham, S. and Turner, G. (2010) Introduction. In S. Cunningham and G. Turner (eds.), *The Media and Communication in Australia* (3rd edn). Sydney: Allen & Unwin, pp. 1–11.

Curran, J. (2010) The Future of Journalism. *Journalism Studies* 11(4): 464–476.

Curran, J. and Leys, C. (2000) Media and the Decline of Liberal Corporatism in Britain. In J. Curran and M.-J. Park (eds.), *Dewesternizing Media Studies*. London: Routledge, pp. 221–236.

Curran, J. and Park, M.-J. (2000) Beyond Globalization Theory. In J. Curran and M.-J. Park (eds.), *Dewesternizing Media Studies*. London: Routledge, pp. 3–18.

Currid, E. (2007) *The Warhol Economy: How Fashion, Art and Music Drive New York City*. Princeton, NJ: Princeton University Press.

Davis, H. and Scase, R. (2000) *Managing Creativity: The Dynamics of Work and Organization*. Buckingham: Open University Press.

de Certeau, M. (1984) *The Practice of Everyday Life*. Berkeley, CA: University of California Press.

De Propris, L. and Hypponen, L. (2008) Creative Clusters and Governance: The Dominance of the Hollywood Film Cluster. In P. Cooke and L. Lazzeretti (eds.), *Creative Cities, Cultural Clusters and Local Economic Development*. Cheltenham, UK: Edward Elgar, pp. 258–286.

De Propris, L., Chapain, C., Cooke, P., MacNeill, S. and Mateos-Garcia, J. (2009) *The Geography of Creativity*. NESTA Interim Report, April. London: National Endowment for Education, Science and the Arts.

De Vany, A. (2004) *Hollywood Economics: How Extreme Uncertainty Shapes the Film Industry*. New York: Routledge.

Dean, J. (2008) Enjoying Neoliberalism. *Cultural Politics* 4(1): 47–72.

Department of Communications and the Arts (1994) *Creative Nation: Commonwealth Cultural Policy*. Canberra: Australian Government Printing Service.

Department of Communications, Information Technology and the Arts (DCITA) (2004) *Digital Content Industry Action Agenda*. Retrieved May 21, 2010, from www.archive.dcita.gov.au/2007/12/digital_content_industry_action_agenda/.

Department of Culture, Media and Sport (1998) *Creative Industries Mapping Document*. London: Department of Culture, Media and Sport. Retrieved May 12, 2010, from http://webarchive.nationalarchives.gov.uk/+/http://www.culture.gov.uk/reference_library/publications/4740.aspx.

Department of Culture, Media and Sport (2001) *Creative Industries Mapping Document 2001*. London: Department of Culture, Media and Sport. Retrieved May 26, 2007, from www.culture.gov.uk/reference_library/publications/4632.aspx.

Department of Culture, Media and Sport (2004) *Government and the Value of Culture*. London: Department of Culture, Media and Sport. Retrieved May 25, 2010, from http://webarchive.nationalarchives.gov.uk/+/http://www.culture.gov.uk/reference_library/publications/4581.aspx/.

Department of Culture, Media and Sport (2007) *Creative Industries Economic Estimates 2007: Statistical Bulletin*. London: Department of Culture, Media and Sport.

Department of Culture, Media and Sport (2008a) *Creative Britain: New Talents for a New Economy*. Report prepared for Department for Business Enterprise and Regulatory Reform and Department for Innovation, Universities and Skills. London: HMSO.

Department of Culture, Media and Sport (2008b) *Supporting Excellence in the Arts – From Measurement to Judgement*. McMaster Report. London: Department of Culture, Media and Sport.

Department of Culture, Media and Sport/Department for Business, Innovation and Skills (DCMS/DBIS) (2009) *Digital Britain: Final Report*. June. London: DCMS/DBIS. Retrieved May 26, 2010, from http://interactive.bis.gov.uk/digitalbritain/.

Department of State Development and Industry (2003) *Creativity is Big Business: A Framework for the Future*. Brisbane: Queensland Government.

Design Institute of Australia (DIA) (2010) *What is a Designer?* Retrieved September 21, 2010, from www.dia.org.au/index.cfm?id=186.

Design Singapore Council (DSC) (2010) *Design for Enterprises*. Retrieved September 21, 2010, from www.designsingapore.org/RunScript.asp?page=76&p=ASP\Pg76.asp.

Deuze, M. (2007) *Media Work*. Cambridge: Polity Press.

Dicken, P. (2003a) 'Placing' Firms: Grounding the Debate on the 'Global' Corporation. In J. Peck and H. W. C. Yeung (eds.), *Remaking the Global Economy*. London: Sage, pp. 27–44.

Dicken, P. (ed.) (2003b) *Global Shift* (4th edn). London: Sage.

Dicken, P. (2007) Economic Globalization: Corporations. In G. Ritzer (ed.), *The Blackwell Companion to Globalization*. Malden, MA: Blackwell, pp. 291–306.

Dirlik, A. (2003) Global Modernity? Modernity in an Age of Global Capitalism. *European Journal of Social Theory* 6(3): 275–292.

Dobb, M. (1973) *Theories of Value and Distribution since Adam Smith*. Cambridge: Cambridge University Press.

Dodgson, M., Gann, D. and Salter, A. (2002) The Intensification of Innovation. *International Journal of Innovation Management* 6(1): 53–83.

Dodgson, M., Gann, D. and Salter, A. (2005) *Think, Play, Do: Technology, Innovation and Organization*. Oxford: Oxford University Press.

Dominguez, V. (2000) Invoking Culture: The Messy Side of 'Cultural Politics'. In G. Bradford, M. Gary and G. Wallach (eds.), *The Politics of Culture: Policy Perspectives for Individuals, Institutions and Communities*. New York: New Press, pp. 20–37.

Donald, S. H. and Gammack, J. (2007) *Tourism and the Branded City: Film and Identity on the Pacific Rim*. Aldershot: Ashgate.

Doremus, P., Keller, W., Pauly, L. and Reuich, S. (1998) *The Myth of the Global Corporation*. Princeton, NJ: Princeton University Press.

Douglas, M. and Isherwood, B. (2000) The Uses of Goods. In M. J. Lee (ed.), *The Consumer Society Reader*. Malden, MA: Blackwell, pp. 73–83.

Doyle, G. (2002) *Understanding Media Economics*. London: Sage.

Drahos, P. and Braithwaite, J. (2002) *Information Feudalism: Who Owns the Knowledge Economy?* London: Earthscan.

du Gay, P. and Pryke, M. (2002) Cultural Economy: An Introduction. In P. du Gay and M. Pryke (eds.), *Cultural Economy: Cultural Analysis and Commercial Life*. London: Sage, pp. 1–19.

Dunleavy, P. and O'Leary, B. (1987) *Theories of the State: The Politics of Liberal Democracy*. Basingstoke: Macmillan.

Dunning, J. (2000) Regions, Globalization and the Knowledge-based Economy: The Issues Stated. In J. Dunning (ed.), *Regions, Globalization and the Knowledge-Based Economy*. Oxford: Oxford University Press, pp. 8–41.

During, S. (1993) Introduction. In S. During (ed.), *The Cultural Studies Reader*. London: Routledge, pp. 1–25.

During, S. (2010) *Exit Capitalism: Literary Culture, Theory and Post-Secular Modernity*. London: Routledge.

Dyson, J. (2010) *Ingenious Britain: Making the UK the Leading High-Tech Exporter in Europe*. Report prepared for the Conservative Party, March.

Eckersley, S. (2008) Supporting Excellence in the Arts: From Measurement to Judgement. *Cultural Trends* 17(3): 183–187.

Eco, U. (1983) *The Name of the Rose*. Trans. W. Weaver. San Diego, CA: Harcourt Brace Jovanovich.

Economist, The (2010) The Growth of the State: Leviathan Stirs Again. January 21. Retrieved July 15, 2010, from www.economist.com/node/15328727.

Elliott, L. and Atkinson, D. (2007) *Fantasy Island*. London: Constable and Robinson.

Ellis, B. E. (1991) *American Psycho*. New York: Vintage.

Eribon, D. (1991) *Michel Foucault*. Trans. B. Wing. Cambridge, MA: Harvard University Press.

Ernst, D. and Kim, L. (2002) Global Production Networks, Knowledge Diffusion, and Local Capacity Formation. *Research Policy* 31: 1417–1429.

Esping-Andersen, G. (1990) *The Three Worlds of Welfare Capitalism.* Cambridge: Polity Press.

European Commission (2005) Principles and Guidelines for the Community's Audiovisual Policy in the Digital Age. Retrieved June 9, 2010, from http://europa.eu/legislation_summaries/audiovisual_and_media/l24223_en.htm.

European Commission (2010) *Green Paper: Unlocking the Potential of the Cultural and Creative Industries.* COM(2010) 183. Brussels: EC.

Evans, G. (2009) Creative Cities, Creative Spaces and Urban Policy, *Urban Studies* 46(5/6): 1003–1040.

Fay, S. (1997) It's Wimbledonisation. *The Independent.* December 28. Retrieved May 27, 2010, from www.independent.co.uk/life-style/its-wimbledonisation-1290844.html.

Featherstone, M. (1991) *Consumer Culture and Postmodernism.* London: Sage.

Ferguson, P. R. (1988) *Industrial Economics: Issues and Perspectives.* Basingstoke: Macmillan.

Fitzgerald, B. (2006) Creative Commons: Accessing, Negotiating and Remixing Online Content. In P. Thomas and J. Servaes (eds.), *Intellectual Property Rights and Communications in Asia.* New Delhi: Sage, pp. 219–225.

Flew, T. (2002) Beyond *ad hocery*: Defining Creative Industries. In M. Volkering (ed.), *Cultural Sites, Cultural Theory, Cultural Policy: Proceedings of the Second International Conference on Cultural Policy Research.* Wellington, New Zealand: Te Papa. January 23–26, pp. 181–191.

Flew, T. (2003) Creative Industries and the New Economy. In G. Argyrous and F. Stilwell (eds.), *Economics as a Social Science: Readings in Political Economy.* Sydney: Pluto Press.

Flew, T (2004a) Media and Communication. In R. Wissler, B. Haseman, S.-A. Wallace and M. Keane (eds.), *Innovation in Australian Arts, Media and Design: Fresh Challenges for the Tertiary Sector.* Sydney: Flaxton Press, pp. 111–122.

Flew, T. (2004b) Creativity, the 'New Humanism' and Cultural Studies. *Continuum: Journal of Media and Cultural Studies* 18(2): 161–178.

Flew, T. (2004c) Creativity, Cultural Studies and Service Industries. *Communication and Critical/Cultural Studies* 1(2): 176–193.

Flew, T. (2005a) Creative Commons and the Creative Industries. *Media and Arts Law Review* 10(4): 257–264.

Flew, T. (2005b) Sovereignty and Software: Rethinking Cultural Policy in a Global Creative Economy. *International Journal of Cultural Policy* 11(3): 243–259.

Flew, T. (2006) The Social Contract and Beyond in Broadcast Media Policy. *Television and New Media* 7(3): 282–305.

Flew, T. (2007) *Understanding Global Media.* Basingstoke: Palgrave Macmillan.

Flew, T. (2008) *New Media: An Introduction* (3rd edn). Melbourne: Oxford University Press.

Flew, T. (2009a) Online Media and User-Created Content: Case Studies in News Media Repositioning in the Australian Media Environment. In T. Flew (ed.), *Communication, Creativity and Global Citizenship: Refereed Proceedings of the Australian and New Zealand Communications Association Annual Conference.* Brisbane, July 8–10. Retrieved February 17, 2010, from www.proceedings.anzca09.org.

Flew, T. (2009b) Democracy, Participation and Convergent Media: Case Studies in Contemporary Online News Journalism in Australia. *Communication, Politics and Culture* 42(2): 87–115.

Flew, T. (2009c) The Cultural Economy Moment? *Cultural Science* 2(1). Available at www.cultural-science.org/journal/index.php/culturalscience/article/view/23/79.

Flew, T. (2010) New Media Policies. In M. Deuze (ed.), *Managing Media Work*. Los Angeles, CA: Sage, pp. 59–72.

Flew, T. (2012) Challenges of Suburban Cultural Research: The Australian 'Creative Suburbia' Project. *International Journal of Cultural Studies* 15(4): (forthcoming).

Flew, T. and Cunningham, S. (1997) Media Policy. In D. Woodward, A. Parkin and J. Summers (eds.), *Government, Politics, Power and Policy in Australia*. Melbourne: Longman Cheshire, pp. 468–487.

Flew, T. and McElhinney, S. (2005) Globalization and the Structure of New Media Industries. In L. Lievrouw and S. Livingstone (2nd eds.), *Handbook of New Media*. London: Sage, pp. 287–306.

Flew, T. and Wilson, J. (2010) Journalism as Social Networking: The Australian *You Decide* Project and the 2007 Federal Election. *Journalism: Theory, Practice and Criticism* 11(2): 131–147.

Florida, R. (2002) *The Rise of the Creative Class*. New York: Basic Books.

Florida, R. (2007) *The Flight of the Creative Class*. New York: Harper Collins.

Florida, R. (2008) *Who's Your City: How the Creative Economy is Making Where to Live the Most Important Decision of Your Life*. New York: Basic Books.

Fogel, R. W. (1999) Catching Up with the Economy. *American Economic Review* 89(1): 1–21.

Footer, M. and Graber, C. B. (2000) Trade Liberalization and Cultural Policy. *Journal of International Economic Law* 3(1): 115–144.

Fortunati, L. and Deuze, M. (2010) Atypical Newswork, Atypical Media Management. In M. Deuze (ed.), *Managing Media Work*. Thousand Oaks, CA: Sage, pp. 111–120.

Foster, P. (2008) Long Tail Theory Contradicted as Study Reveals 10m Digital Music Tracks Unsold. *Times Online*. December 22. Retrieved May 24, 2010, from http://entertainment.timesonline.co.uk/tol/arts_and_entertainment/music/article5380304.ece.

Foucault, M. (1991a) Governmentality. In G. Burchell, C. Gordon and P. Miller (eds.), *The Foucault Effect: Studies in Governmentality*. London: Harvester Wheatsheaf, pp. 87–104.

Foucault, M. (1991b) Politics and the Study of Discourse. In G. Burchell, C. Gordon and P. Miller (eds.), *The Foucault Effect: Studies in Governmentality*. London: Harvester Wheatsheaf, pp. 53–72.

Foucault, M. (1991c) *Remarks on Marx: Conversations with Duccio Trombadori*. Trans. R. J. Goldstein and J. Cascaito. New York: Semiotext(e).

Foucault, M. (2008) *The Birth of Biopolitics: Lectures at the Collège de France 1978–1979*. Ed. M. Senellart. Trans. G. Burchell. Basingstoke: Palgrave Macmillan.

Freedman, D. (2008) *The Politics of Media Policy*. Cambridge: Polity Press.

Friedman, M. and Freidman, R. (1980) *Free to Choose*. New York: Harcourt Brace Jovanovich.

Friedman, T. (2005) *The World is Flat: A Brief History of the Twenty-First Century*. New York: Farrar, Strauss and Giroux.

Friedmann, J. (1995) Where We Stand: A Decade of World City Research. In P. Knox and P. J. Taylor (eds.), *World Cities in a World-System*. New York: Cambridge University Press, pp. 21–47.

Friedmann, J. (2006) The World City Hypothesis. In N. Brenner and R. Keil (eds.), *The Global Cities Reader*. London: Routledge, pp. 67–71.

Friedmann, J. and Wolff, G. (2006) World City Formation: An Agenda for Research and Action. In N. Brenner and R. Keil (eds.), *The Global Cities Reader*. London: Routledge, pp. 57–66.

Frith, S., Cloonan, M. and Williamson, J. (2009) On Music as a Creative Industry. In A. Pratt and P. Jeffcutt (eds.), *Creativity, Innovation and the Cultural Economy*. London: Routledge, pp. 74–89.

Frow, J. (1995) *Cultural Studies and Cultural Value*. Oxford: Oxford University Press.

Fuchs, C. (2008) *Internet and Society: Social Theory in the Information Age*. New York: Routledge.

Galloway, S. and Dunlop, S. (2007) A Critique of Definitions of the Cultural and Creative Industries in Public Policy. *International Journal of Cultural Policy* 13(1): 17–31.

Galperin, H. (1999) Cultural Industries Policy in Regional Trade Agreements: The Case of NAFTA, the European Union and MERCOSUR. *Media, Culture and Society* 21(5): 627–648.

Gamble, A. (2001) Neo-Liberalism. *Capital and Class* 25: 127–134.

Gamble, A. (2004) British National Capitalism since the War: Declinism, Thatcherism and New Labour. In J. Perraton and B. Clift (eds.), *Where are National Capitalisms Now?* Basingstoke: Palgrave Macmillan, pp. 33–49.

García, L. (2002) The Architecture of Global Networking Technologies. In S. Sassen (ed.), *Global Networks, Linked Cities*. New York: Routledge, pp. 39–70.

Garnham, N. (1987) Public Policy and the Cultural Industries. *Cultural Studies* 1(1): 23–37.

Garnham, N. (1990) *Capitalism and Communication*. London: Sage.

Garnham, N. (1995) Political Economy and Cultural Studies: Reconciliation or Divorce? *Critical Studies in Mass Communication* 12(1): 62–71.

Garnham, N. (2005) From Cultural to Creative Industries: An Analysis of the Implications of the 'Creative Industries' Approach to Arts and Media Policy Making in the United Kingdom. *International Journal of Cultural Policy* 11(1): 15–29.

Gellner, E. (1983) *Nations and Nationalism*. Oxford: Basil Blackwell.

Gertler, M. (2003) A Cultural Economic Geography of Production. In K. Anderson, M. Domosh, N. Thrift and S. Pile (eds.), *Handbook of Cultural Geography*. Thousand Oaks, CA: Sage, pp. 131–146.

Giarini, O. (2002) The Globalisation of Services in Economic Theory and Economic Practice: Some Conceptual Issues. In J. R. Cuadrado-Roura, L. Rubalcaba-Bermejo and J. R. Bryson (eds.), *Trading Services in the Global Economy*. Cheltenham, UK: Edward Elgar, pp. 58–77.

Gibson, C. and Kong, L. (2005) Cultural Economy: A Critical Review. *Progress in Human Geography* 29(5): 541–561.

Gibson, M. (2007) *Culture and Power: A History of Cultural Studies*. Oxford: Berg.

Gibson-Graham, J. K. (2003) Poststructural Interventions. In E. Sheppard and T. J. Barnes (eds.), *A Companion to Economic Geography*. Malden, MA: Blackwell, pp. 95–110.

Giddens, A. (1990) *The Consequences of Modernity*. Oxford: Polity Press.

Giddens, A. (1998) *The Third Way*. Cambridge: Polity Press.

Giddens, A. (2003) *Runaway World: How Globalization is Reshaping Our Lives*. New York: Routledge.

Gill, I. and Kharas, H. (2007) *An East Asian Renaissance: Ideas for Economic Growth*. Washington, DC: World Bank.

Girard, A. (1982) Cultural Industries: A Handicap or a New Opportunity for Cultural Development? In UNESCO, *Cultural Industries: A Challenge for the Future*. Paris: UNESCO, pp. 24–39.

Giroux, H. (2005) The Terror of Neoliberalism: Rethinking the Significance of Cultural Politics. *College Literature* 32(1): 1–19.

Glaesar, E. (2000) The New Economics of Urban and Regional Growth. In G. Clark, M. Feldman and M. Gertler (eds.), *The Oxford Handbook of Economic Geography*. Oxford: Oxford University Press, pp. 83–98.

Glyn, A., Armstrong, P. and Harrison, J. (1991) *Capitalism since 1945*. Oxford: Basil Blackwell.

Gordon, C. (1991) Government Rationality: An Introduction. In G. Burchell, C. Gordon and P. Miller (eds.), *The Foucault Effect: Studies in Governmentality*. Hemel Hempstead: Harvester Wheatsheaf, pp. 1–51.

Gordon, I. and McCann, P. (2001) Industrial Clusters: Complexes, Agglomerations, and/or Social Networks? *Urban Studies* 37(3): 513–532.

Gournelos, T. (2009) Puppets, Slaves, and Sex Changes: Mr. Garrison and *South Park*'s Performative Sexuality. *Television and New Media* 10(3): 270–293.

Graber, C. B. (2006) The New UNESCO Convention on Cultural Diversity: A Counterbalance to the WTO? *Journal of International Economic Law* 9(3): 553–574.

Graham, A. and Davies, G. (1997) *Broadcasting, Society and Policy in the Multimedia Age*. Luton: John Libbey Media.

Grant, P. and Wood, C. (2004) *Blockbusters and Trade Wars: Popular Culture in a Globalised World*. Vancouver: Douglas & McIntyre.

Greenhalgh, L. (1998) From Arts Policy to Creative Economy. *Media International Australia* 87: 84–94.

Grodach, C. and Loukaitou-Sideris, A. (2007) Cultural Development Strategies and Urban Revitalization. *International Journal of Cultural Policy* 13(4): 349–370.

Grossberg, L. (2006) Does Cultural Studies Have Futures? Should It? (Or What's the Matter with New York?). *Cultural Studies* 20(1): 1–32.

Grossberg, L., Nelson, C. and Treichler, P. (1992) Cultural Studies: An Introduction. In L. Grossberg, C. Nelson and P. Treichler (eds.), *Cultural Studies*. New York: Routledge, pp. 1–17.

Guala, F. (2006) Critical Notice – Review of *Naissance de la Biopolitique: Cours au Collège de, France, 1978–1979*. *Economics and Philosophy* 22: 429–439.

Gyford, J. (1985) *The Politics of Local Socialism*. London: Allen & Unwin.

Hackett, K., Ramsden, P., Sattar, D. and Guene, C. (2000) *Banking on Culture: New Financial Instruments for Expanding the Cultural Sector in Europe*. Report prepared for the Arts Council England by the North West Arts Board. Final Report, September. London: Gulbenkian Foundation.

Hajer, M. and Laws, D. (2006) Ordering through Discourse. In M. Moran, M. Rein and R. E. Goodin (eds.), *The Oxford Handbook of Public Policy*. Oxford: Oxford University Press, pp. 251–267.

Hall, P. (1966) *The World Cities*. New York: McGraw-Hill.

Hall, P. (1998) C*ities in Civilization: Culture, Innovation and Urban Order*. London: Orion Phoenix.

Hall, S. (1977) Culture, the Media and the 'Ideological Effect. In J. Curran, M. Gurevitch and J. Woollacott (eds.), *Mass Communication and Society*. London: Edward Arnold, pp. 315–348.

Hall, S. (1986) Cultural Studies: Two Paradigms. In R. Collins, J. Curran, N. Garnham, P. Scannell, P. Schlesinger and C. Sparks (eds.), *Media, Culture and Soceity: A Critical Reader*. Sage: London, pp. 33-48.

Hall, S. (1992) Cultural Studies and its Theoretical Legacies. In L. Grossberg, C. Nelson and P. Treichler (eds.), *Cultural Studies*. New York: Routledge, pp. 277-286.

Hall, S. (2005) New Labour's Double Shuffle. *The Review of Education, Pedagogy, and Cultural Studies* 27(3): 319–335.

Hammett, J. and Hammett, K. (eds.) (2007) *The Suburbanization of New York: Is the World's Greatest City Becoming Just Another Town?* New York: Princeton Architectural Press.

Hamnett, C. (2003) Gentrification, Postindustrialism, and Industrial and Occupational Restructuring in Global Cities. In G. Bridge and S. Watson (eds.), *A Companion to the City*. Malden, MA: Blackwell, pp. 331–341.

Hardt, M. and Negri, A. (2000) *Empire*. Cambridge, MA: Harvard University Press.

Hardt, M. and Negri, A. (2005) *Multitude*. London: Penguin.

Harney, S. (2010) Creative Industries Debate – Unfinished Business: Labour, Management, and the Creative Industries. *Cultural Studies* 24(3): 431–444.

Harris, J. (2004) *Britpop! Cool Britannia and the Spectacular Demise of English Rock*. London: Da Capo Press.

Harris, N. (1984) *Of Bread and Guns: The World Economy in Crisis*. Harmondsworth: Penguin.

Hart-Landsberg, M. and Burkett, P. (1998) Contradictions of Capitalist Industrialisation in East Asia: A Critique of 'Flying Geese' Theories of Development. *Economic Geography* 72(2): 87–110.

Hart-Landsberg, M. and Burkett, P. (2003) A Critique of 'Catch-Up' Theories of Development. *Journal of Contemporary Asia* 33(2): 147–171.

Hartley, J. (2003) *A Short History of Cultural Studies*. London: Sage.

Hartley, J. (2004) The 'Value Chain of Meaning' and the New Economy. *International Journal of Cultural Studies* 7(1): 129–140.

Hartley, J. (2005) Creative Industries. In J. Hartley (ed.), *Creative Industries*. Malden, MA: Blackwell, pp. 1–43.

Hartley, J. (2008) *Television Truths*. Malden, MA: Blackwell.

Hartley, J. (2009) From the Consciousness Industry to the Creative Industries: Consumer-Created Content, Social Network Markets, and the Growth of Knowledge. In J. Holt and A. Perren (eds.), *Media Industries: History, Theory, and Method*. Malden, MA: Blackwell, pp. 231–244.

Hartley, J. and Montgomery, L. (2009) Fashion as Consumer Entrepreneurship: Emergent Risk Culture, Social Network Markets, and the Launch of *Vogue* in China. *Chinese Journal of Communication* 2(1): 61–76.

Harvey, D. (1982) *The Limits to Capital*. Oxford: Blackwell.

Harvey, D. (1989) *The Condition of Postmodernity*. Oxford: Blackwell.

Harvey, D. (2005) *A Brief History of Neoliberalism*. Oxford: Oxford University Press.

Harvey, D. (2008) From Managerialism to Entrepreneurialism: The Transformation of Urban Governance in Late Capitalism. In R. L. Martin and P. J. Sunley (eds.), *Economic Geography – Critical Concepts in the Social Sciences. Volume V: Regulating the Economic Landscape*. New York: Routledge, pp. 237–259.

Hawkins, G. (1993) *From Nimbin to Mardi Gras: Constructing Community Arts*. Sydney: Allen & Unwin.

Healy, K. (2002) What's New for Culture in the New Economy? *Journal of Arts Management, Law, and Society* 32(2): 86–103.

Hearn, G. and Pace, C. (2006) Value-Creating Ecologies: Understanding Next Generation Business Systems. *Foresight* 8(1): 55–65.

Heartfield, J. (2000) *Great Expectations: The Creative Industries in the New Economy*. London: Design Agenda.

Heilbroner, R. (2003) Do Machines Make History? In R. C. Scharff and V. Dusek (eds.), *Philosophy of Technology: The Technological Condition*. Malden, MA: Blackwell, pp. 398–404.

Held, D. and McGrew, A. (2002) *Globalisation/Anti-Globalisation*. Cambridge: Polity Press.

Held, D., McGrew, A., Goldblatt, D. and Perraton, J. (1999) *Global Transformations: Politics, Economics and Culture*. Stanford, CA: Stanford University Press.

Henderson, J., Dicken, P., Hess, M., Coe, N. and Yeung, H. W. (2002) Global Production Networks and the Analysis of Economic Development. *Review of International Political Economy* 9(3): 436–464.

Herman, E. S. (1997) The Externalities Effects of Commercial and Public Broadcasting. In P. Golding and G. Murdock (eds.), *The Political Economy of the Media* (Vol. 1). Cheltenham: Edward Elgar, pp. 374–404.

Herman, E. S. and McChesney, R. W. (1997) *The Global Media: The New Missionaries of Global Capitalism*. London: Cassell.

Hesmondhalgh, D. (2007a) *The Cultural Industries* (2nd edn). London: Sage.

Hesmondhalgh, D. (2007b) Creative Labour as a Basis for Critique of Creative Industries Policy. In G. Lovink and N. Rossiter (eds.), *My Creativity Reader: A Critique of Creative Industries*. Amsterdam: Institute of Network Culture, pp. 59–68.

Hesmondhalgh, D. (2008) Cultural and Creative Industries. In J. Frow and T. Bennett (eds.), *SAGE Handbook of Cultural Analysis*. London: Sage, pp. 552–569.

Hesmondhalgh, D. (2009) Politics, Theory and Method in Media Industries Research. In J. Holt and A. Perren (eds.), *Media Industries: History, Theory and Method*. Malden, MA: Wiley-Blackwell, pp. 245–255.

Hesmondhalgh, D. and Pratt, A. (2005) Cultural Industries and Cultural Policy. *International Journal of Cultural Policy* 11(1): 1–13.

Higgs, P. and Cunningham, S. (2008) Creative Industries Mapping: Where Have We Come From and Where Are We Going? *Creative Industries Journal* 1(1): 7–30.

Higgs, P., Cunningham, S. and Pagan, J. (2007) *Australia's Creative Economy: Basic Evidence on Size, Growth, Income and Employment*. CCI Technical Report. Brisbane: Australian Research Council Centre of Excellence for Creative Industries and Innovation (CCI). Retrieved November 21, 2010, from http://eprints.qut.edu.au/8241/.

Higgs, P., Cunningham, S. and Bakhshi, H. (2008) *Beyond the Creative Industries: Mapping the Creative Economy in the United Kingdom*. Technical Report. National Endowment for Science, Technology and the Arts (NESTA). February.

Hirst, P., Thompson, G. and Bromley, S. (2009) *Globalization in Question* (3rd edn). Cambridge: Polity Press.

HM Treasury (2006) *Cox Review of Creativity in Business: Building on the UK's Strengths*. London: HM Treasury.

Hobsbawm, E. J. (1990) *Echoes of the Marseillaise: Two Centuries Look Back on the French Revolution*. London: Verso.

Holden, J. (2009) How We Value Arts and Culture. *Asia Pacific Journal of Arts and Cultural Management* 6(2): 447–456.

Hong Kong Centre for Cultural Policy Research (HK CCPR) (2003) *Baseline Study of Hong Kong's Creative Industries*. Retrieved September 26, 2009, from www.info.gov.hk/gia/general/200309/16/0916249.htm.

Horwitz, R. (1989) *The Irony of Regulatory Reform: The Deregulation of American Telecommunications*. New York: Oxford University Press.

Hoskins, C., McFadyen, S. and Finn, A. (2004) *Media Economics: Applying Economics to New and Traditional Media*. Thousand Oaks, CA: Sage.

Howkins, J. (2001) *The Creative Economy: How People Make Money from Ideas*. London: Allen Lane.

Howkins, J. (2005) The Mayor's Commission on the Creative Industries. In J. Hartley (ed.), *Creative Industries*. Oxford: Blackwell, pp. 117–125.

Hu, A. (2002) Knowledge and Development: The New Catch-Up Strategy. In B. Grewal, L. Xue, P. Sheehan and F. Sun (eds.), *China's Future in the Knowledge Economy: Engaging the New World*. Melbourne/Beijing: Centre for Strategic Economic Studies/Tsinghua University Press, pp. 240–269.

Hui, D. (2006) From Cultural to Creative Industries: Strategies for Chaoyang District, Beijing. *International Journal of Cultural Studies* 9(3): 317–331.

Hunter, I. (1988) *Culture and Government: The Emergence of Literary Education*. Basingstoke: Macmillan.

Hunter, I. (1994) *Rethinking the School*. Sydney: Allen & Unwin.

Hutchinson, D. (2004) Protecting the Citizen, Protecting Society. In R. C. Allen and A. Hill (eds.), *The Television Studies Reader*. London: Routledge, pp. 64–78.

Hutton, W. (2006) *The Writing on the Wall: China and the West in the 21st Century*. London: Little, Brown.

Hutton, W. and Desai, M. (2007) Does the Future Really Belong to China? *Prospect Magazine* 130, January.

Internet World Stats (2010) The Internet Big Picture: World Internet Users and Population Stats. Retrieved January 11, 2010, from www.internetworldstats.com/stats.htm.

Jacobs, J. (1961) *The Death and Life of American Cities*. New York: Vintage.

James, A., Martin, R. L. and Sunley, P. J. (2008) The Rise of Cultural Economic Geography. In R. L. Martin and P. J. Sunley (eds.), *Economic Geography: Critical Concepts in the Social Sciences. Volume IV: The Cultural Economy*. London: Routledge, pp. 3–18.

Jameson, F. (1984) Postmodernism, or the Cultural Logic of Late Capitalism. *New Left Review* 146, July–August: 53–92.

Jayne, M. (2004) Culture that Works? Creative Industries Development in a Working-Class City. *Capital and Class* 28(3): 199–210.

Jayne, M. and Bell, D. (eds.) (2004) *City of Quarters: Urban Villages in the Contemporary City*. Aldershot: Ashgate.

Jeffcutt, P. (2004) Knowledge Relations and Transactions in a Cultural Economy: Analysing the Creative Industries Ecosystem. *Media International Australia* 112: 67–82.

Jenkins, H. (2006) *Convergence Culture: Where Old and New Media Collide*. New York: New York University Press.

Jermyn, H. (2001) *The Arts and Social Exclusion: A Report Prepared for the Arts Council of England*. London, September.

Jin, L. (2002) China: one year into the WTO process. Address to the World Bank by China's Vice-Minister of Finance, October 22. Retrieved June 13, 2007, from http://info.worldbank.org/etools/docs/voddocs/108/208/IMF-WB_address_final.pdf.

Kapur, J. (2009) An 'Arranged Love' Marriage: India's Neoliberal Turn and the Bollywood Wedding Culture Industry. *Communication, Culture and Critique* 2(2): 221–233.

KEA European Affairs (2006) *The Economy of Culture in Europe*. Study prepared for the European Commission (Directorate-General for Education and Culture), October. Retrieved April 4, 2008 from www.ebu.ch/CMSimages/en/BRUDOC_INFO_EN_318_tcm6-48296.pdf.

Keane, M. (2007) *Created in China: The Great New Leap Forward*. London: Routledge.

Keane, M. (2009) The Capital Complex: Beijing's New Creative Clusters. In L. Kong and J. O'Connor (eds.), *Creative Economies, Creative Cities: Asian–European Perspectives*. Dordrecht: Springer Press, pp. 77–95.

Kellner, D. and Pierce, C. (2007) Media and Globalization. In G. Ritzer (ed.), *The Blackwell Companion to Globalization*. Malden, MA: Blackwell, pp.383–395.

Kelly, O. (2003) Art. In J. Lewis and T. Miller (eds.), *Critical Cultural Policy Studies: A Reader*. Malden, MA: Blackwell, pp. 188–191.

Kipnis, A. (2007) Neoliberalism Reified: *Suzhi* Discourse and Tropes of Neoliberalism in the People's Republic of China. *Journal of the Royal Anthropological Institute* 13: 383–400.

Kirchner, S. (1995) Beyond the Two-Party System: A Neoliberal Perspective. *Policy* 11(3): 34–38.

Knell, J. and Oakley, K. (2007) *London's Creative Economy: An Accidental Success?* Provocation Series, Vol. 3, No. 3. London: The Work Foundation London Development Agency. Retrieved June 24, 2008, from www.theworkfoundation.com/assets/docs/publications/63_creative_London.pdf.

Kong, L. (2009) Beyond Networks and Relations: Towards Rethinking Creative Cluster Theory. In L. Kong and J. O'Connor (eds.), *Creative Economies, Creative Cities: Asian–European Perspectives*. Dordrecht: Springer Press, pp. 66–76.

Kong, L., Gibson, C., Khoo, L. and Semple, A. (2006) Knowledge of the Creative Economy: Towards a Relational Geography of Diffusion and Adaptation in Asia. *Asia Pacific Viewpoint* 47(2): 173–194.

Kornberger, M. (2010) *Brand Society: How Brands Transform Management and Lifestyle*. Cambridge: Cambridge University Press.

Korpi, W. (1983) *The Democratic Class Struggle*. London: Routledge & Kegan Paul.

Kotkin, J. (2006) *The City: A World History*. New York: Random House.

Kotkin, J. (2007) What is the New Suburbanism? In A. Chavan, C. Peralta and C. Steins (eds.), *Planetizen: Contemporary Debates in Urban Planning*. Washington, DC: Island Press, pp. 28–33.

Krugman, P. (2003) Where in the World is the 'New Economic Geography'? In G. L. Clark, M. P. Feldman and M. S. Gertler (eds.), *The Oxford Handbook of Economic Geography*. Oxford: Oxford University Press, pp. 49–60.

Laclau, E. and Mouffe, C. (1985) *Hegemony and Socialist Strategy*. London: Verso.

Landry, C. (2000) *The Creative City: A Toolkit for Urban Innovators*. London: Earthscan.

Landry, C. (2005) London as a Creative City. In J. Hartley (ed.), *Creative Industries*. Oxford: Blackwell, pp. 233–243.

Landry, C. and Wood, P. (2003) *Harnessing and Exploiting the Power of Culture for Competitive Advantage*. A Report by Comedia for Liverpool City Council and the Core Cities Group. London: Comedia.

Lash, S. and Urry, J. (1987) *The End of Organized Capitalism*. Cambridge: Polity Press.

Lash, S. and Urry, J. (1994) *Economies of Signs and Space*. London: Sage.

Leadbeater, C. (1999) *Living on Thin Air: The New Economy*. London: Penguin.

Leadbeater, C. (2008) *We-Think: Mass Innovation, Not Mass Production*. London: Profile.

Leadbeater, C. and Miller, P. (2004) *The Pro-Am Revolution: How Enthusiasts are Changing Our Economy and Society*. London: DEMOS.

Lee, M. (1993) *Consumer Culture Reborn: The New Cultural Politics of Consumption*. London: Routledge.

Leo, P. and Lee, T. (2004) The 'New' Singapore: Mediating Culture and Creativity. *Continuum: Journal of Media and Cultural Studies* 18(2): 205–218.

Lessig, L. (2004) *Free Culture: How Big Media Uses Technology and the Law to Lock Down Culture and Control Creativity*. New York: Penguin.

Lewis, J. (1990) *Art, Culture, and Enterprise: The Politics of Art and the Cultural Industries*. London: Routledge.

Lievrouw, L. (2006) New Media Design and Development: Diffusion of Innovations v Social Shaping of Technology. In L. Lievrouw and S. Livingstone (eds.), *The Handbook of New Media: Updated Student Edition*. London: Sage, pp. 246–265.

Lievrouw, L. and Livingstone, S. (2006) Introduction to the Updated Student Edition. In L. Lievrouw and S. Livingstone (eds.), *The Handbook of New Media: Updated Student Edition*. London: Sage, pp. 1–14.

Lipietz, A. (1984) *Mirages and Miracles: The Crises of Global Fordism*. London: Verso.

Litman, J. (2001) *Digital Copyright*. Amherst, NY: Prometheus Books.

Livingstone, S., Lunt, P. and Miller, L. (2007) Citizens and Consumers: Discursive Debates during and after the Communications Act 2003. *Media, Culture and Society* 29(4): 613–638.

Lloyd, C. (2000) Globalization: Beyond the Ultra-Modernist Narrative to a Critical Realist Perspective on Geopolitics in the Cyber Age. *International Journal of Urban and Regional Research* 24(2): 258–273.

Looseley, D. (1995) *The Politics of Fun: Cultural Policy and Debate in Contemporary France*. Oxford: Berg.

Lorenzen, M. and Frederiksen, L. (2008) Why Do Cultural Industries Cluster? Localization, Urbanization, Products and Projects. In P. Cooke and L. Lazzeretti (eds.), *Creative Cities, Cultural Clusters and Local Economic Development*. Cheltenham, UK: Edward Elgar. pp. 155–179.

Löwy, M. (2002) The Revolutionary Romanticism of May 1968. *Thesis Eleven* 68: 95–100.

Lyotard, J.-F. (1988) *The Differend: Phrases in Dispute*. Manchester: Manchester University Press.

Machin, S. and McNally, S. (2007) Tertiary Education Systems and Labour Markets. Paper commissioned by the Education and Training Policy Division, OECD, for the *Thematic Review of Tertiary Education*. January.

MacKenzie, D. and Wacjman, J. (1999) Introductory Essay: The Social Shaping of Technology. In D. MacKenzie and J. Wacjman (eds.), *The Social Shaping of Technology* (2nd edn). Milton Keynes: Open University Press, pp. 3–27.

Mandel, E. (1975) *Late Capitalism*. London: Verso.

Mandel, E. (1983) Consumption. In T. Bottomore, L. Harris, V. G. Kiernan and R. Miliband (eds.), *A Dictionary of Marxist Thought*. Oxford: Blackwell, pp. 92–93.

Marglin, S. and Schor, J. (1990) *The Golden Age of Capitalism*. New York: Oxford University Press.

Marshall, A. (1990) *Principles of Economics* (8th edn). London: Macmillan. (1st edn, 1890.)

Marshall, D. (ed.) (2006) *The Celebrity Culture Reader*. New York: Routledge.

Martin, R. and Sunley, P. (2003) Deconstructing Clusters: Chaotic Concept or Policy Panacea? *Journal of Economic Geography* 3: 3–35.

Marx, K. (1976 [1867]) *Capital*. Volume One. Harmondsworth: Penguin.

Maslow, A. (1943) A Theory of Human Motivation. *Psychological Review* 50(4): 370–396.

Mason, R. (1998) *The Economics of Conspicuous Consumption: Theory and Thought since 1700*. Cheltenham, UK: Edward Elgar.

Mattelart, A. (1994) *Mapping World Communication: War, Progress, Culture*. Trans. S. Emanuel and J. A. Cohen. Minneapolis, MN: University of Minnesota Press.

Mattelart, A. and Piemme, J. (1982) Cultural Industries: The Origin of an Idea. In UNESCO, *Cultural Industries: A Challenge for the Future*. Paris: UNESCO, pp. 51–61.

Max-Neef, M. (1992) Development and Human Needs. In P. Ekins and M. Max-Neef (eds.), *Real-Life Economics: Understanding Wealth Creation*. London: Routledge, pp. 197–213.

McGuigan, J. (1996) *Culture and the Public Sphere*. London: Routledge.

McGuigan, J. (1998) National Government and the Cultural Public Sphere. *Media International Australia* 87: 68–83.

McGuigan, J. (2009a) *Cultural Analysis*. Los Angeles, CA: Sage.

McGuigan, J. (2009b) Doing a Florida Thing: The Creative Class Thesis and Cultural Policy. *International Journal of Cultural Policy* 15(3): 291–300.

McMillan, J. (2002) *Reinventing the Bazaar: A Natural History of Markets*. New York: W. W. Norton & Co.

McNair, B. (2006) *Cultural Chaos: Journalism, News and Power in a Globalised World*. New York: Routledge.

McQueen, H. (2009) An Implosion of Knowledge. *Meanjin* 68(1): 56–61.

McRobbie, A. (1996) All the World's a Stage, Screen or Magazine: When Culture is the Logic of Late Capitalism. *Media, Culture and Society* 18(2): 335–342.

McRobbie, A. (1998) Great Debates in Art and Design Education. In A. McRobbie (ed.), *British Fashion Design: Rag Trade or Image Industry?* London: Routledge, pp. 17–32.

McRobbie, A. (1999) *In the Culture Society: Art, Fashion and Popular Music*. London: Routledge.

McRobbie, A. (2005) Clubs to Companies. In J. Hartley (ed.), *Creative Industries*. Malden, MA: Blackwell, pp. 375–390.

McSmith, A. (2010) *No Such Thing as Society: Britain in the 1980s*. London: Constable.

McWilliam, E. and Hatcher, C. (2004) Emotional Literacy as a Pedagogical Product. *Continuum: Journal of Media and Cultural Studies* 18(2): 179–189.

McWilliam, K. (2008) The Global Diffusion of a Community Media Practice: Digital Storytelling Online. In J. Hartley and K. McWilliam (eds.), *Story Circle: Digital Storytelling around the World*. Malden, MA: Wiley-Blackwell, pp. 37-74.

Melkote, S. R. (2010) Theories of Development Communication. In D. K. Thussu (ed.), *International Communication: A Reader*. London: Routledge, pp. 105–121.

Menger, P. (1999) Artistic Labour Markets and Careers. *Annual Review of Sociology* 25: 541–574.

Meyrowitz, J. (1994) Medium Theory. In D. Crowley and D. Mitchell (eds.), *Communication Theory Today*. Cambridge: Polity Press, pp. 50–73.

Miège, B. (1989) *The Capitalization of Cultural Production*. New York: International General.

Miles, S. and Miles, M. (2004) *Consuming Cities*. Basingstoke: Palgrave Macmillan.

Miller, D. (1995) Consumption as the Vanguard of History: A Polemic by Way of an Introduction. In D. Miller (ed.), *Acknowledging Consumption*. London: Routledge, pp. 1–57.

Miller, T. (1996) The Crime of Monsieur Lang: GATT, the Screen, and the New International Division of Cultural Labour. In A. Moran (ed.), *Film Policy: International, National and Regional Perspectives*. New York: Routledge, pp. 72–84.

Miller, T. (2004) A View from a Fossil: The New Economy, Creativity and Consumption – Two or Three Things I Don't Believe In. *International Journal of Cultural Studies* 7(1): 55–66.

Miller, T. (2008) Anyone for Games? Via the New International Division of Cultural Labour. In H. Anheier and Y. Raj Isar (eds.), *The Cultural Economy – The Cultures and Globalization Series 2*. Los Angeles, CA: Sage, pp. 227–240.

Miller, T. (2009a) Albert and Michael's Recombinant DNA. *Continuum: Journal of Media and Cultural Studies* 23(2): 269–275.

Miller, T. (2009b) Can Natural Luddites Make Things Explode or Travel Faster? The New Humanities, Cultural Policy Studies, and Creative Industries. In J. Holt and A. Perren (eds.), *Media Industries: History, Theory, and Method*. Malden, MA: Wiley-Blackwell, pp. 184–198.

Miller, T. (2010) Michel Foucault, *The birth of biopolitics: lectures at the Collège de France 1978–79*. *International Journal of Cultural Policy* 16(1): 56–57.

Miller, T., Govil, N., McMurria, J. and Maxwell, R. (2001) *Global Hollywood*. London: British Film Institute.

Miller, T. and Yúdice, G. (2002) *Cultural Policy*. London: Sage.

Milner, A. and Browitt, J. (2002) *Contemporary Cultural Theory* (3rd edn). Sydney: Allen & Unwin.

Ministry of Trade and Industry (MTI) (2003) *Economic Contribution of Singapore's Creative Industries*. Singapore: Government of Singapore.

Ministry of Trade and Industry (MTI) (2008) *Creative Industries Singapore*. Retrieved May 2, 2008, from www.ci.sg/strategy.html.

Mitchell, W., Inouye, A. and Blumenthal, M. (2003) *Beyond Creativity: Information Technology, Innovation, and Creativity*. Washington, DC: National Academies Press.

Mizra, M. (2006) The Therapeutic State. *International Journal of Cultural Policy* 11(3): 261–273.

MKW Wirtschaftsforchung GmbH (2001) *Exploitation and Development of the Job Potential in the Cultural Sector in the Age of Digitalisation*. Final Report. Commissioned by the European Commission DG Employment and Social Affairs, June. Retrieved May 15, 2008, from http://ec.europa.eu/culture/pdf/doc924_en.pdf.

Mohun, S. (2003) Consumer Sovereignty. In D. B. Clarke, M. A. Doel and K. M. L. Housiaux (eds.), *The Consumption Reader*. London: Routledge, pp. 139–143.

Mommaas, H. (2004) Cultural Clusters and the Post-Industrial City. *Urban Studies* 41(3): 507–532.

Mommaas, H. (2009) Spaces of Culture and Economy: Mapping the Cultural-Creative Cluster Landscape. In L. Kong and J. O'Connor (eds.), *Creative Economies, Creative Cities: Asian–European Perspectives*. Dordrecht: Springer Press, pp. 45–59.

Montgomery, L. (2009) Spaces to Grow: Copyright, Cultural Policy and Commercially Focused Music in China. *Chinese Journal of Communication* 2(1): 36–49.

Mosco, V. (2009) *The Political Economy of Communication* (2nd edn). London: Sage.

Mulgan, G. (1997) *Connexity: Responsibility, Freedom, Business and Power in the 21st Century*. London: Vintage.

Murdock, G. (1982) Large Corporations and the Control of the Communications Industries. In M. Gurevitch, T. Bennett, J. Curran and J. Woollacott (eds.), *Culture, Society and the Media*. London: Methuen, pp. 118–150.

Murdock, G. and Golding, P. (2005) Culture, Communications and Political Economy. In J. Curran and M. Gurevitch (eds.), *Mass Media and Society* (4th edn). London: Hodder Education, pp. 60–83.

Murray, R. (1971) The Internationalization of Capital and the Nation State. *New Left Review* 67: 84–109.

Murray, R. (1989) Fordism and Post-Fordism. In S. Hall and M. Jacques (eds.), *New Times: The Changing Face of Politics in the 1990s*. London: Lawrence & Wishart.

Murray, S. and Ouellette, L. (eds.) (2004) *Reality TV: Remaking Television Culture*. New York: New York University Press.

Myerscough, J. (1988) *The Economic Importance of the Arts in Britain*. London: Policy Studies Institute.

Mytelka, L. and Smith, K. (2002) Policy Learning and Innovation Theory: An Interactive and Co-Evolving Process. *Research Policy* 31: 1467–1479.

National Endowment for Science, Technology and the Arts (NESTA) (2006) *Creating Growth: How the UK Can Invest in Creative Businesses*. Retrieved May 1, 2008, from www.nesta.org.uk/creating-value-how-the-uk-can-invest-in-new-creative-businesses-2/.

Neff, G., Wissinger, E. and Zukin, S. (2005) Entrepreneurial Labor among Cultural Producers: 'Cool' Jobs in 'Hot' Industries. *Social Semiotics* 15(3): 307–334.

Negus, K. (2002) Identities and Industries: The Cultural Formation of Aesthetic Economies. In P. du Gay and M. Pryke (eds.), *Cultural Economy: Cultural Analysis and Commercial Life*. London: Sage, pp. 115–131.

Negus, K. (2006) Rethinking Creative Production away from the Cultural Industries. In J. Curran and D. Morley (eds.), *Media and Cultural Theory*. London: Routledge, pp. 197–208.

Negus, K. and Pickering, M. (2004) *Creativity, Communication and Cultural Value*. London: Sage.

Neilson, B. and Rossiter, N. (2005) From Precarity to Precariousness and Back Again: Labour, Life and Unstable Networks. *Fibreculture Journal* 5, September. Retrieved March 10, 2008, from http://journal.fibreculture.org/issue5/neilson_rossiter.html.

New Zealand Institute for Economic Research (NZIER) (2002) *Creative Industries in New Zealand: Economic Contribution*. March. Wellington: NZIER.

New Zealand Ministry for Economic Development (NZ MED) (2003) *Benchmark Indicators Report 2003*. Published August 1. Retrieved March 15, 2008, from www.med.govt.nz/templates/MultipageDocumentTOC____1864.aspx.

Nielsén, T. (2004) *Understanding the Experience Economy: A Swedish Perspective on Creativity*. Stockholm: QNB Analys & Kommunikation AB.

Nixon, S. (2003) *Advertising Cultures*. London: Sage.

Nonini, D. (2008) Is China Becoming Neoliberal? *Critique of Anthropology* 28(2): 145–178.

Nordfors, D. (2009) Keynote at the Innovation @ Creative Industries Conference in Berlin. *The Innovation Journalism Blog*. Published June 29. Retrieved November 24, 2010, from www.innovationjournalism.org/blog/2009/06/keynote-at-innovation-creative.html.

Nordic Innovation Centre (NICe) (2006) *In Search of the Experience Economy*. Oslo: Nordic Innovation Centre, March.

Nordic Innovation Centre (NICe) (2007) *A Creative Economy Green Paper for the Nordic Region*. Oslo: Nordic Innovation Centre, September.

Nove, A. (1983) *The Economics of Feasible Socialism*. London: Allen & Unwin.

Oakley, K. (2004) Not So Cool Britannia: The Role of Creative Industries in Economic Development. *International Journal of Cultural Policy* 7(1): 67–77.

O'Connor, J. (1999) Popular Culture, Reflexivity and Urban Change. In J. Verwijnen and P. Lehtuvuori (eds.), *Creative Cities*. Helsinki: University of Art and Design Publishing Unit.

O'Connor, J. (2004) 'A Special Kind of City Knowledge': Innovative Clusters, Tacit Knowledge and the 'Creative City'. *Media International Australia* 112: 131–149.

O'Connor, J. (2007) *The Cultural and Creative Industries: A Review of the Literature*. A Report for Creative Partnerships. London: Arts Council England.

O'Connor, J. (2009) Creative Industries – A New Direction? *International Journal of Cultural Policy* 15(4): 387–402.

O'Connor, J. and Gu, X. (2006) A New Modernity? The Arrival of 'Creative Industries' in China. *International Journal of Cultural Studies* 9(3): 271–283.

O'Connor, J. and Lovatt, A. (1995) Cities and the Night-Time Economy. *Planning Practice & Research* 10(2): 127–134.

Odlyzko, A. (2001) Content is Not King. *First Monday* 6(3), February 5. Retrieved April 6, 2008, from http://firstmonday.org/htbin/cgiwrap/bin/ojs/index.php/fm/article/view/833/742.

O'Keeffe, A. (2009) The Price of Everything. *New Statesman*. February 12. Retrieved March 19, 2009, from www.newstatesman.com/art/2009/02/cultural-scene-money-work.

Olson, S. R. (2004) Hollywood Planet: Global Media and the Competitive Advantage of Narrative Transparency. In R. C. Allen and A. Hill (eds.), *The Television Studies Reader*. New York: Routledge, pp. 111–129.

O'Regan, T. (1998) Thinking about Policy Utility: Some Aspects of Australian Cultural Policy Development in a South African Context. *Critical Arts* 12 (1 & 2): 1–23.

O'Regan, T. (2002) Too Much Culture, Too Little Culture: Trends and Issues for Cultural Policy-Making. *Media International Australia* 102: 9–24.

Organisation for Economic Co-operation and Development (OECD) (1998) *Content as a New Growth Industry*. Paris: OECD.

Organisation for Economic Co-operation and Development (OECD) (2006) *Digital Broadband Content: Digital Content Strategies and Policies*. Working Party on the Information Economy. DSTI/ICCP/IE(2005)/FINAL. Paris: OECD.

Organisation for Economic Co-operation and Development (OECD) (2010) *The Evolution of News and the Internet*. Working Party on the Information Economy. DSTI/ICCP/IE(2009)/14. Paris: OECD.

Ozawa, T., Castello, S. and Phillips, R. (2001) The Internet Revolution, the 'McLuhan' Stage of Catch-up, and Institutional Reforms in Asia. *Journal of Economic Issues* 35(2): 289–298.

Palmer, M. (1996) GATT and Culture: A View from France. In A. van Hemel, H. Mommaas and C. Smithuijsen (eds.), *Trading Culture: GATT, European Cultural Policies and the Transatlantic Market*. Amsterdam: Boekman Foundation, pp. 27–38.

Peck, J. (2005) Struggling with the Creative Class. *International Journal of Urban and Regional Research* 29(4): 740–770.

Peck, J. (2008) Remaking Laissez-Faire. *Progress in Human Geography* 32(1): 3–43.

Perelman, M. (2002) *Steal This Idea: Intellectual Property Rights and the Corporate Confiscation of Creativity*. New York: Palgrave.

Perraton, J. and Clift, B. (2004) So Where are National Capitalisms Now? In J. Perraton and B. Clift (eds.), *Where are National Capitalisms Now?* Basingstoke: Palgrave Macmillan, pp. 195–261.

Peston, R. (2009) Total and the Wimbledon Effect. *BBC News – Peston's Picks*. February 2. Retrieved May 27, 2010, from www.bbc.co.uk/blogs/thereporters/robertpeston/2009/02/total_and_the_wimbledon_effect.html.

Peterson, R. A. (1976) The Production of Culture: A Prolegomenon. In R. A. Peterson (ed.), *The Production of Culture*. Thousand Oaks, CA: Sage, pp. 7–22.

Picard, R. (1989) *Media Economics: Concepts and Issues*. Newbury Park, CA: Sage.

Pink, D. (2006) *A Whole New Mind: Why Right-Brainers Will Rule the World*. New York: Reed Elsevier.

Porter, M. (1998) Clusters and the New Economics of Competition. *Harvard Business Review* 76(6): 77–91.

Porter, M. (2000) Locations, Clusters, and Company Strategy. In G. Clark, M. Feldman and M. Gertler (eds.), *The Oxford Handbook of Economic Geography*. Oxford: Oxford University Press, pp. 253–274.

Potts, J. (2007) Art and Innovation: An Evolutionary Economic View of the Creative Industries. *UNESCO Observatory* 1(1): 1–18.

Potts, J., Cunningham, S., Hartley, J. and Ormerod, P. (2008) Social Network Markets: A New Definition of the Creative Industries. *Journal of Cultural Economics* 32(2): 167–185.

Power, D. (2009) Culture, Creativity and Experience in Nordic and Scandinavian Cultural Policy. *International Journal of Cultural Policy* 15(4): 445-460.

Power, D. and Scott, A. (2004) A Prelude to Cultural Industries and the Production of Culture. In D. Power and A. J. Scott (eds.), *Cultural Industries and the Production of Culture*. London: Routledge, pp. 3–18.

Pratt, A. (1997) *The Cultural Industries Sector: Its Definition and Character from Secondary Sources on Employment and Trade, 1984–1991*. Research Papers in Environmental and Spatial Analysis, No. 41. Department of Geography and Environment, London School of Economics, July.

Pratt, A. (2004a) Mapping the Cultural Industries: Regionalization – the Example of South East England. In D. Power and A. J. Scott (eds.), *Cultural Industries and the Production of Culture*. London: Routledge, pp. 19–36.

Pratt, A. (2004b) The Cultural Economy: A Call for a Spatialized 'Production of Culture' Perspective. *International Journal of Cultural Studies* 7(1): 117–128.

Pratt, A. (2005) Cultural Industries and Public Policy. *International Journal of Cultural Policy* 11(1): 31–44.

Pratt, A. (2008) Creative Cities: The Cultural Industries and the Creative Class. *Geografiska Annaler: Series B – Human Geography* 90(2): 107–117.

Pratt, A. (2009a) The Creative and Cultural Economy and the Recession. *Geoforum* 40(1): 495–496.

Pratt, A. (2009b) Innovation and Creativity. In T. Hall, P. Hubbard and J. R. Short (eds.), *The SAGE Companion to the City*. London: Sage, pp. 138–153.

Preston, G. C.-H. (2009) Review of G. Bloustein et al. (eds.), *Sonic Synergies*. *Media International Australia* 132: 142–143.

Productivity Commission (2000) *Broadcasting: Final Report*. Canberra: Ausinfo.

Progressive Policy Institute (2002) 'Coopetition' in the New Economy: Collaboration among Competitors. The New Economy Index: What's New about the New Economy. Retrieved April 7, 2008, www.neweconomyindex.org/section1_page07.html.

Pusey, M. (2009) 25 Years of Neo-Liberalism in Australia. In R. Manne and D. McKnight (eds.), *Goodbye to All That: On the Failure of Neo-Liberalism and the Urgency of Change*. Melbourne: Black Inc. Agenda, pp. 125–146.

Quiggan, J. (2009) Australia and the Global Financial Crisis. In R. Manne and D. McKnight (eds.), *Goodbye to All That: On the Failure of Neo-Liberalism and the Urgency of Change*. Melbourne: Black Inc. Agenda, pp. 147–180.

Quiggan, J. (2010) *Zombie Economics: How Dead Ideas Still Walk Among Us*. Princeton, NJ: Princeton University Press.

Quiggan, J. and Potts, J. (2008) Economics of Non-market Innovation and Digital Literacy. *Media International Australia* 128: 144–150.

Raboy, M. (2002) Media Policy in the New Communications Environment. In M. Raboy (ed.), *Global Media Policy in the New Millennium*. Luton: University of Luton Press.

Rennie, E. (2003) 'Trespassers are Welcome': Access and Community Television Policy. *Javnost (The Public)* 10(1): 49–62.

Rifkin, J. (2000) *The Age of Access*. London: Penguin.

Ritzer, G. (2006) *McDonaldization: The Reader*. Thousand Oaks, CA: Pine Forge Press.

Roach, C. (1997) The Western World and NWICO: United They Stand? In P. Golding and P. Harris (eds.), *Beyond Cultural Imperialism: Globalisation, Communication and the New International Order*. London: Sage, pp. 94–116.

Robertson, R. (1992) *Globalization*. London: Sage.

Robertson, R. (2007) Theories of Globalization. In G. Ritzer (ed.), *The Blackwell Companion to Globalization*. Malden, MA: Blackwell, pp. 125–143.

Robinson, K. (2001) *Out of Our Minds: Learning to be Creative*. Oxford: Capstone.

Rogers, E. M. (2003) *Diffusion of Innovations* (6th edn). New York: Free Press.

Romer, P. (1990) Endogenous Technological Change. *Journal of Political Economy* 98(5): 71–102.

Roodhouse, S. (2006) *Cultural Quarters: Principles and Practice*. Bristol: Intellect Press.

Ross, A. (2007) Nice Work If You Can Get It: The Mercurial Career of Creative Industries Policy. In G. Lovink and N. Rossiter (eds.), *MyCreativity Reader: A Critique of Creative Industries*. Amsterdam: Institute of Network Cultures, pp. 17–39.

Ross, A. (2008) The New Geography of Work: Power to the Precarious? *Theory, Culture and Society* 25(7–8): 31–49.

Ross, A. (2009) On the Digital Labor Question. Presentation to *The Internet as Playground and Factory*, Institute for Distributed Creativity, New School for Social Research, New

York, September 29. Retrieved June 1, 2010, from https://lists.thing.net/pipermail/idc/2009-November/004039.html.

Rossiter, N. (2006) *Organized Networks: Media Theory, Creative Labour, New Institutions*. Amsterdam: Institute of Network Cultures.

Rowse, T. (1985) *Arguing the Arts: The Funding of the Arts in Australia*. Melbourne: Penguin.

Ryan, B. (1992) *Making Capital from Culture*. Thousand Oaks, CA: Sage.

Santagana, W. (2004) Creativity, Fashion and Market Behaviour. In D. Power and A. J. Scott (eds.), *Cultural Industries and the Production of Culture*. New York: Routledge, pp. 75–90.

Sassen, S. (2000) Whose City Is It? Globalization and the Formation of New Claims. In F. J. Lechner and J. Boli (eds.), *The Globalization Reader*. Malden, MA: Blackwell, pp. 70–76.

Sassen, S. (2002) Locating Cities on Global Circuits. In S. Sassen (ed.), *Global Networks, Linked Cities*. London: Routledge, pp. 1–36.

Sassen, S. (2006) *Cities in a World Economy*. Thousand Oaks, CA: Pine Forge Press.

Schiller, H. I. (1991) Not Yet the Post-Imperialist Era. *Critical Studies in Mass Communication* 8(1): 13–28.

Schlesinger, P. (1991) Media, the Political Order and National Identity. *Media, Culture and Society* 13(3): 297–308.

Schlesinger, P. (1997) From Cultural Difference to Political Culture: Media, Politics and Collective Identity in the European Union. *Media, Culture and Society* 19(3): 369–391.

Scholte, J. A. (2005a) *Globalization: A Critical Introduction*. Basingstoke: Palgrave Macmillan.

Scholte, J. A. (2005b) *The Sources of Neoliberal Globalization*. United Nations Research Institute for Social Development. Overarching Concerns Programme Paper No. 8, October.

Schudson, M. (1994) Culture and the Integration of National Societies. *International Social Science Journal* 6(1): 63–80.

Schulze, G. (2003) International Trade. In R. Towse (ed.), *A Handbook of Cultural Economics*. Cheltenham, UK: Edward Elgar, pp. 269–275.

Schultz, J. (1994) Media Convergence and the Fourth Estate. In J. Schultz (ed.), *Not Just Another Business: Journalists, Citizens and the Media*. Sydney: Pluto Press, pp. 15–34.

Schumpeter, J. A. (1942) *Capitalism, Socialism and Democracy*. New York: Harper & Row.

Schuster, J. M. (2002) Sub-National Cultural Policy – Where the Action Is? Mapping State Cultural Policy in the United States. *International Journal of Cultural Policy* 8(2): 181–196.

Schwengel, H. (1991) British Enterprise Culture and German *Kulturgesellschaft*. In R. Keat and N. Abercrombie (eds.), *Enterprise Culture*. London: Routledge, pp. 136–150.

Scott, A. J. (2000) *The Cultural Economy of Cities*. Thousand Oaks, CA: Sage.

Scott, A. J. (2003) Economic Geography: The Great Half-Century. In G. L. Clark, M. P. Feldman and M. S. Gertler (eds.), *The Oxford Handbook of Economic Geography*. Oxford: Oxford University Press, pp. 18–44.

Scott, A. J. (2004) Cultural-Products Industries and Urban Economic Development: Prospect for Growth and Market Contestation in Global Context. *Urban Affairs Review* 39(1): 461–90.

Scott, A. J. (2005) *On Hollywood: The Place, the Industry*. Princeton, NJ: Princeton University Press.

Scott, A. J. (2006) Entrepreneurship, Innovation and Industrial Development: Geography and the Creative Field Revisited. *Small Business Economics* 26(1): 1–24.

Scott, A. J. (2008a) Cultural Economy: Retrospect and Prospect. In H. Anheier and Y. R. Isar (eds.), *The Cultural Economy*. Los Angeles, CA: Sage, pp. 307–323.

Scott, A. J. (2008b) *Social Economy of the Metropolis: Cognitive-Cultural Capitalism and the Global Resurgence of Cities*. Oxford: Oxford University Press.

Scott, A. J., Agnew, J., Soja, E. and Storper, M. (2001) Global City-Regions. In A. J. Scott (ed.), *Global City-Regions: Trends, Theory, Policy*. Oxford: Oxford University Press, pp. 11–30.

Screen Production and Development Association (SPADA) (2004) Survey of Screen Production in New Zealand 2004. Retrieved April 24, 2008, from www.spada.co.nz/resources/research/research.html.

Seaman, B. (2000) Arts Impact Studies: A Fashionable Excess. In G. Bradford, M. Gary and G. Wallach (eds.), *The Politics of Culture: Policy Perspectives for Individuals, Institutions and Communities*. New York: New Press, pp. 266–285.

Shim, D. (2008) The Growth of Korean Cultural Industries and the Korean Wave. In C. Beng Huat and K. Iwabuchi (eds.), *East Asian Pop Culture: Analysing the Korean Wave*. Hong Kong: Hong Kong University Press, pp. 15–32.

Shorthose, J. (20004a) Accounting for Independent Creativity in the New Cultural Economy. *Media International Australia* 112: 150–161.

Shorthose, J. (2004b) The Engineered and the Vernacular in Cultural Industries Quarters. *Capital and Class* 28(3): 159–178.

Simmel, G. (2003 [1902]) The Philosophy of Fashion. In D. B. Clarke, M. A. Doel and K. M. L. Housiaux (eds.), *The Consumption Reader*. London: Routledge, pp. 238–245.

Sinclair, J. (2010) Advertising. In S. Cunningham and G. Turner (eds.), *The Media and Communication in Australia* (3rd edn). Sydney: Allen & Unwin, pp. 189–206.

Singer, J. (2010) Journalism in a Network. In M. Deuze (ed.), *Managing Media Work*. Thousand Oaks, CA: Sage, pp. 103–110.

Siune, K. and Hulten, O. (1998) Does Public Broadcasting Have a Future? In D. McQuail and K. Siune (eds.), *Media Policy: Convergence, Concentration and Commerce*. London: Sage, pp. 23–37.

Siwek, S. (2006) *Copyright Industries in the US Economy – The 2006 Report*. Washington, DC: International Intellectual Property Alliance.

Skidelsky, R. (2000) *John Maynard Keynes. Vol. 3, Fighting for Britain 1937–1946*. London: Papermac.

Sklair, L. (2002) *Globalization: Capitalism and its Alternatives*. Oxford: Oxford University Press.

Slater, D. (2002) Capturing Markets from the Economists. In P. du Gay and M. Pryke (eds.), *Cultural Economy: Cultural Analysis and Commercial Life*. London: Sage, pp. 59–77.

Slater, D. (2003) Cultures of Consumption. In K. Anderson, M. Domosh, S. Pile and N. Thrift (eds.), *Handbook of Cultural Geography*. London: Sage, pp. 147–163.

Slater, T. (2006) The Eviction of Critical Perspectives from Gentrification Research. *International Journal of Urban and Regional Research* 30(4): 737–757.

Smiers, J. (2004) A Convention on Cultural Diversity: From WTO to UNESCO. *Media International Australia* 111: 81–96.

Smith, C. (1998) Secretary of State's Foreword. In *Creative Industries Mapping Document*. London: Department of Culture, Media and Sport. Retrieved May 12, 2010, from http://webarchive.nationalarchives.gov.uk/+/http://www.culture.gov.uk/reference_library/publications/4740.aspx.

Smythe, D. (1995) On the Audience Commodity and its Work. In O. Boyd-Barrett and C. Newbold (eds.), *Approaches to Media: A Reader*. London: Arnold, pp. 222–228.

Sparks, C. (2007) *Globalization, Development and the Mass Media*. London: Sage.

Stevenson, D. (2000) *Art and Organisation*. Brisbane: University of Queensland Press.

Stevenson, D. (2004) 'Civic Gold' Rush: Cultural Planning and the Politics of the 'Third Way'. *International Journal of Cultural Policy* 10(1): 119–131.

Stiglitz, J. (2002) *Globalization and its Discontents*. London: Allen Lane.

Stiroh, K. (1999) Is There a New Economy? *Challenge* 42(4): 82–101.

Storey, J. (1999) *Cultural Consumption and Everyday Life*. London: Arnold.

Storper, M. (1997) *The Regional World*. London: Guildford Press.

Storper, M. and Christopherson, S. (1987) Flexible Specialization and Regional Industrial Agglomerations: The Case of the U.S. Motion-Picture Industry. *Annals of the Association of American Geographers* 77: 260–282.

Storper, M. and Scott, A. J. (2009) Rethinking Human Capital, Creativity and Urban Growth. *Journal of Economic Geography* 9(1): 147–167.

Storper, M. and Venables, A. (2004) Buzz: Face-to-Face Contact and the Urban Economy. *Journal of Economic Geography* 4(2): 351–370.

Stratton, J. (2009) The Murderous State: The Naturalisation of Violence and Exclusion in the Films of Neoliberal Australia. *Cultural Studies Review* 15(1): 11–32.

Streeter, T. (1995) *Selling the Air: A Critique of the Policy of Commercial Broadcasting in the United States*. Chicago: University of Chicago Press.

Stretton, H. (1987) *Political Essays*. Melbourne: Georgian House.

Strinati, D. (2004) *An Introduction to Theories of Popular Culture*. London: Routledge.

Swedish Industrial Design Foundation (2010) *The Design Ladder*. Retrieved September 21, 2010, from www.svid.se/English/About-design/The-Design-ladder/.

Swyngedouw, E. (2003) The Marxian Alternative: Historical-Geographical Materialism and the Political Economy of Capitalism. In E. Sheppard and T. J. Barnes (eds.), *A Companion to Economic Geography*. Malden, MA: Blackwell, pp. 41–59.

Taylor, C. W. (1991) *The Ethics of Authenticity*. Cambridge, MA: Harvard University Press.

Taylor, P. J. (2004) *World City Network: A Global Urban Analysis*. London: Routledge.

Taylor, P. J., Walker, D. R. F. and Beaverstock, J. V. (2002) Firms and Their Global Service Networks. In S. Sassen (ed.), *Global Networks, Linked Cities*. New York: Routledge, pp. 93–115.

Terranova, T. (2004) *Network Culture: Politics for the Information Age*. London: Pluto Press.

Thomas, A. O. (2006) *Transnational Media and Contoured Markets: Redefining Asian Television and Advertising*. New Delhi: Sage.

Thompson, G. (2003) *Between Hierarchies and Markets: The Logic and Limits of Network Forms of Organization*. Oxford: Oxford University Press.

Thompson, J. (1991) *Ideology and Modern Culture*. Cambridge: Polity Press.

Thompson, J. (1995) *The Media and Modernity: A Social Theory of the Media*. Cambridge: Polity Press.

Thrift, N. (2005) *Knowing Capitalism*. London: Sage.

Throsby, D. (1992) Artists as Workers. In R. Towse and A. Khakee (eds.), *Cultural Economics*. Berlin: Springer Verlag, pp. 201–208.

Throsby, D. (2001) *Economics and Culture*. Cambridge: Cambridge University Press.

Throsby, D. (2008a) Modelling the Cultural Industries. *International Journal of Cultural Policy* 14(3): 217–232.

Throsby, D. (2008b) The Concentric Circles Model of the Cultural Industries. *Cultural Trends* 17(3): 147–164.

Tian, X. (2007) *Managing International Business in China*. Cambridge: Cambridge University Press.

Timberlake, M. and Ma, X. (2007) Cities and Globalization. In G. Ritzer (ed.), *The Blackwell Companion to Globalization*. Malden, MA: Blackwell, pp. 254–271.

Tomlinson, J. (2007) Cultural Globalization. In G. Ritzer (ed.), *The Blackwell Companion to Globalization*. Malden, MA: Blackwell, pp. 352–366.

Towse, R. (1996) *The Economics of Artists' Labour Markets*. London: Arts Council of England.

Towse, R. (2003a) Introduction. In R. Towse (ed.), *A Handbook of Cultural Economics*. Cheltenham, UK: Edward Elgar, pp. 1–14.

Towse, R. (2003b) Cultural Industries. In R. Towse (ed.), *A Handbook of Cultural Economics*. Cheltenham, UK: Edward Elgar, pp. 170–176.

Towse, R. (2010) *A Textbook of Cultural Economics*. Cambridge: Cambridge University Press.

Toynbee, J. (2000) *Making Popular Music: Musicians, Creativity and Institutions*. London: Arnold.

Trend, D. (1997) *Cultural Democracy: Politics, Media, New Technology*. Albany, NY: State University of New York Press.

Tsai, H.-H., Lee, H.-Y. and Yu, H.-C. (2008) Developing the Digital Content Industries in Taiwan. *Review of Policy Research* 25(2): 169–188.

Turnbull, S. (2008) Mapping the Vast Suburban Tundra: Australian Comedy from Dame Edna to *Kath and Kim*. *International Journal of Cultural Studies* 11(1): 15–32.

United Nations Commission for Trade, Aid and Development (UNCTAD) (2004) *Creative Industries and Development*. TD(XI)/BP/13, Eleventh Session, Sao Paolo, June 13–18. Retrieved June 15, 2009, 2010, from www.unctad.org/en/docs/tdxibpd13_en.pdf.

United Nations Commission for Trade, Aid and Development (UNCTAD) (2008) *Creative Economy Report 2008*. United Nations: Geneva.

United Nations Educational, Scientific and Cultural Organization (UNESCO) (1982) *World Conference on Cultural Policies: Final Report*. Paris: UNESCO.

UNESCO (2003) *Culture, Trade and Globalisation: Questions and Answers*. Paris: UNESCO. Retrieved June 4, 2008, from www.unesco.org/culture/industries/trade/htmleng.

UNESCO (2004) *UNESCO and the Issue of Cultural Diversity – Review and Strategy 1946–2004*. Division of Cultural Policies and Intercultural Dialogue. Paris: UNESCO, September.

UNESCO (2005) *Convention on the Protection and Promotion of the Diversity of Forms of Cultural Expression*. Paris: UNESCO, October 20.

UNESCO (2006) *Understanding Creative Industries: Cultural Statistics for Public Policy-Making*. Paris: UNESCO. Retrieved May 30, 2010, from http://portal.unesco.org/culture/en/ev.php-URL_ID=29947&URL_DO=DO_TOPIC&URL_SECTION=201.html.

UNESCO (2009) *The 2009 UNESCO Framework for Cultural Statistics (FCS)*. Montreal: UNESCO Institute for Statistics.

Vaidhyanathan, S. (2001) *Copyrights and Copywrongs: The Rise of Intellectual Property and How It Threatens Creativity*. New York: New York University Press.

Veblen, T. (1994 [1899]) *The Theory of the Leisure Class*. Introduction by R. Lekachman. New York: Penguin.

Vestheim, G. (1996) Models of Cultural Policy: The Scandinavian Experience. *Culture and Policy* 7(1): 157–176.

Waitt, G. and Gibson, C. (2009) Creative Small Cities: Rethinking the Creative Economy in Place. *Urban Studies* 46(5–6): 1223–1246.

Wang, J. (1996) *High Culture Fever: Politics, Aesthetics and Ideology in Deng's China*. Berkeley, CA: University of California Press.

Wang, J. (2004) The Global Reach of a New Discourse: How Far Can 'Creative Industries' Travel? *International Journal of Cultural Studies* 7(1): 9–19.

Wang, J. (2008) *Brand New China: Advertising, Media and Commercial Culture*. Cambridge, MA: Harvard University Press.

Warren, B. (1971) The Internationalization of Capital and the Nation State: A Comment. *New Left Review* 67: 83–88.

Warsh, D. (2006) *Knowledge and the Wealth of Nations: A Story of Economic Discovery*. New York: W. W. Norton & Co.

Wasko, J. (2003) *How Hollywood Works*. London: Sage.

Wasko, J. (2004) The Political Economy of Communications. In J. Downing, D. McQuail, P. Schlesinger and E. Wartella (eds.), *The SAGE Handbook of Media Studies*. Thousand Oaks, CA: Sage, pp. 309–330.

Waters, M. (2001) *Globalization* (2nd edn). London: Routledge.

Webb, J., Schirato, T. and Danaher, G. (2002) *Understanding Bourdieu*. Sydney: Allen & Unwin.

Weiss, L. (1997) Globalization and the Myth of the Powerless State. *New Left Review* 225: 3–27.

Weiss, L. (2003) Introduction: Bringing Domestic Institutions Back. In L. Weiss (ed.), *States in the Global Economy: Bringing Domestic Institutions Back In*. Cambridge: Cambridge University Press, pp. 1–33.

Westbury, M. and Eltham, B. (2010) Cultural Policy in Australia. In M. Davis and M. Lyons (eds.), *More Than Luck: Ideas Australia Needs Now*. Sydney: Centre for Policy Development, pp. 40–44.

Wilentz, S. (2008) *The Age of Reagan: A History, 1974–2008*. New York: HarperCollins.

Williams, R. (1958) *Culture and Society, 1780–1950*. Harmondsworth: Penguin.

Williams, R. (1976) *Keywords: A Vocabulary of Culture and Society*. London: Fontana.

Williams, R. (1981) *Culture*. London: Fontana.

Williams, R. (1989) Politics and Policies: The Case of the Arts Council. In R. Williams, *The Politics of Modernism: Against the New Conformists*. London: Verso, pp. 141–150.

Williams, R. (1990) *Television: Technology and Cultural Form* (2nd edn). London: Routledge.

Williams, R. and Edge, D. (1996) The Social Shaping of Technology. *Research Policy* 25(4): 865–899.

Winseck, D. (2002) The WTO, Emerging Policy Regimes and the Political Economy of Transnational Communication. In M. Raboy (ed.), *Global Media Policy in the New Millennium*. Luton: University of Luton Press, pp. 19–38.

Winseck, D. (2008) The State of Media Ownership and Media Markets: Competition or Concentration and Why Should We Care? *Sociology Compass* 2(1): 34–47.

Winseck, D. (2011) Political Economy of the Media and the Transformation of the Global Media Industries. In D. Inseck and D. Y. Jin (eds.), *Political Economies of the Media: The Transformation of the Global Media Industries*. London: Bloomsbury (forthcoming).

Winston, B. (1998) *Media Technology and Society – A History: From the Telegraph to the Internet*. London: Routledge.

Withers, G. (2003) Broadcasting. In R. Towse (ed.), *A Handbook of Cultural Economics*. Cheltenham, UK: Edward Elgar, pp. 102–113.

Wood, T. (2010) Good Riddance to New Labour. *New Left Review* 62 (March-April): 5–28.

Woods, N. (2002) Global Governance and the Role of Institutions. In D. Held and A. McGrew (eds.), *Governing Globalization*. Cambridge: Polity Press, pp. 25–45.

Work Foundation, The (2007) *Staying Ahead: The Economic Performance of the UK's Creative Industries*. London: The Work Foundation. Retrieved May 1, 2008, from www.thework-foundation.com/products/publications/azpublications/creativeindustries.aspx.

World Bank (2008) *Knowledge for Development – Knowledge Assessment Methodology*. Washington, DC: World Bank. Retrieved May 13, 2008, from web.worldbank.org/WBSITE/EXTERNAL/WBI/WBIPROGRAMS/KFDLP/.

Worldwatch Institute (2007) *State of the World 2007: Our Urban Future*. Washington, DC: Worldwatch Institute.

Wright, P. (1985) *On Living in an Old Country: The National Past in Contemporary Britain*. London: Verso.

Wright, S., Newbign, J., Kieffer, J., Holden, J. and Bewick, T. (eds.) (2009) *After the Crunch*. London: Creative & Cultural Skills/Counterpoint.

Wu, Q. (2006) Creative Industries and Innovation in China. *International Journal of Cultural Studies* 9(3): 263–266.

Wuwei, L. (2011) *How Creativity is Changing China*, trans. Michael Keane. London: Bloomsbury Academic.

Wyszomirski, M. J. (2008) The Local Creative Economy in the United States of America. In H. Anheier and Y. R. Isar (eds.), *The Cultural Economy*. Los Angeles, CA: Sage, pp. 199–212.

Yeatman, A. (1998) Activism and the Policy Process. In A. Yeatman (ed.), *Activism and the Policy Process*. Sydney: Allen & Unwin, pp. 16–35.

Yeung, H. W. (2004) *Chinese Capitalism in a Global Era: Towards Hybrid Capitalism*. London: Routledge.

Yeung, H. W. and Lin, G. (2003) Theorising Economic Geographies of Asia. *Economic Geography* 79(2): 107–128.

Yusuf, S. and Nabeshima, K. (2005) Creative Industries in East Asia. *Cities* 22(2): 109–122.

Zelizer, B. (2004) *Taking Journalism Seriously: News and the Academy*. Thousand Oaks, CA: Sage.

Zhang, X. (2006) From Institution to Industry: Reform of Cultural Institutions in China. *International Journal of Cultural Studies* 9(3): 297–306.

Zhang, X. (2008) Interview. In T. Flew (ed.), *New Media: An Introduction* (3rd edn). Melbourne: Oxford University Press.

Zheng, J. (2010) The 'Entrepreneurial State' in 'Creative Industries Cluster' Development in Shanghai. *Journal of Urban Affairs* 32(2): 143–17.

Index

Fortunati, L., 110
Foucault, Michel, 3, 7, 10–11, 179–82, 191
'Fourth Estate', 161
FOX Network, 119
France, 159–60
Frankfurt School, 4
Frederiksen, L., 139
Freedman, Des, 162–3, 177, 188
Freeman, Christopher, 124
French Revolution (1789), 159
Friedman, J., 142–3
Friedman, Milton, 132, 166, 187, 190
Friedman, R., 132
Friedman, Thomas, 135
Frith, S., 17, 148, 157
Frow, J., 88
Fuchs, S., 177, 190

galleries, 13, 19, 83, 97
Galperin, H., 170
Gamble, Andrew, 188
Gans-Moore, L., 187
García, L., 142
Garnham, Nicholas, 13, 16, 19–20, 22–3, 91, 100
de Gaulle, Charles, 160
'gay index', 155
Gellner, Ernest, 159
General Agreement of Trade in Services (GATS) 35,
    129–30, 169
Gibson, C., 42, 156
Gibson, Mark, 4, 8
Giddens, Anthony, 133–4
Gill, I., 46
Glaesar, Edward, 155
'GLAM' sector, 13, 19, 83
global brands, 113
global capitalism, 7, 40, 135
global cities, 142, 144
global financial crisis (2007), 29–30, 34, 109
globalisation, 6–7, 133–38, 169–70
    and cities, 138–41
    cultural consequences of, 145
    definitions of, 133
    and Marxism, 135
    and neo-liberalism, 177, 188
    promotion of cultural trade, 127
    promotion of global integration, 142
    spread of consumer culture, 113
Golding, P., 117
Goldman, William, 99
Goldwyn, Samuel, 120
Google Inc., 123

Gordon, C., 182
Gordon, I., 150
Graber, C.B., 129–31
Graham, A., 161
Grant, P., 128
graphic design, 85
Green, J., 165
Grodach, C., 40
gross domestic product (GDP) by world region, 46
Grossberg, L., 166
Gu, X., 50
Guala, F., 180
Gyford, J., 15

Hall, Peter, 142, 145
Hall, Stuart, 2, 4, 8, 17
Hardt, Michael, 106, 135
Harney, S., 106
Harris, Nigel, 135, 139
Hart-Landsberg, M. 47
Hartley, John, 4, 192
Harvey, David, 167, 177, 181, 189
Hawkins, J., 167
Hayek, Friedrich von, 187–9
Healy, Kieran, 168
Heilbroner, Robert, 123
Held, David, 133–4
Henderson, J., 134, 137
heritage industry, 13, 28
Herman, E.S., 113
Hesmondhalgh, David, 5, 18, 30, 88, 90–1, 97, 99,
    106–8, 120–1, 177, 188
Higgs, P., 87, 92–6
high culture 27, 88, 115; see also cultural economics
higher education, 31, 100–1
    within the creative industries, 7–8
    see also tertiary education
Hirschman, Albert, 146
Hirst, P., 135, 137
Hoggart, Richard, 2
Holden, John, 88
Hong Kong, 4
    creative cultural production in, 44
    economic integration with China, 44
    strategies to develop creative economies in, 42
    transition to a high-income country, 45
Horkheimer, M., 113, 184
Horwitz, Robert, 163, 167
Hoskins, C., 18, 118–19, 128
Howard, John, 51
Howkins, J., 87
Hunt, Jeremy, 21

Hunter, Ian, 3
Hutchinson, D., 161
Hutton, Will, 50, 165
Hypponen, L., 148

imperfectly competitive markets, 118
income inequality, 47
Independent Film and Television Alliance
    (IFTA), 39
industrial capitalism, 40, 154
industrial design, 85
industrial organisation theory, 117–18
industrial production, 114, 123
industrialisation
    of cities, 138
    of culture, 4
information society, 13, 44; *see also* knowledge
    economies
Innis, Harold, 123
innovation
    adoption of, 125
    clusters of, 124
    and the dynamics of the creative industries, 30
    non-incremental, 125
    policy for, 171–3
    types of, 124
innovator's dilemma, 125
intellectual property, 10, 20, 26, 28, 34, 87, 174
    in developing countries, 57–8
interior design, 85
International Conference on Creative Industries and
    Innovation (2005), 49
International Intellectual Property Alliance (IIPA),
    39–40
International Monetary Fund (IMF), 166, 169, 188
International Non-Governmental Organisations
    (INGOs), 134
international treaties and laws, 134, 137
Internet, 5, 26, 123, 127
    Chinese censorship of, 49
    global usage of, 134
    illegal downloads and copyright protection, 127, 174
    innovation enabled by, 171
    proliferation of information on, 173
Isherwood, B., 114

Jackson, Peter, 52
Jacobs, Jane, 41, 154
Jameson, Fredric, 8
Jenkins, H., 175
Jermyn, H., 168–9
Johns, J., 157

Johnson, Boris, 30, 153
Jowell, Tessa, 22, 28

Kapur, J., 178
KEA European Affairs, 36–7
Keane, M., 48
Kelly, O., 167
Keynes, John Maynard, 160, 189
Keynesian economics, 167, 188–9
Kim, L., 137
Kipnis, A., 189
Kirchner, S., 178
Knell, J., 152–3
knowledge economies, 14, 19, 29, 38, 177, 192
knowledge-intensive industries, 19
Kong, L., 42, 44, 147
Kotkin, Joel, 156
Kozul-Wright, Z., 56–7, 122

Laclau, Ernesto, 189
l'action socioculturelle, 160
laissez-faire versus state intervention, 180
Landry, C., 144–6, 151
Lash, S., 19, 184
late capitalism, 8
Leadbeater, Charles, 14, 171, 174
Leary, R., 18, 86
Lee, M., 96, 112–13
Lee, T., 44
Leo, P., 44
Lessig, L., 175–6
liberalism, 189
libraries, 13, 19, 83, 97
Lievrouw, L., 124–5
Lin, G., 46
Lipietz, Alain, 190
Litman, J., 175
Livingstone, Ken, 16, 151
Livingstone, S., 124
Li Wuwei, 192
localisation of businesses, 139
London *see under* United Kingdom
Lorenzen, M., 139
Loukaitou-Sideris, A., 40
Lowy, Michael, 186
Lyotard, Jean-François, 185

Ma, X., 144
McCann, P., 150
McChesney, R.W., 113
'McDonaldization' of society, 113
McElhinney, S., 135, 187

symbolic goods, 87
symmetrical ignorance, 120

Taiwan, creative industries in, 42, 44
taxonomies for creative industries, 87–8
Taylor, Charles, 102
Taylor, P.J., 142–3
technological development, 164–5
    adoption in social systems, 124–5
    and the capitalist market economy, 123
telecommunications industry, 19
television industry, 134, 185; *see also* broadcast media
tertiary education, 107–8
textile, clothing and footwear (TCF) industries, 84, 87
Thatcher, Margaret, 14, 168, 188
theatres, 97
Theory of the Leisure Class, 114
Thomas, A.O., 165
Thompson, John, 187–8
'Third Way', the, 4, 14, 17, 178
'Three T's' index, 41, 155
Thrift, N., 145
Throsby, David, 27, 36, 87, 115–16
Timberlake, M., 144
Tomlinson, John, 145
tourism industry, 13, 36, 40, 83
Towse, Ruth, 5, 115, 166
Transnationality Index, 157
Trend, D., 167
Turner, B., 189

United Kingdom
    Arts Council of England, 22
    Arts Council of Great Britain, 14, 160
    arts policy, 160
    Browne Review of Higher Education Funding (2010), 31
    Coalition government (formed 2010), 21, 28, 30, 153, 168; 'Big Society' project, 168
    Conservative government (1979–97), 14–17, 21
    Council for the Encouragement of Music and the Arts, 159
    Cox Review of Creativity in Business (2006), 15, 23, 110
    creative industries in, 10, 12–13, 17–19; development of, 10, 21; employment in, 94–5; in post-industrial cities, 14–15; promotion of, 14; redistribution of, 22; value to the economy, 9, 12–13, 28; 'Wimbledonisation' effect, 31
    cultural policies, 9–13, 15–16, 20
    Department for Business, Innovation and Skills, 23

United Kingdom *cont.*
    Department of Culture, Media and Sport (DCMS), 9, 11–12, 21, 24; classification of creative industries, 10, 12–13, 17–20, 24, 83, 86–7; *Creative Britain: New Talents for the New Economy* (2008), 23; *Creative Industries Mapping Document* (2001), 9–10, 17–18, 20–2; *Digital Britain* report (2009), 23; Regional Cultural Consortia, 21
    Film Council, abolition of, 28
    Labour government (1997–2010), 2–4, 9, 11, 13–14, 17, 21–2, 28, 183; and local councils, 15; and the 'Third Way', 14, 17
    London: as a creative city, 22, 150–4; Greater London Council (GLC), 16; Greater London Enterprise Board (GLEB), 16; Olympic Games (2012), 151; predominance in UK creative industries, 22
    McMaster Report (2008), 22
    music industry, 14, 17
    National Endowment for Science, Technology and the Arts (NESTA), 23–4, 26–8, 167; classification of creative industries, 24–5, 89–90, 92–3; *Creating Growth* report (2006), 23–4; model of creative industries, 25
    'New Labour' project, 2–4, 11, 13, 18, 22, 28–9, 168, 181, 183, 188; redefinition of Labour Party, 14; and the 'Third Way', 14, 17, 178
    Northern Rock, 28
    Ofcom (Office of Communications), 163
    Peacock Review of Public Broadcasting (2005), 168
    public sector debt, 31
    Regional Arts Boards, 21
    Regional Development Agencies, 21, 28
    regionalisation agenda, 21
    Royal Bank of Scotland, 28
    treatment of intellectual property, 34
    Work Foundation, 23–4, 36; 'concentric circles of industries' model, 26, 36, 87–8; *Staying Ahead* report (2007), 23, 27–8
United Nations, 52, 134
    Conference on Trade and Development (UNCTAD), 2, 4, 33, 52, 54, 57, 93, 98, 125; definition of creative industries, 54; High-Level Panel on Creative Industries, 53; model of the creative industries, 56; Transnationality Index (TNI), 136
    Copenhagen Agreement on Climate Change, 134